Daniel Braga Nascimento

Citizenship and Residence by Investment

An analysis of EU and International Law in investment migration programmes

PETER LANG
Berlin · Bruxelles · Chennai · Lausanne · New York · Oxford

Bibliographic Information published by the Deutsche Nationalbibliothek
The Deutsche Nationalbibliothek lists this publication in the Deutsche Nationalbibliografie; detailed bibliographic data is available in the internet at http://dnb.d-nb.de.

Library of Congress Cataloging-in-Publication Data
Names: Braga Nascimento, Daniel, 1990- author
Title: Citizenship and residence by investment : an analysis of eu and international law in investment migration programmes / Daniel Braga Nascimento.
Description: 1st edition. | New York : Peter Lang Publishing Inc, 2026. | Series: Erlanger schriften zum öffentlichen recht, 21928460 ; 15 | Includes bibliographical references and index.
Identifiers: LCCN 2025049491 (print) | LCCN 2025049492 (ebook) | ISBN 9783631942154 hardback | ISBN 9783631942857 pdf | ISBN 9783631942864 epub
Subjects: LCSH: Citizenship—Law and legislation | Naturalization—Law and legislation | Emigration and immigration law | Investments, Foreign—Law and legislation
Classification: LCC K3275 .B73 2026 (print) | LCC K3275 (ebook)
LC record available at https://lccn.loc.gov/2025049491
LC ebook record available at https://lccn.loc.gov/2025049492

Zugl.: Erlangen-Nürnberg, Univ., Diss., 2025

Cover illustration: Historisches Siegel der Universität Erlangen-Nürnberg.

DE-29
ISSN 2192-8460
ISBN 978-3-631-94215-4 (Print)
ISBN 978-3-631-94285-7 (ePDF)
ISBN 978-3-631-94286-4 (ePUB)
DOI 10.3726/b23176

Published by Peter Lang GmbH, Berlin, Germany

info@peterlang.com

www.peterlang.com

Contact for General Product Safety Regulation (GPSR): gpsr@peterlang.com

Contents

Figures

Tables

Abstract

Citizenship by investment and residence by investment are forms of acquiring citizenship and residence due to an injection of money into a country. Born in the Caribbean countries, the practice of selling citizenship arrived in Europe and has sparked particular attention in the case of Malta. However, more than twenty Member States have residence by investment schemes in their legislation. In recent years, European institutions have argued, against citizenship by investment, that these programmes lack a genuine link (a proper connection between the state and the investor), pose different risks (money laundering, corruption, security, lack of transparency), and should be phased out. This dissertation seeks to answer the following question: To what extent do residency and citizenship by investment programmes comply with European and international law? Using case studies, legislation, and principles of European law, analysis of case law from the CJEU and international courts (the ICJ and arbitral tribunals), and national legislation from Malta and Portugal, the dissertation is divided into three chapters. The first chapter describes the law in Portugal and Malta. Respective laws relate to residence by investment (*ARI – Autorização de Residência por Investimento*) in Portugal and citizenship by investment (*Naturalization by Exceptional Contributions*, formerly the "*Individual Investor Programme*") in Malta. The second chapter deals with responses from European institutions, such as the European Commission and the European Parliament, and addresses EU law (principle of sincere cooperation, EU Citizenship). The last chapter considers international law using the *Nottebohm* case, and examines public international law, as well as examples of other naturalisation policies that would be at risk if the theory of the genuine link was understood as a requirement and not as guidance. Finally, the dissertation presents possible pathways for institutions and policymakers to follow.

Keywords: citizenship; EU citizenship; genuine link; investment; residence

Zusammenfassung:

Staatsbürgerschaft durch Investition und Aufenthaltstitel durch Investition sind Formen des Erwerbs der Staatsbürgerschaft und eines Aufenthaltstitels durch Geldzufluss in ein Land. Die Praxis des Verkaufs der Staatsbürgerschaft, die in den karibischen Ländern entwickelt wurde, wurde auch in Europa begründet und erregte im Fall von Malta besondere Aufmerksamkeit. Allerdings haben mehr als 20 Mitgliedstaaten Regelungen für den Erwerb der Staatsbürgerschaft durch Investitionen in ihrer Gesetzgebung. In den letzten Jahren haben europäische Institutionen gegen die Staatsbürgerschaft durch Investitionen argumentiert, dass diesen Programmen ein sog. "*genuine link*" (eine ordnungsgemäße Verbindung zwischen dem Staat und dem Investor) fehlt, dass sie verschiedene Risiken bergen (Geldwäsche, Korruption, Sicherheit, mangelnde Transparenz) und dass sie auslaufen sollten. Diese Dissertation versucht, die folgende Frage zu beantworten: Inwieweit entsprechen Programme für Aufenthaltstitel und Staatsbürgerschaften durch Investitionen dem europäischen und internationalen Recht? Anhand von Fallstudien, Gesetzgebung und Grundsätzen des europäischen Rechts, einer Analyse der Rechtsprechung des EuGH und internationaler Gerichte (Internationaler Gerichtshof und Schiedsgerichte) sowie der nationalen Gesetzgebung Maltas und Portugals ist die Dissertation in drei Kapitel unterteilt. Das erste Kapitel beschreibt das Recht in Portugal und Malta. Die jeweiligen Gesetze beziehen sich auf den Aufenthalt durch Investitionen (*ARI – Autorização de Residência por Investimento*) in Portugal und die Staatsbürgerschaft durch Investitionen (*Naturalization by Exceptional Contributions*, früher das „*Individual Investor Programme*") in Malta. Das zweite Kapitel befasst sich mit den Reaktionen europäischer Institutionen wie der Europäischen Kommission und des Europäischen Parlaments und behandelt das EU-Recht (Grundsatz der loyalen Zusammenarbeit, EU-Bürgerschaft). Im letzten Kapitel wird das Völkerrecht anhand des Falls *Nottebohm* betrachtet und das Völkerrecht sowie Beispiele für andere Einbürgerungsregelungen, die gefährdet wären, wenn die Theorie des "genuine link" als Voraussetzung und nicht als Empfehlung verstanden würde, untersucht. Schließlich werden in der Dissertation mögliche Wege aufgezeigt, denen Institutionen und politische Entscheidungsträger folgen können.

Schlüsselwörter: Staatsbürgerschaft; EU-Staatsbürgerschaft; "*genuine link*"; Investition; Aufenthaltstitel

Acknowledgements

I thank my supervisor Prof Dr Anuscheh Farahat, for the precise feedback and guidance and unconditional support throughout all my projects during the PhD. Thanks also to the team in Erlangen-Nuremberg and the broader family from the Faculty of Law, Master's in Human Rights, and PhD in Human Rights and Business programmes. Conducting the PhD at FAU also improved my skills through the Language Centre, the Writing Center, and the Career Center. Thank you to the Welcome Center who made the journey in Germany smoother at every stage.

My researcher training was also helped by the two years during which I taught seminars on international migration law and decolonising human rights on the Human Rights MA. I had thirty international students who taught me a lot about intercultural communication and dialogue related to research in the two fields.

I am also grateful for the several scholars with whom I had the chance to discuss my research individually. I am likewise thankful for the seminars in Bergen (Netherlands), with the Amsterdam migration law team, and in Brussels (Free University of Brussels) at the PhD seminar of the Odysseus Network of EU Migration and Asylum Law.

Thank you to the Friedrich Ebert Stiftung for the PhD scholarship.

Finally, and most importantly, thank you to my parents, who have supported me unconditionally throughout my journey, my partner for the words of encouragement and love, and all my friends who have given me the strength to write a PhD, partly during a pandemic, in another country and in a language other than that allocated me by the lottery of birth.

Abbreviations

AG	Advocate General
AML	Anti-money laundering
CBM	Citizenship by Merit
CCD	Customer Due Diligence
CFR	Charter of Fundamental Rights of the European Union
CJEU	Court of Justice of the European Union
CMVM	Portuguese Securities Market Commission
EC	European Commission
ECtHR	European Court of Human Rights
ECR	European Court Reports
EP	European Parliament
EU	European Union
FATF	Financial Action Task Force
FDI	Foreign Direct Investment
FJCP	Federation of Jewish Communities of Spain
ICJ	International Court of Justice
IIP	Individual Investor Programme
MS	Member State
OCCRP	Organized Crime and Corruption Reporting Project
OECD	Organization for Economic Co-operation and Development
TEU	Treaty on the European Union
TFEU	Treaty on the Functioning of the European Union
UDHR	Universal Declaration of Human Rights

Table of Cases

Alphabetical list of all cases

International Arbitration

Flegenheimer Case – Decision No. 182, Reports of International Arbitral Awards (20 September 1958)
Iran–United States Conciliation Commission
Iran v. United States, Case No. 32-A/18-FT, 5 Iran–US Claims Tribunal Reporter 251
Italian-United States Conciliation Commission:
Mergé Case (United States v. Italy) 14 R.I.A.A.
Franco-Italian Conciliation Commission:
Rambaldi Claim (France v. Italy) 13 R.I.A.A. 786 (1957)
Mengui Claim (France v. Italy) 13 R.I.A.A. 801 (1958)
Lombroso Claim (France v. Italy) 13 R.I.A.A. 84 (1958)

Court of Justice of the European Union (CJEU)

European Court of Justice. Commission of the European Communities v Council of the European Communities. European Agreement on Road Transport, (Case 22-70) [1971]
European Court of Justice, Case, European Commission vs Republic of Malta, (C-181/23) [2023]
European Court of Justice, Case, European Commission vs Republic of Malta, (C-181/23) [2023] Opinion of Advocate General Collins, delivered on 4 October 2024

European Court of Justice. Case, Federal Republic of Germany v European Parliament and Council of the European Union, (C-380/03), [2006], ECR 2006 I-11573
European Court of Justice. Gerardo Ruiz Zambrano v Office national de lémploi (ONEm) [2001] ECR 2011 I-01177
European Court of Justice. Ingrid Boukhalfa vs Bundesrepublik Deutschland (Case C-214/94) [1996] ECR 1996 I-02253
European Court of Justice. Janko Rottmann v Freistaat of Bayern (C-135/08) [2010], ECR 2010 I-01449
European Court of Justice. JY v Wiener Landesregierung (C-118-20) [2022], ECLI:EU:C:2022:34
European Court of Justice. M. G. Tjebbes and Others v Minister van Buitenlandse Zaken (C-221/17) [2019] ECLI:EU:C:2019:189
European Court of Justice. Mario Vicente Micheletti v Delegación del Gobierno em Cantabria (Case C-369/90) [1992] ECR I-4239
European Court of Justice. Rudy Grzelczyk v Centre public d'aide sociale d'Ottignies-Louvain-la-Neuve (Case C-184/99), [2001] EU:C:2001:458

International Court of Justice (ICJ)

Liechtenstein vs. Guatemala (Nottebohm) [1955] Judgement of 6 April 1955

Permanent Court of International Justice (PCIJ)

S.S. "Lotus" (France v Turkey) [1927] Rep Series A, No 10, 18

Table of Cases

Alphabetical list of all cases

International Arbitration

Flegenheimer Case – Decision No. 182, Reports of International Arbitral Awards (20 September 1958)

Iran–United States Conciliation Commission

Iran v. United States, Case No. 32-A/18-FT, 5 Iran–US Claims Tribunal Reporter 251

Italian-United States Conciliation Commission:

Mergé Case (United States v. Italy) 14 R.I.A.A.

Franco-Italian Conciliation Commission:

Rambaldi Claim (France v. Italy) 13 R.I.A.A. 786 (1957)

Mengui Claim (France v. Italy) 13 R.I.A.A. 801 (1958)

Lombroso Claim (France v. Italy) 13 R.I.A.A. 84 (1958)

Court of Justice of the European Union (CJEU)

European Court of Justice. Commission of the European Communities v Council of the European Communities. European Agreement on Road Transport, (Case 22-70) [1971]

European Court of Justice, Case, European Commission vs Republic of Malta, (C-181/23) [2023]

European Court of Justice, Case, European Commission vs Republic of Malta, (C-181/23) [2023] Opinion of Advocate General Collins, delivered on 4 October 2024

European Court of Justice. Case, Federal Republic of Germany v European Parliament and Council of the European Union, (C-380/03), [2006], ECR 2006 I-11573
European Court of Justice. Gerardo Ruiz Zambrano v Office national de lémploi (ONEm) [2001] ECR 2011 I-01177
European Court of Justice. Ingrid Boukhalfa vs Bundesrepublik Deutschland (Case C-214/94) [1996] ECR 1996 I-02253
European Court of Justice. Janko Rottmann v Freistaat of Bayern (C-135/08) [2010], ECR 2010 I-01449
European Court of Justice. JY v Wiener Landesregierung (C-118-20) [2022], ECLI:EU:C:2022:34
European Court of Justice. M. G. Tjebbes and Others v Minister van Buitenlandse Zaken (C-221/17) [2019] ECLI:EU:C:2019:189
European Court of Justice. Mario Vicente Micheletti v Delegación del Gobierno em Cantabria (Case C-369/90) [1992] ECR I-4239
European Court of Justice. Rudy Grzelczyk v Centre public d'aide sociale d'Ottignies-Louvain-la-Neuve (Case C-184/99), [2001] EU:C:2001:458

International Court of Justice (ICJ)

Liechtenstein vs. Guatemala (Nottebohm) [1955] Judgement of 6 April 1955

Permanent Court of International Justice (PCIJ)

S.S. "Lotus" (France v Turkey) [1927] Rep Series A, No 10, 18

Introduction

Back in 1997, Mastercard launched the slogan, "There are some things money can't buy. For everything else, there's Mastercard." Opponents of the idea of selling citizenship for an amount of money would add to the Mastercard list of things money cannot buy: Citizenship. Basically, money should not buy citizenship, they would say. On the other hand, the advocates who believe does not pose a problem would rather say that you can buy citizenship and pay with one click and your Mastercard. Welcome to the world of investor's residence and citizenship programmes.

Besides the Mastercard slogan, Karl Marx had already stated that with commodification, market logic impregnates all domains of human life.[1] The market logic has certainly arrived for citizenship. At first, one can see a win-win logic: states profit by receiving a large amount of money that can be invested in infrastructure, education, or whatever. On the other side, the investor profits from mobility rights and all the other rights that derive from citizenship. What could then be the problem with selling residence and citizenship? For the European Commission, a lack of a genuine link is one of the main problems with citizenship by investment (CBI).[2] But even

1 Marx, K., On the Jewish Question, in Marx-Engels-Reader, R. C. Tucker, Editor 1972, Norton: New York. P. 24–51

2 European Commission, Investor citizenship schemes: European Commission opens infringements against Cyprus and Malta for "selling" EU Citizenship. Available on: https://ec.europa.eu/commission/presscorner/detail/en/ip_20_1925 Access on: 06/04/2023

when citizenship for sale is beneficial (in economic terms) for all, conferring citizenship "should serve purposes very different from boosting the treasury."[3]

Although one could think that citizenship by investment is a new phenomenon, it is important to say that this is not true, as Caribbean countries already began to grant citizenship for sums of money back in the 1980s. On the other hand, discretionary naturalisation due to noteworthy cultural, athletic, or scientific achievements, or attainments of other kinds is also present in 22 of 27 EU Member States.[4] The European Parliament Research Service stated that EU Member States earned EUR 9.2 billion from investment migration routes between 2008 and 2018.[5] Investment migration relates to two different legal categories: residence by investment (RBI) and citizenship by investment. On the website of the Investment Migration Council,[6] under the tab "What is investment migration?" they explain that investment migration is a form of "legal migration used by over 80 sovereign states globally."[7] Investment migration "comprises various citizenship and residence by investment programmes which allow individuals to gain citizenship or residence rights in return for investments in their host countries."[8] This simplistic definition can be challenged by Kristin Surak's observation that,[9] at first glance, the phrase

3 Tanasoca, A. (2016). Citizenship for Sale: Neomedieval, not Just Neoliberal? *European Journal of Sociology / Archives Européennes De Sociologie*, *57*(1), 169–195. doi:10.1017/S0003975616000059

4 Dzankic, J., Investment-based citizenship and residence programmes in the EU. RSCAS EUI Working Papers, 2015. 2015/08: p. 5–6

5 European Parliament Research Service (EPRS), "Avenues for EU action on citizenship and residence by investment schemes" (2021).

6 The Investment Migration Council (IMC) is a forum for investment migration, bringing together stakeholders in the field. It is based in Geneva and it is an impact focused Swiss based (non-profit) membership organisation and registered with the European Commission Joint Transparency Register Secretariat (ID 337639131420-09).63. Council, I.-I.M. About the IMC. 2022; Available from: https://investmentmigration.org/about/about-the-imc/. Accessed 20 October 2023.

7 Investment Migration Council, What is Investment Migration? 2022; Available on: https://investmentmigration.org/about/what-is-investment-migration/, accessed 20 October 2022.

8 Investment Migration Council, What is Investment Migration? 2022; Available on: https://investmentmigration.org/about/what-is-investment-migration/ accessed 20 October 2022.

9 Surak, Kristin. Investment Migration: Empirical Developments in the Field and Methodological Issues in Its Study, in Citizenship and Residence Sales Rethinking the

investment migration can be misleading. This is because neither "investment" nor "migration" accurately captures what lies beneath the concept. For example, although investments are considered in applications for many programmes, it is not the only requirement, and other possibilities may be included. In Malta, a EUR 10,000 donation to charity is a requirement; and in Portugal, there is an allowance for donating to the public good or charitable causes. Second, investment migration does not equate to direct migration.[10] If we take the UN Department of Economic and Social Affairs (UN DESA)'s definition of international migration as a parameter, for example, investors who stay in their home countries and only visit the country for which they hold the residence permit or passport as investors for leisure would not be migration according to this concept.

Although no investment programme provides statistics on how many investors actually migrate to the new country, most participants do not migrate to the country but rather use the new passport or residence permit to facilitate life projects: sending children to study abroad,[11] or possessing the security of being able to leave their country of origin, as a plan B.[12] These

---

Boundaries of Belonging Edited by Dimitry Kochenov and Kristin Surak. Cambridge: Cambridge University Press, 2023

10 Despite numerous definitions of the concept of migration, here I apply the example of the International Organization for Migration's definition as "The movement of persons away from their place of usual residence and across an international border to a country of which they are not nationals." For statistical purposes, the United Nations Department of Economic and Social Affairs (UN DESA) defines an "international migrant" as "any person who changes his or her country of usual residence" (Recommendations on Statistics of International Migration, Revision 1 (1998) para. 32). The UN DESA definition excludes movements that are due to "recreation, holiday, visits to friends and relatives, business, medical treatment or religious pilgrimages" (ibid.). in IOM, International Migration Law: Glossary on Migration, 2019, page 113

11 Surak, Kristin. Investment Migration: Empirical Developments in the Field and Methodological Issues in Its Study, in Citizenship and Residence Sales Rethinking the Boundaries of Belonging Edited by Dimitry Kochenov and Kristin Surak. Cambridge: Cambridge University Press, 2023, page 28.

12 Surak, Kristin, Millionaire Mobility and the Sale of Citizenship (2020) 47 (1) Journal of Ethnic and Migration Studies 166; Kristin Surak and Yusuke Tsuzuki, "Are Golden Visas a Golden Opportunity? Assessing the Economic Origins and Outcomes of Residence by Investment Programmes" (2021) 47(15) *Journal of Ethnic and Migration Studies* 3367

are examples, not from statistics, but from interviews that Kristin Surak discovered during her research into the reasons for acquiring a passport through investment.[13]

Looking at an overview of law firm websites dealing with investment migration, one sees a menu of possibilities through an advertisement that shows the benefits of various programmes in different parts of the world. Whereas on one hand, it is easy to find investment options through simple searches on websites of law firms specialising in migration by investment, on the other hand exact numbers of how many people have naturalised through this criterion are scarce or not disclosed by the countries that have adopted these schemes. Therefore, one of the challenges in investment migration is data. It is not clear how many people have applied for residence by investment or citizenship by investment in recent decades. In 2021, a European Parliamentary Research Service study estimated that between 2001 and 2019, around 132,000 people were granted residence or citizenship in the European Union thanks to Citizenship by Investment or Residence by Investment.[14] In the case of Citizenship by Investment in Malta and Cyprus, over 50 % and 40 % respectively of beneficiaries have been Russian nationals. In contrast, Residence by Investment is of little interest for Russian nationals, except the Latvian Residence by Investment, where most of applicants are Russian. In 2021, most approvals in the EU for Residence by Investment were from Greece, Spain, and Portugal, and the number of Russian applicants was lower.[15] Data from service providers also reveals the average age of applicants is between 35 and 45.[16]

Scholarly discourse on the topic has subsequently emerged and asserted that citizenship is not a commodity that can be traded,[17] emphasising the

---

13 Surak, Kristin, Millionaire Mobility and the Sale of Citizenship (2020) 47 (1) Journal of Ethnic and Migration Studies

14 European Parliamentary Research Service, Avenues for EU action on citizenship and residence by investment schemes. 2021

15 European Parliament, Russia's war on Ukraine: Reassessing "citizenship by investment" schemes 2022; Available on: https://www.europarl.europa.eu/RegData/etudes/ATAG/2022/729385/EPRS_ATA(2022)729385_EN.pdf.

16 Investment Migration Council, *About the IMC*. 2022; Available from: https://investmentmigration.org/about/about-the-imc/

17 Shachar, A. Citizenship for Sale?, in The Oxford Handbook of Citizenship 2017, Oxford University Press: Oxford

European Union's lack of competence in naturalisation matters,[18] among other arguments. The normative debate is still open because the schemes still exist, and arguments also exist for their cessation, regulation, and improvement. What is interesting in this debate is the disciplinary divide. While most jurists clarify that it is not a violation of some law (e.g. EU law) to sell residency or citizenship, most political scientists defend the political aspect of citizenship and claim that citizenship by investment changes citizenship's meaning, making it a commodity. Disciplines approached the issue with different lenses and could not be put on the same level as the benchmarks for each of the disciplines are different. The European institutions also have their views on the matter, as do the Member States. Whose standpoint should prevail, that of Member States or that of the European institutions? This dissertation will demonstrate that both sides present compelling arguments that must be carefully weighed, and that a straightforward response cannot adequately encompass all the complexities inherent in the practices of selling residency permits and citizenship.

0.1 State of the Art

Citizenship and its connection with investment or skills is a new field of research. Back in 2006, Ayelet Shachar discussed the "race for talent" regarding country schemes to attract highly skilled professionals.[19] The term coined by Shachar means that countries use residence permits in a facilitated way to attract people with the skills and/or money to fulfil open vacancies in strategic and demanding areas of the labour market or to contribute large amounts of money to the economy via investment, in exchange for a residence permit or citizenship. The implications of the state being a "head hunter" for highly skilled labour for the fabric of communities also shows how requirements are eased for desired migrants.[20] Shachar contributes a chapter in *The Oxford*

---

18 Sarmiento, Daniel; Van den Brink, Martijn. EU Competence and Investor Migration in Citizenship and Residence Sales

19 Shachar, A. "The Race for Talent: Highly Skilled Migrants and Competitive Immigration Regimes," *N.Y.U.L. Reviwq* 148 (2006)

20 Strumia, F. New-generation Skilled Migration Policies and the Changing Fabric of Membership: Talent as Output and the Headhunting State. IMC Working Papers, 2016/4 (Investment Migration Working Papers)

Handbook of Citizenship on the normative arguments for and against citizenship by investment.[21] A comprehensive overview of different categories of citizenship by investment is also offered by Jelena Dzankic.[22]

It has been said already that these citizen-investors have an interest in the polity that is "purely instrumental," that is, linked to the mobility rights attached to passports,[23] and the attendant "economic or financial benefits."[24] Furthermore, "how the global stratification system reproduces inequalities by focusing on the institutional nature of citizenship as an ascriptive characteristic that is increasingly becoming commodified, as those with inferior statuses try to move up in the global hierarchy" has been explored by Manuela Boatca.[25] The concept of meritocracy and how it influences the discourses on citizenship by investment has been explored by Odile Ammann.[26]

The sale of citizenship in Cyprus has been scrutinised under EU law by Sofya Kudryashova.[27] She asked whether the requirement to permanently own residential property in Cyprus results in a violation of the free movement of capital under EU law and whether the possibility of revocation of Cypriot nationality for non-compliance with the aforementioned requirement violates EU citizenship case law. Her findings were that the requirement to permanently own residential property in Cyprus violated Article 63 of the

---

21 Shachar, A. Citizenship for Sale?, in The Oxford Handbook of Citizenship 2017, Oxford University Press: Oxford

22 Dzankic, Jelena, The Global Market for Investor Citizenship. 1 ed. Politics of Citizenship and Migration. 2019: Palgrave Macmillan.

23 Bauböck, R. Global, European and National Questions about the Price of Citizenship. EUI Working Paper RSCAS 2014ª (Should Citizenship be for Sale?)

24 Magni-Berton, R. Citizenship for Those Who Invest into the Future of the State is not Wrong, the price is the problem. EUI Working Paper RSCAS, 2014 (Should Citizenship be for Sale?)

25 Boatca, M. Commodification of Citizenship: Global Inequalities and the Modern Transmission of Property, in Overcoming Global Inequalities, C.C.-D. Immanuel Wallerstein, Christian Suter, Editor 2015, Paradigm Publishers.

26 Ammann, O., Passports for Sale: How (un) meritocratic are Citizenship by Investment Programmes? European Journal of Migration and Law, 2020, 22, p. 309–337

27 Kudryashova, Sofia. The Sale of Conditional EU Citizenship: The Cyprus Investment Programme under the Lens of EU law. IMC Working Papers, 2019 (Investment Migration Working Papers)

Treaty on the Functioning of the European Union (TFEU).[28] Regarding the second question, "the revocation of Cypriot nationality and EU citizenship as a result of non-compliance with the condition to retain the investment in the Republic forever is illegitimate and unjustifiable, as it leads to the revocation of Union citizenship based on the exercise of the rights it grants access to and leaves the investor's entire family unprotected and with no other alternative but to leave the territory of the Union."[29]

Analysts have examined different movements in investment migration. Luuk van der Baaren and Hanwei Li have shown how investment migration works between China and Portugal,[30] and golden visas in Portugal have received much scholarly attention in the last 10 years. Sofia Gaspar and Fernando Haro,[31] for example, have shown that Chinese investors in search of residence permits are just a part of a broader Chinese investment pattern in Portugal. China is the largest investor in Portugal and represented 3.3 % of Portuguese GDP between 2011 and 2015.

Kristen Surak has written extensively on the growth of citizenship by investment programmes,[32] as well as on inequality and investment migration.[33] She highlights the literature's broad "South to North" focus, whereas the investment migration industry's largest number of applicants are currently actually "South-South." Examples include Iranians buying citizenship in Caribbean countries to facilitate mobility in the Middle East. By numbers,

---

28 Within the framework of the provisions set out in this Chapter, all restrictions on the movement of capital between Member States and between Member States and third countries shall be prohibited. European Union, "Treaty on the Functioning of the European Union," (1958).

29 Kudryashova, Sofia. The Sale of Conditional EU Citizenship: The Cyprus Investment Programme under the Lens of EU law. IMC Working Papers, 2019 (Investment Migration Working Papers)

30 Li, L.v.d. B.a.H, Wealth Influx, Wealth Exodus: Investment Migration from China to Portugal. IMC Working Papers, 2018/1 (Investment Migration Working Papers)

31 Gaspar, Sofia; de Haro, Fernando (2020) Buying Citizenship? Chinese Golden Visa Migrants in Portugal. International Migration, Vol. 58 (3)

32 Surak, K. Global Citizenship 2.0 The Growth of Citizenship by Investment Programs. IMC Working Papers, 2016/3 (Investment Migration Working Papers)

33 Surak, K. Millionaires and Mobility: inequality and Investment Migration Programs, in Money Matters in Migration, W. M. Tesseltje de Lange, Annette Schrauwen, Editor. 2021, Cambridge University Press: Cambridge.

Turkey is the top issuer of citizenship by investment in the world, while Malaysia ranks first in granting residence by investment.[34]

In contrast to what some law firms advertise,[35] Martijn van den Brick has shown that rights granted to investors who acquire residence permits are modest in EU law.[36] Many law firms advertise that investors will have rights of considerable importance when acquiring residence by investment. In reality, EU rights from which investors can benefit when buying residence by investment are modest, because investors may only travel in the Schengen area for up to 90 days in a 180-day period, and they are not granted the right to work or live permanently in another Member State. The acquisition of permanent residence "based on national law through investment or otherwise, does not bring the third-country national within the scope of the Directive for as long as the requirements in the Directive have not been satisfied."[37]

EU interference in the naturalisation laws of Members States has been discussed by Daniel Sarmiento.[38] He argues that cases in which EU law can interfere in Member States' laws on nationality concern restrictions of EU

---

34 Surak, Kristin. Investment Migration: Empirical Developments in the Field and Methodological Issues in Its Study, in Citizenship and Residence Sales Rethinking the Boundaries of Belonging Edited by Dimitry Kochenov and Kristin Surak. Cambridge: Cambridge University Press, 2023, page 68

35 "Fast-track to permanent residency in the EU in 4 weeks," 2016, https://www.artoncapital.com/industry-news/press-releases/fast-track-permanent-residency-eu-4-weeks/.

36 Brink, M.v.d., Investment Residence and the concept of residence in EU law: interactions, tensions, and opportunities. IMC Working Papers, 2017 (Investment Migration Working Papers)

37 Brink, M.v.d., Investment Residence and the concept of residence in EU law: interactions, tensions, and opportunities. IMC Working Papers, 2017 (Investment Migration Working Papers) Here by the Directive it is meant the Council Directive 2003/109/EC of 25 November 2003 concerning the status of third-country nationals who are long-term residents. The requirements for a Member State to grant long-term resident status to third-country nationals are: legally and continuously residence within its territory for five years immediately prior to the submission of the relevant application; stable and regular resources which are sufficient to maintain himself/herself and the members of his/her family, without recourse to the social assistance system of the Member State concerned; sickness insurance in respect of all risks normally covered for his/her own nationals in the Member State concerned; member States may require third-country nationals to comply with integration conditions, in accordance with national law.

38 Sarmiento, D., EU Competence and the Attribution of Nationality in Member States. IMC Working Papers, 2019/2 (Investment Migration Working Papers)

rights, but not cases in which the attribution of nationality is a source of EU rights for the individual. The EU can "only introduce measures in this area of national law on the grounds of Article 352 TFEU, and even in this case, it must comply with strict requirements, such as the existence of a genuine need to improve the goals of the Treaties, as well as a unanimous vote in the Council."[39]

Furthermore, how the principles of proportionality and sincere cooperation relate to investment migration have been discussed by Matjaž Tratnik and Petra Weingerl,[40] and Elena Prats has attempted to use contractual law to argue against the citizenship by investment model in the Maltese case.[41]

Dimitry Kochenov[42] and Elena Basheska have argued that the European Commission's position – in arguing against citizenship by investment and by requiring a genuine link, if not consistent with EU law or international law – expresses a "purely nationalist and problematic understanding of citizenship, by a deeply politicised European Commission, where the matters of legality are hijacked by the blood nationalist interest." They also express their surprise at this twist, considering the Union's history and the values it seeks to promote.

Luca Mavelli argues that the sale of citizenship is not only about commodification but part of a neoliberal political economy of belonging.[43] From the discipline of sociology, Ana Tanasoca reflects on how the sale of noble titles in the past can produce arguments extended by analogy to the sale of citizenship.[44] The critique of citizenship by investment is also highlighted by

39 Sarmiento, D., EU Competence and the Attribution of Nationality in Member States. IMC Working Papers, 2019/2 (Investment Migration Working Papers)

40 Weingerl, M.T.a. P. Investment Migration and State Autonomy: a Quest for the Relevant Link. IMC Working Papers, 2019/4 (Investment Migration Working Papers)

41 Prats, E. Are Citizenship by Investment Programs Legitimate? Suggesting Some Assessment Methods, in Money Matters in Migration, W. M. Tesseltje de Lange, Annette Schrauwen, Editor 2021, Cambridge University Press: Cambridge

42 Kochenov, D. Citizenship. 2019 Cambridge: The MIT Press

43 Mavelli, L. Citizenship for Sale and the Neoliberal Political Economy of Belonging. International Studies Quarterly (2018. *62*: p. 482–493)

44 Tanasoca, A. Citizenship for Sale Neomedieval, not just Neoliberal? European Journal of Sociology, 2016. *57*: p. 169–195

Ayelet Schahar and Ran Hirschl, who say that "cash-for-passports" affect the most "sacrosanct non-market good: membership in a political community."[45]

The genuine link has also received attention from Peter Spiro, who refers to the *Nottebohm*[46] case as a jurisprudential illusion.[47] For Rayner Thwaits, the *Nottebohm* case is a "dead letter" or a "one-off" confined to the facts of the case.[48] Martijn van den Brick explains that the crux of the *Nottebohm* case is not about granting EU citizenship to citizens with a genuine link, but about other countries recognising citizenship when there is no genuine link.[49]

Most literature on investment migration has emerged since 2013, when the citizenship-by-investment scheme in Malta came into being, and a few years after the initiation of various residency-by-investment schemes across the European Union following the 2008 economic crisis. In-depth analysis of European and international law in relation to these schemes is still lacking. No doctoral thesis has been written on the subject that involves case studies and jurisprudential analysis of the Court of Justice of the European Union (CJEU), arbitral tribunals, and international courts (i.e. the International Court of Justice [ICJ]). This dissertation aims to fill this gap and contribute to the field of investment migration from a legal perspective.

0.2 Research Problem

Many countries worldwide, including Member States of the European Union, have legislative schemes that grant a residence permit or citizenship in exchange for an investment from the applicant. The practice originated in the Caribbean and reached the European Union in 2013, with Malta, Cyprus, and Bulgaria granting citizenship to third-country nationals. As

45 Shachar, A.; Hirschl, Ran. On Citizenship, States, and Markets, 2014. Journal of Political Philosophy, Volume 22, 2, Pages 231–57

46 For a full explanation of the Nottebohm case, please refer to chapter three, where the case is analysed in detail.

47 Spiro, P., Nottebohm and Genuine Link: Anatomy of a Jurisprudential Illusion. IMC Working Papers, 2019 (Investment Migration Working Papers)

48 Thwaits, Rayner. The Life and Times of the Genuine link (2018) 49 Victoria University Law Review 645, 657

49 Van den Brick, Martijn, Revising Citizenship within the European Union: Is a Genuine Link Requirement the Way Forward?, 2020, EUI Working Papers 2020/76 Robert Schuman Centre for Advanced Studies, GLOBALCIT

for the practice of residence by investment, more than half of the Member States have investment routes that guarantee applicants a residence permit as an investor, and the right to live and work in the country.

Since 2014, the European Commission, the European Parliament, and the literature on the topic have begun responding to such legislation by criticising the practice and arguing that these practices do not comply with European or international law. The criticism based in European law is that of a violation of the principle of sincere cooperation, which appears in Article 4 of the Treaty on the European Union. As far as international law is concerned, the genuine link theory, which is not a definition of nationality but a suggested requirement of its inter-state recognition from the *Nottebohm* case (1955) at the ICJ, has served as a justification for European institutions to say that investors have no ties to the countries that grant them citizenship. Therefore, since the genuine link theory would apply to European law, a normative battle is ongoing based on the defence that to grant citizenship, a genuine link is required on the part of the applicant and the state that naturalises them. It is very interesting that the European Commission has not filed infringement procedures against all the Member States that offer residence permits by investment, but has done so against Malta, the only case of citizenship by investment still in operation in the European Union. Bulgaria and Cyprus abandoned their schemes after criticism.

One of the main criticisms in Europe is that citizenship granted by a Member State also grants European citizenship, which implies the right to live, work, and have diplomatic defence in all Member States (27 countries of the European Union). On the other hand, naturalisation has always been the competence of the Member States. According to the conferral principle (Articles 4 and 5 Treaty on European Union [TEU]), this is an exclusive competence of Member States. No sentence in the Treaties refers to naturalisation being the competence of the European Union, which is why clues have been sought in the CJEU's decisions about possible interference by European law in matters of naturalisation.

0.3 Research Question

Bearing in mind that competence for naturalisation is of competence of the Member States of the European Union established by the principle of conferral in the European Union Treaties, the question is to what extent residence and citizenship by investment are consistent with the legislation and jurisprudence of European law and international law.

0.4 Methodology

As a scholar in the field of migration who has worked in the academic and professional field of migration law since 2015, encountering the literature on citizenship and residency by investment was a watershed. While inclusive migration policies that grant residence or citizenship have always been well regarded, the topic of investment migration reveals arguments against inclusion. Moreover, while most migrants face a Kafkaesque process of understanding the bureaucratic strings of applying for residency or naturalisation, the field of investment migration presents an easier, faster, and more efficient process: a red carpet for special migrants. I subsequently decision to delve into the following enquiry: what role does law play in this discourse?

I understand legal doctrine as a hermeneutic and explanatory discipline in Mark van Hoecke's typology.[50] I have used a wide range of normative sources in my research, such as the Treaties (TFEU, TEU), general principles of EU law (sincere cooperation), authoritative sources (CJEU and ICJ cases), transcriptions of European Parliament debates, and both legal and social scientific scholarship. In the first chapter, I discuss the descriptive part of the law in Portugal and Malta. I use several sources specific to the respective legal systems: in Portugal, *leis, portarias, despachos,* and meetings of the Parliament *(Reunião Plenária)*; in Malta, the Citizenship Act, reports from the Individual Investor Programme (IPP) regulator, and Legal Notices. Focusing on two cases has helped me to understand the nuances and depths of two schemes in different categories: citizenship by investment and residence by investment.

Against this background, I have focused on two legal systems: those of Portugal and Malta. In the first chapter, I introduce the two models of attraction. In one case, the Portuguese scheme (*ARI – Autorização de Residência por Investimento*) launched in 2012 and is still in force. In the other case, the

---

50 Van Hoecke, Mark. Legal Doctrine: Which Method (s) for what Kind of Discipline? In Methodologies of Legal Research Which Kind of Method for What Kind of Discipline? (2013) Oxford: Hart Publishing, page 11

first and only remaining country to grant citizenship by investment within the European Union is Malta. Regarding Malta, I delimitate my focus to only the IPP and the Citizenship for Exceptional Services Regulations. This delineation is important, as some countries – including Malta and Portugal – have hosted more than one investment migration programme over time, and some have more than one option operating at the same time, which is often overlooked by the literature.[51] Malta already had seven different residence by investment programmes, and Portugal and Malta both offered residence by purchasing real estate in the 1980s.[52] My choice to include two case studies at the very beginning of the dissertation also responds to the wider literature, which highlights that understanding the impact and outcomes of investment migration requires more detailed understanding of how these programmes work in practice, something that attracted little academic interest until 2023.[53]

In the second chapter, I present the responses of the European institutions, along with the literature's discussion regarding institutions' arguments against the schemes: the principle of sincere cooperation; the genuine link theory; the lack of transparency; money laundering; and corruption. The chapter is structured chronologically, focusing on the actions of two institutions: the Commission and the Parliament. I cover the period from 2014 to 2023. Chapter two demonstrates that while naturalisation falls within the competence of Member States, the evolution of jurisprudence on EU citizenship in European law has led to numerous constraints on Member States' nationality practice. Consequently, these constraints have resulted in increased interference by EU law in the citizenship law of Member States.

---

51 Surak, Kristin. Investment Migration: Empirical Developments in the Field and Methodological Issues in Its Study, in Citizenship and Residence Sales Rethinking the Boundaries of Belonging Edited by Dimitry Kochenov and Kristin Surak. Cambridge: Cambridge University Press, 2023, page 30

52 Surak, Kristin, Citizenship and Residence by Investment Schemes – State of Play and Avenues for EU Action, in Meenakshi Fernandes et al., "Avenues for EU action on citizenship and residence by investment schemes" (2022) European Parliamentary Research Service Annex II.

53 Surak, Kristin. Investment Migration: Empirical Developments in the Field and Methodological Issues in Its Study, in Citizenship and Residence Sales Rethinking the Boundaries of Belonging Edited by Dimitry Kochenov and Kristin Surak. Cambridge: Cambridge University Press, 2023, page 26

Having found that these programmes are consistent with the law, regarding the validity, meaning, and scope of domestic rules that conflict with EU law,[54] I began to conduct in-depth research on the *Nottebohm* case, the primary case used by European institutions to argue for a genuine link between the country and the investor. In light of the Portuguese and Maltese cases, chapter three, the final chapter, I present the conclusion that the genuine link is not a requirement, but merely a matter for guidance for Member States in their naturalisation policies. To assume that the *Nottebohm* case should impose a requirement on all Member States regarding their naturalisation law is to misunderstand the case, which mostly concerns diplomatic protection and has less to do with requirements for the acquisition of nationality. Given that citizenship and residency obtained through investment fall under the competence of Member States, and considering that jurisprudence at both the EU and international levels does not strongly advocate for the requirement of a genuine link as a universal standard for naturalisation policies, I then present criticisms of the practice of granting citizenship or residence by an amount of money, as well as possible pathways to accommodate such critiques, and legal arguments on the future of investment migration.

---

54 Van Hoecke, Mark. Legal Doctrine: Which Method (s) for what Kind of Discipline? In Methodologies of Legal Research Which Kind of Method for What Kind of Discipline? (2013) Oxford: Hart Publishing

What is Residence and Citizenship by Investment?

Citizenship by investment and residence by investment schemes allow third-country nationals to obtain residence or citizenship in a host country in exchange for a financial contribution. These schemes are part of a larger array of means of securing residence and citizenship by transferring economic capital, including entrepreneurial and business visas and discretionary economic citizenship.[55] While entrepreneurial programmes require the applicant to manage the business, in the case of residence by investment, economic capital is most important to the application, rather than talent, know-how, or business skills. In Kristin Surak's binary conception,[56] whereas entrepreneurial programmes have an "active" investment in the form of a business presence, residence by investment is a passive investment: a mere bank transfer. Around sixty countries in the world have CBI or RBI policies. Additionally, some countries have begun to grant citizenship by financial contributions in a discretionary manner. In Austria, Comoros, Panama, and Vanuatu, there is no standardised procedure defined for granting citizenship via an extraordinary economic contribution. This is highly criticised by scholars who question why European institutions do not also attack these schemes in the way they oppose citizenship by investment and residence by

55 Section 21 of the German Act on the Residence, Economic Activity and Integration of Foreigners in the Federal Territory would be an example where the migrant invests 250,000 into the country to create a business.

56 Surak, Kristin. Investment Migration: Empirical Developments in the Field and Methodological Issues in Its Study, in Citizenship and Residence Sales Rethinking the Boundaries of Belonging Edited by Dimitry Kochenov and Kristin Surak. Cambridge: Cambridge University Press, 2023, page 30

investment.[57] Citizenship by investment, like RBI and entrepreneurial visas, involves a clear list of application requirements, such as timeframe, cost, investment options, and due diligence. It grants the applicant full membership of a polity, otherwise known as citizenship.

Several Member States have established regimes with the goal of attracting rich individuals by granting them residence in exchange for an investment. The investment varies according to the country, including government bonds, real estate, and bank deposits. For a few thousand euros, the applicant acquires residence rights, which can be converted later into permanent residence and often even into citizenship. The two schemes are included under the umbrella term "investment migration," also known as immigrant investor programmes and economic citizenships programmes.

Although they have only received prominent attention since 2013, schemes to purchase residency or citizenship in exchange for a contribution have existed since ancient Greece.[58] Citizenship was also for sale in pre-modern Europe; the practice preceded the year 1500. Maarten Prak has highlighted, however, that the older and contemporary practices differ heavily. First, in early modern Europe, the numbers were higher and even middle class and sometimes working-class people would buy citizenship. Today, the target is the rich. Second, residence was expected, and new citizens would be required to participate in a range of community activities under the ideology of local republicanism.[59] Nowadays, Portugal requires seven days of residence in the first year and fourteen in subsequent years.

Also, it must be said that residence by investment was not born in Europe, although European practice attracts international attention because it gives mobility rights (for 90 days) to other countries in the European Union. The origins

---

57 Kochenov, D. B., Elena, It's All about Blood, Baby! The European Commission's Ongoing Attack against Investment Migration in the Context of EU Law and International Law. Working Paper no. 161 The Centre on Migration, Policy & Society, 2022

58 Surak, Kristin. Citizenship and Residence by investment schemes – State of play and avenues for EU action. Anex II in Avenues for EU action on citizenship and residence by investment schemes: European added value assessment. Meenakshi Fernandes, Cecilia Navarra, and David de Groot with María García Muñoz, 2021

59 Prak, Maarten. Citizenship for Sale in Pre-modern Europe. In Citizenship and Residence Sales Rethinking the Boundaries of Belonging Edited by Dimitry Kochenov and Krisitn Surak, Cambridge 2023, page 222

of residence by investment lie in the 1980s in Hong Kong, when Hong Kong citizens began to buy citizenship from small Pacific, Caribbean, and Latin American states as a form of security before the return to Chinese rule.[60] Following this demand, the United States and Australia added the possibility of residence permits granted for passive investments to their pre-existing business and entrepreneur visas.[61] Most programmes born in the EU occurred after the 2008 financial crisis, which particularly hit smaller countries, so the idea of attracting money via residence or citizenship was therefore attractive,[62] although affluent countries as well as small countries applied the practice. Justin Lindeboom and Sophie Meunier hypothesise that several Member States conceived of these programmes in the wake of the financial crisis as an additional incentive to attract foreign capital into their ailing economies.[63]

Data from the Investment Migration Council reveals that over 93 % of investment migration programmes are located in so-called rich nations, with high-income countries accounting for 63 % and upper-middle-income countries accounting for 30 %. Chinese nationals "account for approximately 80 % of applicants to any residence programme in the world. However, the industry has seen an increase in business coming from India, Vietnam, Russia, South Africa, and Nigeria, in addition to the US and the UK."[64]

In 2011, only three Member States had residency or citizenship by investment programmes. In 2023, ten Member States (Cyprus, Estonia, Greece, Spain, Hungary, Italy, Latvia, Luxemburg, Malta, and the Netherlands) offered schemes

60 Surak, Kristin. Investment Migration: Empirical Developments in the Field and Methodological Issues in Its Study, in Citizenship and Residence Sales Rethinking the Boundaries of Belonging Edited by Dimitry Kochenov and Kristin Surak. Cambridge: Cambridge University Press, 2023, page 34

61 Surak, Kristin. Investment Migration: Empirical Developments in the Field and Methodological Issues in Its Study, in Citizenship and Residence Sales Rethinking the Boundaries of Belonging Edited by Dimitry Kochenov and Kristin Surak. Cambridge: Cambridge University Press, 2023, page 34

62 Parker, O., Commercializing Citizenship in Crisis EU: the Case of Immigrant Investor Programmes. Journal of Common Market Studies, 2016. **55**: p. 332–348.

63 Lindeboom, Justin & Meunier Sophie, In the shadow of the Euro Crisis Foreign Direct Investment and Investment Migration Programmes in the European Union, in Citizenship and Residence Sales Rethinking the Boundaries of Belonging Edited by Dimitry Kochenov and Kristin Surak, 2023, Cambridge, page 448

64 Investment Migration Council, Transitioning to a Regulated Environment Yearbook 2021/2022, 4, Editor. 2021

granting residence permits on the basis of investments. Ireland and Portugal phased out their schemes on 15 and 16 February 2023, respectively. What explains the growth in CBI and RBI schemes in the EU? First, the need for some Member States to create alternative sources of revenue, especially after the 2008 financial crisis. Second, the presence of newly wealthy individuals from emerging economies. Kristin Surak has shown that in 2000,[65] 7 % of ultra-high-net-worth individuals (people with an equivalent of EUR 857,500 to EUR 25.7 million in investable assets) came from emerging economies. This figure had grown to 25 % by 2015. And the trend is for these numbers to increase.

Table 1. Citizenship and Residence by Investment in EU Member States

Source: government websites[66]

[65] Surak K., "What Money Can Buy: Citizenship by Investment on a Global Scale," In Fassin D., ed. Deepening Divides: How Borders and Boundaries Drive Our World Apart. Pluto Press, 2020

[66] Here, Portugal is shown as phased out only because it has phased out most of the programme's investment options, although it still remains after the changes implemented in 2023.

Their prices and requirements are presented in Table 2.

Table 2. Main Programmes of Residence by Investment in the European Union

Country	Law	Investment	Requirement
Bulgaria	Law on Foreigners, Article 24 (19), Article 24 (20)	€ 310,000 in property or company shares, or 127,000 million in poorer regions and jobs for five Bulgarian citizens	Temporary residence (physical presence requirement: 6 months and 1 day)
Cyprus	Regulation 6 (2) of the Aliens and Immigration Regulations	Property purchase of at least € 300,000 and deposit of € 300,00 in a Cypriot bank, and income of at least €300.000 per year	Permanent residence (physical presence requirement: 1 day)
Estonia	Aliens Act, Article 192	Investment of € 65,000	Temporary residence (physical presence requirement: 183 days)
Greece	Law No. 4251 on Immigration and Social Integration Code and other provisions, Article 20	Investment of € 250,000 in property	Temporary residence (physical presence requirement: no formal requirement, but cannot apply for citizenship)
Italy	Provisional budget of the State for 2017 and multi-annual budget for the triennial period 2017–2019 para 152–159	Annual payment of taxes in the amount of € 100,000	Temporary residence physical presence requirement: no formal requirement
Latvia	Immigration Law, Section 23	Invest € 35,000 in a company that pays at least € 40,000 in taxes; or investment of €150,000 in a company that employs at least fifty people; or investment of € 250,00 in property; or € 280,000 of liabilities with a Latvian credit institution; or a € 250,000 deposit in a Latvian bank	Temporary residence (physical presence requirement: 6 consecutive months)

(Continued)

Table 2. (Continued)

Country	Law	Investment	Requirement
Malta	Malta Residence and Visa Programme	Own property valued at € 275,000 in Malta (€ 220,000 in the south of Malta; € 250,00 in Gozo), or rent property at a minimum of € 9600 per annum (€ 8750 in the south of Malta and Gozo)	Temporary residence (physical presence requirement: no formal requirement)
Spain	Law 14/2013, on the assistance to investors and their internationalisation and Act 25/2015 on the Internationalisation of the Spanish Economy	€ 2 million investment in Spanish debt bonds, or €1 million in Spanish banks or companies, or property purchase of at least € 500,000	Temporary residence (physical presence requirement: no required minimum)

Source: Passport Index, J Dzankic, [69]

The crux in these types of residence is that they offer investors the possibility to acquire residence status without going through the normal requirements by which ordinary migrants would have to prove eligibility, regarding language and time of residence, for instance. Residence by investment programmes in the EU differ from other residence permits in two ways: (a) the ultimate purpose is to attract money; (b) investors receive the status without being residents and without fulfilling the requirements that ordinary migrants need to go through.[67] In Portugal, for example, investors only need to be present for seven days during the first year and fourteen days during each subsequent period of two years.[68] If the golden visa is retained for five years, there is the possibility of transforming the temporary residence permit into a permanent residence permit, with the requirement of passing a basic Portuguese language test and six years of lawful residence.[69] This means that holding a

67 Van den Brink, Martijn, Investment Residence and the Concept of Residence in EU Law: Interactions, Tensions, and Opportunities. IMC Working Papers, 2017(Investment Migration Working Papers)

68 Portugal. Applying for Residence in Portugal Article 90-A – Residence Permit for Investment Purposes. 2022; Available from: https://imigrante.sef.pt/en/solicitar/residir/art90-a/.

69 Portugal, Portuguese Nationality Act Law 37/81, of 3 October. 1981

Golden Visa residence permit from Portugal for five years can satisfy the legal requirements for permanent residence in Portugal without actually having to spend five years in the country.

Regarding rights, those who purchase residence by investment in a Member State that is part of the Schengen zone will be able to move freely within the Schengen zone without a visa for 90 days in a 180-day period.[70] As CBI and RBI are not present in European legislation on legal migration, a grey area has been established through the inclusion of these programmes on a continent with a unique union of states.

1.1 Description of the Two Case Studies

This section aims to describe how third-country nationals can acquire either a residence title in the case of an investment in the country (Portugal) or citizenship by investment, that is, the purchase of citizenship by means of a money transfer (Malta).

The two cases are interesting because Portugal has become a real "success," as data shows that from October 2012 to January 2023, 11,628 investment visas were sold,[71] an average of three golden visas per day. In addition to the nearly 12,000 visas, another 18,962 residence permits were issued to family members of the principal investors.[72] It can be said then that in Portugal, 23,628 people received Portuguese residence by investment within this timeframe. The main beneficiaries are nationals from China (5,258), Brazil (1,178), the United States of America (558), Turkey (547), and South Africa (508).[73] These numbers relate only to the 11,628 primary beneficiaries, as more data regarding family members was not revealed by the Portuguese government. Portugal has more applications for golden visas than all other EU countries

[70] Van den Brink, Martijn, Investment Residence and the Concept of Residence in EU Law:
Interactions, Tensions, and Opportunities. IMC Working Papers, 2017(Investment Migration Working Papers)

[71] Autorização de Residência para Investimento, Serviço de Estrangeiros e Fronteiras, in https://www.sef.pt/pt/Documents/JAN_2023_ARI_CUMULATIVO.pdf, Access on 13 February, 2023.

[72] Ibid., 1.

[73] Ibid., 1.

(such as Greece and Spain) with similar schemes in total. Although they are not the same, they do provide a right of residence through some form of investment. The Maltese case proves illustrative because it is the only example that hasn't been repealed since the European Commission's criticism. The Commission attacked the schemes by saying that they promote corruption and money laundering, violate the principle of sincere cooperation, and fail to comply with the principle of a genuine link,[74] a principle originating from the International Court of Justice through the *Nottebohm* case. Previously, Bulgaria and Cyprus also had citizenship by investment schemes but closed their programmes in 2020 (Cyprus) and 2022 (Bulgaria) after requests from the European Commission and because of corruption scandals reported by the media.

Another connection between the two case studies is the fact that both countries see themselves as countries of emigration; although numbers of immigrants have risen over recent decades, the policy remains protectionist.[75] This is a common phenomenon in southern Europe, where countries have changed from being countries of emigration to countries of immigration, but the changes are not reflected in policy.[76]

Residence by investment (Portugal) and citizenship by investment (Malta) are comparable because both legal statuses (residence and citizenship) are granted based on the applicant's ability to pay a large amount of money. The amount invested is important because it is the main link between the investor and the country that is offering residency or citizenship. However, there are several differences between residence by investment in an EU Member State and the sale of passports. Whereas in citizenship by investment, the naturalisation process is faster and lacks

---

74 The principle of the genuine link corresponds to the idea that states were not required to recognise the grant of nationality made by another state where the individual did not enjoy a genuine link with the conferring state. Nottebohm Case (Liechtenstein vs Guatemala) 1955, International Court of Justice

75 By protectionist I mean action and legislation of a government to reduce immigration with the argument of protecting national jobs.

76 Russell King, Anthony Fielding & Richard Black, "The international migration turnaround in Southern Europe," in Southern Europe and the New Immigrations, eds. R. King & R. Black, Sussex Academic Press, Brighton, 2007, pp. 1–25

many requirements besides the investment, in residence by investment, there is a pathway to investor citizenship, but this depends on proving other requirements. These requirements vary from country to country. Some require physical presence, and this period can be from one day (Latvia) to seven days in the first year (Portugal), to half the period of the residence permit (the United States). Another important difference is the fact that residence rights are confined to the Member State where the person has the residence permit.

The permit entitles its holder to travel freely across other countries in the Schengen area for no more than 90 days in a 180-day period. For example, a person holding Portuguese citizenship receives the rights of EU citizenship, including free movement (the right to relocate to another EU country), consular protection, and electoral rights. On the other hand, a holder of a permanent residence permit (*AR permanente*) receives residence and employment rights in Portugal only, with the possibility of limited free travel (max. 90 days) in the rest of the EU. Second, in order to naturalise, the holder of an investor residence permit must maintain their resident status for several years. Furthermore, an investor does also not automatically acquire the rights of the status of long-term resident. Third-country nationals must have legally resided for a continuous period of five years in one of the Member States to which the Directive is applied in order to be entitled to long-term residence status and they must also fulfil the Directive's other requirements: they must have stable and regular resources, health insurance, and not pose a threat to public policy or security.[77]

To better understand this, the forthcoming pages are dedicated to explaining how these schemes work in detail. The Portuguese scheme is introduced first.

1.2 The case of Portugal (Residence by Investment)

While walking the streets of Chiado, a busy downtown neighbourhood of Lisbon, visitors from all over the world come cross a real estate agency

---

77 Articles 4–6 of Directive 2003/109/EC concerning the status of third-country nationals who are long-term residents [2004]

advertising Portuguese residence permits with a picture of the Portuguese passport. What is interesting is the "non-habitual residents" definition that the company uses, which already gives the impression that these investors are non-habitual residents. Indeed, the Portuguese residence permit by investment requests that the applicant stay only seven days for the first year on Portuguese soil. But what are the other requirements, and how does the procedure work in practice? This chapter describes precisely how the Portuguese golden visa works in practice.

While the European Union has only experienced three Member States with citizenship by investment programmes (Malta, Cyprus, and Bulgaria), offering residence visas by investment is a much more widely used practice across the Union.[78] There are a total of twenty-four investor residence programmes across twenty-three Member States[79]. This group can be divided into countries that have stipulated their investment rules directly in immigration and nationality law, and countries that have stipulated the rules beyond foreign entry laws. Austria, Bulgaria, Croatia, Cyprus, the Czech Republic, Estonia, France, Germany, Greece, Hungary, Ireland,[80] Latvia, Lithuania, Malta, the Netherlands, Portugal,[81] Romania, and Spain are part of the first group. Belgium, Italy, Poland, Slovakia, and Slovenia have programmes but the laws which govern them are not part of the laws regulating entry and stay of aliens. Table 2.3 provides an overview of all residence by investment programmes in the European Union.

---

78 Christians, Allison, Buying in: Residence and Citizenship by Investment, 2017, 62 Saint Louis University Law Journal 51.

79 Note that this does not include countries with discretionary naturalisation on grounds of national interest. Austria would be an example with Article 11(4) and 10(6) of the Naturalisation Act, where naturalisation is granted in the interest of the country in the fields of science, commerce, the arts or sport.

80 In February 2023, Ireland also axed its golden visa scheme – the Immigrant Investor Programme – which offered Irish residence in return for a €500,000 donation or three-year annual €1 million investment in the country.

81 The Portuguese programme was suspended in February 2023 and returned afterwards with stricter options of investment.

Table 3. Residence by Investment in the EU

Country	Law	Investment	Status obligation
Austria	Niederlassungs- und Aufenthaltsgesetz – NAG, § 44	Minimum of EUR 40,000	Temporary residence
Belgium	"Professional Card" programme	Not specified	Temporary residence (not specified)
Bulgaria	Law on Foreigners, Article 24 (19), Article 24 (20)	€ 310,000 in property or company shares, or € 127,000 million in poorer regions and jobs for five Bulgarian citizens	Temporary residence (physical presence requirement: 6 months and 1 day)
Croatia	Aliens Act, Articles 76–78	Owning a trade company (min. value € 13,200) or investing €26,400; employing three Croatian citizens in both cases	Temporary residence (physical presence requirement: over 6 months)
Cyprus	Regulation 6 (2) of the Aliens and Immigration Regulations	Property purchase of at least € 300,000 and deposit of € 300,000 in a Cypriot bank, and income of at least € 300,000 per year	Permanent residence (physical presence requirement: 1 day)
Czech Republic	Act on the Residence of Foreign Nationals, section 31	Establishment of a limited company with minimum capital of € 7300 and possess fifty times the minimum monthly subsistence	Temporary residence (physical presence requirement: 6 months and 1 day)
Estonia	Aliens Act, Article 192	Investment of € 65,000	Temporary residence (physical presence requirement: 183 days)
France	Decree 2009-114 of 11 September 2009	€ 10 million and fifty jobs in France	Temporary Residence (physical presence requirement: over 6 months)

(Continued)

Table 3. (Continued)

Country	Law	Investment	Status obligation
Germany	Section 21 of the Act on the Residence, Economic Activity and Integration of Foreigners in the Federal Territory of Germany	Amount not specified: economic interest of the state, regional need, positive effects on the economy	Temporary residence (physical presence requirement: over 6 months)
Greece	Law No. 4251 on Immigration and Social Integration Code and other provisions, Article 20	Investment of € 250,000 in property	Temporary residence (physical presence requirement: no formal requirement, but cannot apply for citizenship)
Hungary	The Hungarian investment Immigration Programme	Investment of € 300,000 in five-year securities or treasury bonds	Permanent after 6 months (physical presence requirement: 180 days, notification of absences of over 6 months)
Italy	Provisional budget of the State for 2017 and multi-annual budget for the triennial period 2017–2019, para 152–159	Annual payment of taxes in the amount of € 100,000	Temporary residence (physical presence requirement: no formal requirement)
Latvia	Immigration Law, Section 23	Invest € 35,000 in a company that pays at least € 40,000 in taxes; or investment of € 150,000 in a company that employs at least fifty people; or investment of € 250,000 in property; or € 280,000 of liabilities with a Latvian credit institution; or a € 250,000 deposit in a Latvian credit institution; or a € 250,000 deposit in a Latvian bank	Temporary residence (physical presence requirement: 6 consecutive months)

Country	Law	Investment	Status obligation
Lithuania	Law on the Legal Status of Aliens, Article 45	Register a company whose capital is at least € 28,000 and own at least € 14,000 of capital	Temporary residence (physical presence requirement: over 6 months)
Malta	Malta Residence and Visa Programme	Own property valued at € 275,000 in Malta (€ 220,000 in the south of Malta; € 250,000 in Gozo), or rent property at a minimum of € 9600 per annum (€ 8750 in the south of Malta and Gozo)	Temporary residence (physical presence requirement: no formal requirement)
Netherlands	Decree of September 23, 2013 establishing the entry into force of the Modern Migration Act	Invest € 1,25 million in a company located in the Netherlands	Temporary residence (physical presence requirement: over 6 months)
Poland	Poland Aliens Act, Article 53	Amount not specified: economic activity beneficial to Poland	Temporary residence (physical presence requirement: over 6 months)
Portugal	Law 29/12 of 08/09/2012	Creation of ten jobs, or transfer of 250,000 euros to artistic/ cultural activities or 500,000 euros to non-real estate collective investment organisations or incorporation of a commercial company with headquarters in Portugal	Temporary residence (physical presence requirement: 7 days in the first year and 14 days in the subsequent years)
Romania	Emergency Ordinance No. 194 from 12 December 2002, Article 43	Invest € 70,000 in a limited company, or € 100,000 in a stock company, or create ten jobs in a limited company or fifteen jobs in a stock company	Temporary residence (physical presence requirement: over 6 months)

(Continued)

Table 3. (Continued)

Country	Law	Investment	Status obligation
Slovakia	Act No. 414/2011 on Residence of Aliens and Amendment and Supplementation of Certain Act, Article 22	Amount no specified: permits for investors and businesspeople, on a case-by-case basis	Temporary residence (physical presence requirement: over 6 months)
Slovenia	Slovenia Aliens Act, Article 20, Article 51	Amount not specified: permits for investors and businesspeople, in the interest of the state	Temporary residence (physical presence requirement: over 6 months)
Spain	Law 14/2013, on the assistance to investors and their internationalisation and Act 25/2015 on the Internationalisation of the Spanish Economy	€ 2 million investment in Spanish debt bonds, or € 1 million in Spanish banks or companies, or property purchase of at least € 500,000	Temporary residence (physical presence requirement: no required minimum)

Source: Derived from Dzankic[82] (2019) with updates based on national legislation until September 2024

The scheme in Portugal has undergone several changes over the 10 years in which it has applied. The legislation that has enabled the *Autorização de Residência por Investimento* (ARI-golden visa) is located in different legal categories in Portugal (e.g. *Lei, Despachos, Propostas de Lei*) and understanding the Portuguese legal system is part of understanding the enactment of the golden visas and how they actually work in terms of requirements and procedure.

1.2.1 The Context of the Drafting of the Law That Created the Portuguese Golden Visa

The Portuguese golden visa was created during a turbulent economy time. In 2008, the United States of America was hit by a financial crisis that also arrived in Europe and led to a crisis in 2010–2011. In response, Portugal applied austerity policies.[83] Alongside reductions in public expenditure,

82 Džankić, Jelena. Dzankic, Jelena, The Global Market for Investor Citizenship. 1 ed. Politics of Citizenship and Migration. 2019: Palgrave Macmillan, page 200–203.

83 Blyth, M. (2013) Austerity: the History of a Dangerous Idea. Oxford University Press, New York

foreign investment becomes an important resource. One cannot understand the Portuguese golden visa without the context of the financial crisis amid which it was created.

As a law proposed by the government on 22 March 2012, it was sent to the Committee on Constitutional Affairs, Rights, Freedoms and Guarantees, the competent committee. Importantly, the proposal was not only about the golden visas, but also implementation of EU Directives on immigration.[84] This changed Law No. 23/2007, which concerns the legal regime for the entry, stay, exit, and expulsion of foreigners from national territory. In the Committee report, the golden visas were only a proposal for a one-off change. This would provide the possibility to create a mechanism allowing third-country nationals to invest in Portugal under certain conditions, in exchange for a residence permit.[85] The report mentioned that the goal of the legal change was the "objectives of stimulating economic diplomacy pursued by the Government."[86]

One of three forms of investment that could ensure a residence permit for five years was the acquisition of real estate worth at least EUR 750,000.00,

---

84 Among the implementation of Directives were part of the proposal: a) rules and procedures to be applied by Member States for the return of third-country nationals who are illegally present on national territory (Directive 2008/115/EC of the European Parliament and of the Council of 16 December 2008, "Return Directive"), which, while respecting fundamental rights, should harmonise the rules that already exist in this area. b) conditions of entry and residence of third-country nationals for the purposes of highly qualified employment (Council Directive 2009/50/EC of 25 May, 2009, the "Highly Qualified Employment Directive") and the enshrinement of the legal requirements under the system for granting the "EU Blue Card." This is a specific title that creates a special entry and residence system for highly qualified third-country nationals. c) amendments are based on the criminalisation of the illegal employment of foreign nationals (Directive 2009/52/EC of the European Parliament and of the Council of 18 June 2009, the "Sanctions Directive"). d) application of the long-term resident status of third-country nationals enjoying international protection (Directive 2011/51/EU of the European Parliament and of the Council of 11 May 2011 amending Council Directive 2003/109/EC), as defined in Council Directive 2004/83/EC of 29 April, transposed into national law by Law No. 27/2008 of 30 June. In Assembleia da República, Comissão de Assuntos Constitucionais, Direitos, Liberdades e Garantias. Parecer da Proposta de Lei n. 50/XXI/1 (Gov), 2012.

85 Assembleia da República, Comissão de Assuntos Constitucionais, Direitos, Liberdades e Garantias. Parecer da Proposta de Lei n. 50/XXI/1 (Gov), 2012.

86 Presidência do Conselho de Ministros de Portugal, Proposta de Lei 50/XII, 2012

which was reduced upon the law's adoption to EUR 500,000.00.[87] The other two proposals that could secure a residence permit were the transfer of capital equal to or greater than EUR 1 million, and the creation of at least thirty jobs.[88] During the *trauvax préparatoires* of the law that implemented the residence by investment, the *Alto Comissariado para a Imigração e Diálogo Intercultural* (High Commissariat for Immigration and Intercultural Dialogue) stated that the new law's innovations in creating new residence permits should be welcomed, because they would allow "foreign investment in order to attract investment, fighting, namely, the serious unemployment of national citizens and immigrants, given that one of the requirements is the creation of more than thirty jobs in national territory, without prejudice to the concern that there must be strict control of this type of title due to the risks arising from the 'call effect' of criminal networks."[89,90] The importance of very high-level due diligence and care, in order to avoid recruiting people with criminal involvement, was not highlighted in the proposal but was added later by the High Commissioner. The Chinese League in Portugal also made several suggestions in a letter sent on 25 May 2012, such as that the investment amount of EUR 750,000.00 was too high and that the length of stay in Portugal was inadequate for the business activity of Chinese entrepreneurs.[91]

The proposed amendment to Law No. 50 was then sent to Parliament, which approved and enacted it on 25 July 2012. Thus Law No. 29/2012 entered into force on 8 September 2012. Article 3, paragraph d of the law defined "investment activity" as any activity carried out personally or through a company,[92] which, as a rule, leads to the achievement of at least one of the following situations in the national territory and for a minimum period of five years: (a) Transfer of capital equal or superior to EUR 1 million;

---

87 Presidência do Conselho de Ministros, Proposta de Lei n. 50/XII.

88 Presidência do Conselho de Ministros, Proposta de Lei n. 50/XII, page 8, Article 3, d

89 "No tocante à Autorização de Residência para Atividade de Investimento," importa chamar a atenção para a necessidade de um controlo rigoroso na concessão deste tipo de títulos por força dos riscos decorrentes do "efeito chamada" de redes criminosas"

90 Alto Comissariado para a Imigração e Diálogo Intercultural, Ofício n. 605 – Audição do Conselho Consultivo para os assuntos da Imigração (COCAI), 10 April 2012.

91 Liga dos Chineses em Portugal, Contributo à Proposta de Lei n. 50/XII, 25 May, 2012

92 Artigo 3-*d*) "Atividade de investimento" qualquer atividade exercida pessoalmente ou através de uma sociedade que conduza, em regra, à concretização de, pelo menos, uma das seguintes situações em território nacional e por um período mínimo de cinco

(b) Creation of at least thirty jobs; (c) Acquisition of real estate worth EUR 500,000 or more.[93] The conditions for the application of the special regime – the minimum investment, the minimum period of stay, and the means of proof – were defined by an order (*Despacho*) from the government members responsible for foreign affairs and internal administration.

The order (*Despacho*) has a procedural focus on how the investment visa should be processed. For example, Article 4 establishes the minimum time requirement for investment activity as follows: "The minimum time requirement of five years for the maintenance of investment activities is counted from the date of the granting of the residence permit."[94] Also, a minimum residence time requirement was also implemented in Article 5: "For the purposes of renewing a residence permit, the applicants referred to in Article 2 must demonstrate that they have complied with the following minimum periods of stay in national territory: (a) 30 days in the first year (b) 60 days in the following and subsequent two-year periods."[95] Later on, Article 6 states that the proof of permanence within national territory is achieved through presentation of a valid passport.[96]

To prove the requirements of Article 3(1)(a), applicants had to present (a) a statement from a financial institution authorised to carry out its activity within the national territory, attesting that it is the sole or first holder of the capital; or (b) an updated certificate from the commercial registry proving that the applicant holds shares in a company. In order to prove the requirements of Article 3(1)(b) – creation of jobs – the applicant had to present updated social security certificates from the new employees. Lastly, to prove

---

anos: *i*) Transferência de capitais no montante igual ou superior a 1 milhão de euros; *ii*) Criação de, pelo menos, 30 postos de trabalho; Law No. 29/2012 of 09/08/2012. iii) Aquisição de bens imóveis de valor igual ou superior a 500 mil euros.

93 Law No. 29/2012, which changed Law No. 23/2007 (conditions and procedures for the entry, stay, exit and removal of foreign citizens from Portuguese territory)

94 Gabinetes dos Ministros de Estado e dos Negócios Estrangeiros e da Administração Interna. Despacho n. 11820-A/2012, 03/09/2012.

95 Gabinetes dos Ministros de Estado e dos Negócios Estrangeiros e da Administração Interna. Despacho n. 11820-A/2012, 03/09/2012

96 Gabinetes dos Ministros de Estado e dos Negócios Estrangeiros e da Administração Interna. Despacho n. 11820-A/2012, 03/09/2012

the requirements of Article 3(1)(c) – purchase of property – applicants had to present an updated certificate from the land registry office.[97]

The 2012 order also determined to set up a monitoring group that would implement the provisions set out in the order. This monitoring group, comprised of the director-general of Consular Affairs and the Portuguese Communities, the national director of the Foreigners and Borders Service (SEF), and the president of the Portuguese Agency for Investment and Foreign Trade, worked towards introducing improvements and adaptations to the special regime of residence permits for investment – for example, through visa exemptions within national territory. This aimed to improve the regime's competitiveness.

The next year, a new Order was published. The new order (*Despacho n. 1661-A/2013*) implemented two important changes. The first was to reduce the number of jobs that investment had to promote. Whereas in the initial order it was 30, the new order reduced this to ten positions. In addition, the requirement to remain within Portuguese territory was also reduced. Having been 30 days in the first year and 60 days for following years, the new order reduced this to a mere 7 days in the first year and 14 days in following years.[98] This is a total of 63 days over five years. Apparently, reducing both the time of effective residence within Portuguese territory and the number of jobs created by investment activity would make the Portuguese investment visa more competitive in relation to over 20 other national investment visas in force in the European Union in 2013.

The next changes would occur two years later, in 2015, after corruption scandals involving the golden visas were published in November 2014.[99] The Portuguese Public Prosecutor (*Ministério Público*) had indicted seventeen people and four companies – including the director of the SEF (Foreigners and Borders Service), on charges of passive corruption, influence peddling,

---

97 Gabinetes dos Ministros de Estado e dos Negócios Estrangeiros e da Administração Interna. Despacho n. 11820-A/2012, 03/09/2012.

98 Gabinetes dos Ministros de Estado e dos Negócios Estrangeiros e da Administração Interna, Despacho n. 1661-A/2013

99 Observador. Vistos Gold: 11 detidos por suspeitas de corrupção. Available in: https://observador.pt/2014/11/13/diretor-nacional-sef-detido-por-suspeitas-de-corrupcao-na-atribuicao-dos-vistos-gold/ Access on: 27 March, 2023

money laundering, in – among other things – the allocation of golden visas.[100] In order to include alternative investments besides real estate purchases, to curtail the possibility of corruption, on 19 February 2015 the government approved changes to expand the scheme. The change was made through Law No. 63/2015, on 30 June. The new model extended the scope of golden visas to other types of investments besides real estate: urban rehabilitation, science, innovation, technology, and even cultural investment.

The next section explains the eight modalities of investment that were possible when a third-country national wanted to be granted an ARI *(autorização de residencia por investimento)*, meaning temporary residence in Portugal granted through investment.

1.2.2 The Options of Investment

As introduced earlier, on 8 October 2012 Portugal adopted the so-called "Residence Permit for Investment Activity" (ARI), a legislative innovation that enabled third-country nationals to receive a temporary residence permit to reside in Portugal as long as an investment was made in the country. This investment could be the purchase of real estate worth a minimum of EUR 500,000, capital transfers superior to EUR 1 million, or the creation of at least ten jobs. Besides these three options, five other modalities were listed in the law and will be presented below. For illustration, small fictional cases are presented to simulate the procedure.

The favoured way of acquiring a residence permit was through real estate property purchases; this corresponded to 10,668 of 11,628 residence permits and resulted in over EUR 6 billion in investment.[101] Using the hypothetical example of a Chinese national, who could contact a Portuguese real estate agency directly from China and would need to acquire a property for a minimum of EUR 500,000. After making the purchase, they would receive a residence permit enabling visa-free travel to Portugal. Among the benefits, they could live and work legally in Portugal, acquire permanent residency after five years, and the possibility of obtaining Portuguese citizenship after

---

100 Nota para Comunicação Social: Vistos Gold – Acusação. Available in: https://www.ministeriopublico.pt/sites/default/files/documentos/pdf/nota_comunicao_social_vistos_gold-acusacao.pdf Access on: 27 March, 2023

101 Ibid. 1

five years. Their family would also be able to come as the residence permit was extended to dependent family members. In theory, the process seems like a fast-track to citizenship, but the scheme also encountered real administrative problems. After issue, the residence permit was supposed to be renewed every two years. In October 2022, the Immigration Authority of Portugal had a backlog of 19,000 renewal requests, amounting to 60 % of all the golden visas.[102] This meant that many investors had expired residence permits, making travel abroad impossible.

The second most popular way to acquire residence through investment was also property purchase. Besides property purchases on constructions completed at least 30 years previously or located in urban rehabilitation areas, investors were supposed to execute rehabilitation works on the acquired real estate for an overall amount equal to or greater than EUR 350,000. The main difference between the first and second models is that the first did not obligate the investor to conduct restoration work, nor did it specify the age of the property. This second model focused on restoring old properties: it issued a total of 1,516 residence permits with an overall investment of EUR 545,279,076.42 between October 2012 and January 2023.[103] As for all investors in Portugal, there was a minimum residence requirement. In the hypothetical case of a Brazilian with four other family members, they would be required to live in Portugal for seven days in their first year and another fourteen days in consecutive years. While physical presence was one of the duties, the investment visa offered many benefits to its holder, such as living and working in Portugal, free movement in the Schengen area for 90 days in a 180-day period, and after five years of legal residence, the possibility of acquiring Portuguese citizenship through naturalisation.

The other six options of investment were less relevant numerically. They demonstrate that the creation of jobs via investment or scientific research was not as attractive as real estate property. An overview of the types of investment follows here:

(a) The transfer of capital in the amount equal or superior to EUR 1.5 million;

---

102 Eco. Mais de 60 % dos "vistos gold" estão caducados, 2023. Available in: https://eco.sapo.pt/2022/10/13/mais-de-60-dos-vistos-gold-estao-caducados/ Access on: February 2023

103 Ibidem 1

(b) The creation of at least ten jobs;
(c) The acquisition of real estate worth EUR 500,000 or more;
(d) The acquisition of real estate, the construction of which concluded at least 30 years previously or located in urban rehabilitation areas, and the execution of rehabilitation works on the acquired real estate, in an overall amount equal to or greater than EUR 350,000;
(e) Capital transfers in the amount equal to or greater than EUR 500,000, applied in research activities developed by public or private scientific research institutions, integrated within the national scientific and technological system;
(f) Capital transfers in an amount equal to or greater than EUR 250,000, to be applied in investment or support for artistic production, recovery or maintenance of national cultural heritage, through central and peripheral direct administration services, public institutes, entities that are part of the public business sector, public foundations, private foundations with public utility status, intermunicipal entities, entities that are part of the local business sector, municipal associative entities and public cultural associations, which carry out attributions in the area of artistic production, recovery or maintenance of national cultural heritage;
(g) Capital transfers in the amount equal to or greater than EUR 500,000, aimed at the acquisition of investment units in investment funds or venture capital funds aimed at the capitalisation of companies established under Portuguese legislation, whose maturity, at the time of investment, is at least five years; at least 60 % of the value of the investment is made in commercial companies based within national territory;
(h) Capital transfers in an amount equal to or higher than EUR 500,000, aimed at the incorporation of a commercial company with a head office in the national territory, in conjunction with the creation of five permanent jobs, or an increase in the share capital of a commercial company with a head office in the national territory, already existing, with the creation or maintenance of jobs, with a minimum of five permanent jobs, and for a minimum period of three years.[104]

Data released by the *Serviço de Estrangeiros e Fronteiras* shows that some options had one or only seven investors between October 2012 and January 2023:

---

104 ARI – Autorização de Residência para Atividade de Investmento, Serviço de Estrangeiros e Fronteiras. Available in: https://www.sef.pt/pt/pages/conteudo-detalhe.aspx?nID=62, Access on: 13 February, 2023.

Table 4. Investment Options for Portuguese Golden Visa

Subparagraph and investment	Number of ARIs (golden visas) issued
Subparagraph 1 – transfer of capital	535
Subparagraph 2 – creation of job positions	22
Subparagraph 3 – purchase of property	9,152
Subparagraph 4 – purchase of property	1,516
Subparagraph 5 – research activities	1
Subparagraph 6 – artistic production	6
Subparagraph 7 – commercial companies	389
Subparagraph 8 – commercial company + jobs	7

Source: Serviço de Estrangeiros e Fronteiras, 2023[105]

The number of golden visas steadily increased after the programme was launched. However, in 2015, numbers dropped significantly due to corruption cases reported in the media.[106] After that, numbers continued to rise. The applicants represent another important feature: they may have become Portuguese. All applicants who completed five years of legal residence in Portugal, could legally apply for Portuguese citizenship as long as they met the other requirements. For example, applicants from 2013 or 2015 have already completed five years. However, data on how many investors have become Portuguese citizens is not available. The next section explains the legal path and requirements in Portuguese naturalisation law.

1.2.3 The Way to Citizenship: Naturalisation When in Possession of a Golden Visa

Is acquiring Portuguese citizenship through a golden visa really so simple? First and foremost, it is essential to comprehend the standard procedure for obtaining citizenship in Portugal. Since the seventeenth century, Portugal's favoured tradition for granting citizenship has been via the principle of *ius soli*,

---

105 Ibidem 1

106 In 2014, 11 people were arrested under the Labyrinth Operation (Operação Labirinto), including employees of state on suspicion of corruption, influence peddling, and money laundering in the granting of ARIs (golden visas). The scandals made the Minister of Internal Affairs Miguel Macedo renounce and the suspension of the scheme until March 2015.

meaning that people born on Portuguese territory were automatically granted Portuguese nationality. This changed in 1981 with the Nationality Act, in the context of large numbers of Portuguese emigrants[107] and the passage of new legislation that gave preference to the *ius sanguinis* principle, meaning that nationality was granted on the basis of Portuguese ancestry. The 1981 Act was amended in 2006, created new ways to acquire citizenship through *ius soli* but meanwhile reinforcing the *ius sanguinis* principle. Lastly, the Organic Law No. 2/2018 improved the inclusion of immigrants of second and third generations. For example, the required time for parents' legal residence in Portugal was reduced from five to two years, so that individuals born in Portuguese territory with foreigner parents who do not declare that they want Portuguese citizenship, may be Portuguese by origin, provided that at birth, one parent had resided in Portugal for at least two years.[108] The legislation sought to give primacy to the principle of the will of the interested parties and to reduce bureaucracy in the respective processes. Finally, the possibility of having two or more nationalities has been available in Portugal since 1981.[109]

The two main principles governing acquisition of Portuguese nationality are *ius sanguinis* and *ius soli*, although preference is given to *ius soli*. Descendants of Portuguese people who are not in Portuguese territory at birth are required to declare their wish to be Portuguese or to have their birth registered in the Portuguese registry. By contrast, the *ius soli* principle is not automatic. Besides being born in Portuguese territory, the applicant in case of foreign parents, must have one parent who is a resident in Portugal for at least five years prior to the application.[110] Persons not Portuguese by birth can become Portuguese by naturalisation. For naturalisation to occur, two prerequisites must be satisfied: an expression of intent made by the applicant to the Ministry of Justice (Article 7(1) of the Nationality Act) and legal requirements must be satisfied. These are presented in Article 6 (requirements) of the Portuguese Nationality Act: (a) be of age or emancipated under Portuguese Law; (b) have resided lawfully in Portuguese territory for a minimum of

---

107 Gil, Ana Rita. Princípios de Direito da Nacionalidade. O Direito, 142 (2010)

108 Lei Orgânica n. 2/2018

109 Gil, Ana Rita; Piçarra, Nuno. Report on Citizenship Law Portugal. February 2020, European University Institute (GLOBALCIT)

110 Portuguese Nationality Act, Article 6, paragraph 2, a.

six years; (c) have sufficient knowledge of the Portuguese language;[111] (d) have not been convicted of a crime punishable under Portuguese Law with imprisonment of three years or more.[112] Interestingly, the wording "have resided lawfully," according to Article 15 of the Nationality Act, means that "for the purpose of the preceding articles, legal residents in Portuguese territory are persons who live in the country, with their situations regularised before Portuguese authorities, under any of the titles, visas or permits prescribed by the immigration and asylum regimes."[113] As the investor residence permit is part of the "immigration regime," as per Article 90-A of the Foreigners Act, the requirements for legal residence for investors would comply with the words "have resided lawfully." As an investor, one would meet requirement "b" by living in the country for 37 days instead of six years, because an investor is required by law to reside for seven days in the first year and 14 days in subsequent years (7+14+14+14+14=37 days). This would mean that taking an annual two-week vacation in Portugal would comply with the requirement, while benefiting from free movement in the Schengen zone.

Regarding requirement "c," having sufficient knowledge of the Portuguese language, the requirement is necessary for investors as they submit to general rules on naturalisation. As Brazilians are the second largest group of investors in Portuguese golden visas, this requirement also applies to them, even though Portuguese is their mother tongue. All other nationals from China, Russia, South Africa, and Turkey would need to prove knowledge of the Portuguese language at the A2 level of the Common European Framework for Languages. Requirement "d" highlights the importance of a proper background check on investors. One needs to highlight here that until 2006, besides the four requirements of Article 6 of the Nationality Act, naturalisation through length of residence still required a connection with the Portuguese community, the effectiveness of which was evaluated at the administration's discretion. Today, in contrast, the law considers that residence and knowledge of

---

111 Required knowledge of the Portuguese language means the minimal skills indispensable for interacting with the Portuguese community. It corresponds to the A2 level of the Common European Framework of Reference for Languages.

112 Portuguese Nationality Act, Article 6, paragraph 1

113 Portuguese Nationality Act, Article 15

the Portuguese language are sufficient indicators of an effective connection with the national community.[114]

1.2.4 The National Debate on the Golden Visas

The scheme received several critiques within Portugal. One of the main opponents of the golden visas is Transparency International Portugal. In 2017, for instance, the NGO launched the brochure "golden visas: Investment or money laundering," which exposed the risks of the scheme, such as corruption and money laundering. In 2018, they asked for information from the Ministry of Internal Administration (*Ministério da Administração Interna*) in order to publicise the countries of origin of applicants for golden visas and the number of visas rejected, among other things. As Transparency Portugal received no answer, they complained to the Commission for Access to Administrative Documents and the Administrative Court of the Lisbon Circuit (*Comissão de Acesso a Documentos Administrativos e ao Tribunal Administrativo do Círculo de Lisboa*). Only at the end of 2019 (11 December) did the Ministry of Internal Administration, through the Aliens and Borders Service, send the data.

In addition to calling for the termination of the golden visas programme, Transparency International Portugal delineated eleven criteria that should be considered in the event of the programme's continuation:

(a) preparation of a cost-benefit assessment report, targeting not only the economic aspect, but also the risks of money laundering and financing terrorism;
(b) assessment of risks and vulnerabilities and creation of a mitigation plan;
(c) elaboration of a manual of procedures for the attribution of golden visas;
(d) creation of a mechanism for independent oversight and monitoring of the process of granting golden visas, with the participation of civil society, producing periodic reports, available publicly and free of charge;
(e) involvement and accountability of agents who act as intermediaries (lawyers or consultants hired to advise on obtaining visas, among other things), as well as of the economic agents benefited (such as financial institutions or real estate agents), who should observe strict due diligence standards and verification requirements regarding investors;

114 Ibidem 17

(f) granting money laundering prevention obligations to the *Serviço de Estrangeiros e Fronteiras* (SEF)[115] for better control of applicants and invested funds;
(g) strengthening the information collected and making information publicly available on applicants and beneficiaries of golden visas (already granted and to be granted), especially those who are politicians in their home countries: Politically Exposed Persons (PEP);
(h) applicants must indicate on their application if they have PEP status and should be subject to penalties for the crime of misrepresentation if they fail to do so;
(i) the state must maintain a public and freely accessible list of PEPs who have been granted a golden visa, which must indicate the criteria by which it was granted;
(j) making available all information about the mechanism, namely the entire audit report of the Inspectorate General of the Internal Administration on the procedure for granting residence permits for investment activity of the Foreigners and Borders Service;
(k) tighter criteria for granting visas and family reunification;
(l) registration of companies through which real estate is purchased in order to obtain a visa, similarly to what is done with companies that create jobs;
(m) independent evaluations of real estate acquired for the purpose of granting golden visas, involving the Institute of Registration and Notary Affairs and the Tax and Customs Authority, in order to detect and punish fraudulent overvaluations of real estate for the purpose of facilitating the granting of visas.[116]

Requirement "g" would be an important mechanism, because more than 50 % of people who have received golden visas in Portugal since 2012 are from the world's top thirty money laundering jurisdictions, according to analysis by Investigate Europe.[117] Given the high incidence of corruption in the investors' home countries, checking the origin of the funds used to purchase the golden

115 Portuguese Foreigners and Borders Service
116 International, Transparency. Vistos Gold: Investimento ou Branqueamento? 2018: Available in: https://transparencia.pt/vistos-gold/, Access on: 13 February, 2023
117 Europe, Investigate. Augusto, Dieogo; Bersi, Eurydice; Pena, Paulo. Golden Visas: Europe for Sale?, Investigate Europe, 2023. Available in: https://www.investigate-europe.eu/en/2023/golden-visas-europe-for-sale/, Access on: 14 February, 2023.

visas would be justified. Besides that, Transparency International handed out 'Not so Golden Visa Kits' with information about the scheme to political decision-makers (governors and deputies) from public administration and the sectors most involved in the golden visa policies.

Movements against golden visas are not only found in the NGO sphere, but also across the legislative spectrum. A draft bill from the Left Bloc (*Bloco de Esquerda*) aimed to eliminate the Residence Permit for Investment Activity programme in Portugal. The draft bill (*Projeto de Lei N. 920/XXI/3)* highlighted that the programme has been associated with corrupt practices, money laundering, and other fiscal and criminal offences.[118] For the MEP Ana Gomes, the golden visas are "a scheme to import corruption and organised crime into the European Union."[119] The draft bill also expresses frustration with the fact the programme was presented to "create jobs" but in practice became a failure as the main investment focused on the purchase of real estate investment. This would also "contribute to high-intensity real estate speculation and help to create, in this way, structural problems in the way we conceive the organization of cities."[120] Political reflection also pointed out the difference in treatment for investors applying for the golden visa and receiving fast procedures, whereas migrants in Portugal who work in the country, and pay social security contributions and taxes, face a huge bureaucratic ordeal for their regularisation, where uncertainty, waiting, postponements, and bureaucracy are standard.[121]

The discrimination argument reinforces the reflection of the previous paragraph, which was also posed by the Left Bloc *(Bloco de Esquerda)*. While for some migrants "everything is facilitated by the possession of material goods, without even caring about their origin and nature," for the second category of migrants "people who bring with them only their labour power and upon whom the law and administrative practice impose successive obstacles and restrictions to entry and stay in our country."[122] Lastly, the Bloc affirmed, "This distinction of rights and obligations discriminates positively against those

---

118 Esquerda, Bloco, Projeto de Lei N. 920/XIII/3, 2018
119 Esquerda, Bloco, Projeto de Lei N. 920/XIII/3, 2018
120 Esquerda, Bloco, Projeto de Lei N. 920/XIII/3, 2018
121 Esquerda, Bloco, Projeto de Lei N. 920/XIII/3, 2018
122 Esquerda, Bloco, Projeto de Lei N. 920/XIII/3, 2018

who have money and negatively against those who do not. It is not appropriate for a democratic rule of law that effectively respects human rights."[123]

On 17 June 2022, the draft bill was rejected by the votes of PS (*Partido Socialista*), PSD (*Partido Social Democrata*), and *Chega* e *Iniciativa Liberal.* PCB (*Partido Comunista Português*), BE (*Bloco de Esquerda*), PAN (*Pessoas-Animais-Natureza*) and *Livre* voted in favour. The rejected draft bill focused on the difference in the treatment of migrants, the risks involved in golden visas (money laundry, corruption), and the increasing cost of housing due to the large investments made by foreigners in Lisbon and Porto.

In 2023, the same political party, Left Bloc (*Bloco de Esquerda*), presented a new draft law[124] in order to prohibit the sale of houses to citizens with permanent residence abroad. Inspired by Canada, the legislation would combat the rising price of housing in Portugal. The project referred to the 80 % increase in the price of housing between 2010 and 2022, and the legislation would apply to people who hold a residence visa on the basis of Article 3(1)(d) and Article 90-A of Law No. 23/2007 of 4 July 2007, as amended (golden visas). This was a direct attempt to ban the possibility of investors acquiring residence permits based on real estate purchases. The draft bill also excluded the following categories: (a) Portuguese citizens with their own permanent residence outside Portugal; (b) Immigrants who hold a permanent residence permit under the terms of Articles 76 to 80 of Law No. 23/2007 of 4 July 2007, in its current wording; (c) Persons covered by the protection granted by Law No. 27/2008, of 30 June 2008, and Law No.67/2003, of 23 August 2003, both in their current wording; (d) Foreign citizens who acquire real estate, in joint ownership, with their spouse or common-law partner; (e) Real estate transactions in low-density territories.[125] The project was rejected in a vote on 19/05/2023 at Plenary Meeting no. 130. The following parties voted against the project: PS, PSD, CH, IL. Political parties with abstentions: PCP, PAN, L. Only political party that voted in favour: BE.[126]

---

123 Esquerda, Bloco, Projeto de Lei N. 920/XIII/3, 2018

124 Esquerda, Bloco, Projeto de Lei N. 510/XV/1, 2023

125 Esquerda, Bloco, Projeto de Lei N. 510/XV/1, 2023

126 Parliamentary Activities, Portuguese Parliament, 2024, Available on: https://www.parlamento.pt/ActividadeParlamentar/Paginas/DetalheIniciativa.aspx?BID=152344 Access on: 01/11/2024

1.2.5 The Changes from Decreto Lei n. 14/2021

The *Decreto Lei* n. 14/2021 which came into force on 1 January 2022 changed some requirements of the residence by investment programme. The changes can be understood as a reaction from the government to the critiques regarding the housing crisis mentioned in the previous section. Therefore, a restriction on real estate investments necessary for the concession of the golden visa to territories in the interior of the country, Madeira, and the Azores was implemented. Residential real estate investment in Porto, Lisbon, and the Algarve would not be allowed for the granting of a golden visa. One of the main justifications for the restriction of real estate investment in major Portuguese cities is the impact of the investment on the real estate market. The programme was created at a time when the country still lacked foreign investment and was emerging from one of the worst crises in Portuguese history.

But with the development of tourism and the incentive for foreigners to buy property, there was a considerable increase in prices for both purchase and rent. This put pressure on local residents to move out of the centres, because of the high profits to be made from selling. However, it is questionable whether the golden visas had a direct link to the increase in the real estate market. For example, for every 100 properties transacted, only 3 % were dedicated to ARI (Residence Permit for Investment Activity).[127] This is a low number, and the golden visas market relates to real estate worth EUR 500,000, meanwhile the average purchase of Portuguese people with recourse to credit was around EUR 355,000. "We are talking about completely different segments,"[128] said Hugo Santos Ferreira, a spokesperson for real estate promoters and investors.

It was not only critiques regarding money laundry, corruption, and housing prices that were posed regarding the golden visas. In early 2022, an expected

---

[127] Larguesa, Antônio. "Vistos gold não têm nada a ver com o aumento dos preços das casas," dizem investidores imobiliários. 2022. Available in: https://eco.sapo.pt/entrevista/vistos-gold-nao-tem-nada-a-ver-com-o-aumento-dos-precos-das-casas-dizem-investidores-imobiliarios/, Access on: 14 February, 2023.

[128] Larguesa, Antônio. "Vistos gold não têm nada a ver com o aumento dos preços das casas," dizem investidores imobiliários. 2022. Available in: https://eco.sapo.pt/entrevista/vistos-gold-nao-tem-nada-a-ver-com-o-aumento-dos-precos-das-casas-dizem-investidores-imobiliarios/, Access on: 14 February, 2023.

event raised questions about the beneficiaries of the golden visas: the war in Ukraine and Russians acquiring residence permits.

1.2.6 The War in Ukraine and Russian-Portuguese

The war in Ukraine impacted applicants for golden visas who hold Russian nationality. From October 2012 to December 2022, at least 431 golden visas were granted to Russian citizens and only twelve applications were denied. Of these, twenty-one enjoy permanent residency and it is not publicly known how many have already obtained Portuguese citizenship. Russia almost always ranks in the top five countries whose citizens are granted golden visas. On 25 February 2022, a series of restrictions on Russia was announced by the European Union, including the total suspension of the processing of golden visas and citizenship by investment to people holding Russian nationality.

In Portugal in February 2022, the former minister of foreigner affairs, Augusto Santos Silva, announced the suspension of golden visas for Russian and Belarusian citizens. At the EU level, the Council agreed on 31 August to suspend the EU and Russian visa facilitation agreement from 2007. The visa application fee was also raised from EUR 35 to EUR 80, due to the need to present additional documentary evidence, increased visa processing times, and more restrictive rules for the issuance of multiple-entry visas.

This step was applauded by Transparency International Portugal as an important move against corruption. However, the decision by some Member States to ban Schengen[129] short-term visas being granted to Russians was criticised by legal scholars as "outdated, illegal and [a move] that should be dropped."[130]

1.2.7 The (Near) End of the Scheme in 2023: Turbulence and Uncertainty for Portugal's Golden Visa Programme

On 16 February 2023, the Portuguese government announced the end of the golden visas. As part of a bigger announcement, "*Pacote Habitação*," related

---

129 Prime Minister of Finland, Sanna Marin, asked for an EU ban for Russian citizens from Schengen affirming that "It's not right that at the same time as Russia is waging an aggressive, brutal war of aggression in Europe, Russians can live a normal live, travel in Europe, be tourists. It's not right."

130 Ganty, S. Why Banning Russians from Schengen is Unlawful, 2022; Available in: https://verfassungsblog.de/banning-russians/ Access on: 14 February, 2023

to housing, the golden visas were mentioned as one reason house prices had risen in the preceding 10 years. The new changes were publicly discussed for one month so that, in the end, they could be approved definitively, some by the government, others through a legal proposal to the parliament. This did not come as a surprise, as the Prime Minister Antonio Costa had already, in November 2022, declared the possibility of ending the golden visas[131] with the argument that at that point, the programme was no longer justified. In his announcement, Costa said that the end is "the elimination of the granting of new golden visas."[132] As for the golden visas already granted and their renewal, they would not be affected by the scheme's end. The prime minister also stated that, "In the case of exclusively real estate investments, there will only be a renewal if the investments are for the owner's own and permanent residence or if the property is leased permanently on the rental market."[133] There was no limitation on the price of the lease, only the addition of the obligation to put the property on the renting market. This requirement would also mean that there would be a ban on new licences for Airbnb and other short-term holiday rentals.

But what would happen to the other categories of investment, for example, the creation of jobs or cultural investment? The prime minister answered that "there will be no disruption, there will be a reclassification to another legal figure."[134] It is noteworthy that at no point in the announcement of the new package was there reference to the European Commission's calls for the ending of golden visas in the European Union. The five reasons presented by the government included golden visas in the "fight against real estate speculation."

---

131 Nunes, Flávio (2023), Costa admite acabar com os vitos gold. Available in: https://eco.sapo.pt/2022/11/02/primeiro-ministro-admite-acabar-com-os-vistos-gold/ Access on: 23rd February, 2023.

132 Costa, Antonio, 16/02/2023, Conferência de imprensa do Conselho de Ministros. Available in: https://www.youtube.com/watch?v=iuGquiU7BAo&t=881s Access on: 23 February, 2023

133 Costa, Antonio, 16/02/2023, Conferência de imprensa do Conselho de Ministros. Available in: https://www.youtube.com/watch?v=iuGquiU7BAo&t=881s Access on: 23 February, 2023

134 Costa, Antonio, 16/02/2023, Conferência de imprensa do Conselho de Ministros, time 59:00. Available in: https://www.youtube.com/watch?v=iuGquiU7BAo&t=881s Access on: 23rd February, 2023

In response to the announcement, the Chief Executive of the Investment Migration Council said that "The real issue is electing politicians that have a patriotic duty to protect their countries sovereignty and serve their electorate rather than bow down to the demands of eurocrats in Brussels and Paris (OECD), because that is exactly what is happening."[135] A clear message regarding the competence debate is whether the European Commission or other organisations have the competence to legislate or influence naturalisation or immigration pathways within Member States. On 19 May 2023, the Assembly of the Portuguese Republic debated the end of the golden visas, and members of parliament expressed their opinion on ending the programme.

Perhaps in response to the criticism, the same Portuguese government that declared its intention to close the programme has reversed its decision and stated that it will not close the programme but only eliminate two ways of acquiring the visa: by purchase of any property and by bank transfer. The government wants to retain the following investment options:

Subparagraph 2: creation of at least ten jobs

Subparagraph 5: Scientific research contributions (EUR 500,000)

Subparagraph 6: Cultural heritage/artistic production (EUR 250,000)

Subparagraph 7: Venture capital/Investment funds (EUR 500,000)

Subparagraph 8: Business investment that creates or maintains at least five jobs

The final decision on the new law's wording was scheduled for a session on 19 July 2023. With the decision agreed, the programme terminated only real estate investments and capital transfers in October 2023 with the publication of Law 56/2023. As shown in the previous paragraph, the other five types of investment would continue, with venture capital/investment funds expected to be the option favoured by investors.[136]

Therefore, the investment scheme in exchange for a residence permit remains in force in 2024 and offers five investment options: (a) creation of ten jobs; (b) transfer of capital equal to or greater than EUR 500,000, applied

135 Lécuyer, Bruno. LinkedIn Post on 18th February, 2023

136 Get Golden Visa Research Team, 2024 Report regarding Portugal's Golden Visa Funds in a Post-Real Estate Era, available on: https://media.licdn.com/dms/document/media/D4D1FAQGw26LTGIeEXw/feedshare-document-pdf-analyzed/0/1706712693685?e=1717027200&v=beta&t=dvlNL3VwNFoDdxuJyePPkGgOlUrr7d2zXk-RKa-VqlXI, Access on: 16.05.2024

in research activities developed by public or private scientific research institutions, integrated in the national scientific and technological system; (c) transfer of capital equal to or greater than EUR 250,000, applied in investment or support for artistic production, recovery or maintenance of national cultural heritage, through central and peripheral direct administration services, public institutes, entities part of the public business sector, public foundations, private foundations with public utility status, intermunicipal entities, entities part of the local business sector, or municipal associative entities and public cultural associations that pursue attributions in the area of artistic production, recovery or maintenance of national cultural heritage; (d) capital transfers of EUR 500,000 or more, intended for the acquisition of units in investment funds or venture capital funds aimed at capitalising companies set up under Portuguese law, whose maturity, at the time of the investment, is at least five years; also, at least 60 % of the value of the investments is made in commercial companies based in Portugal; (e) transfer of capital equal to or greater than EUR 500,000, intended for the incorporation of a commercial company based in Portugal, combined with the creation of five permanent jobs, or to reinforce the share capital of an already incorporated commercial company based in Portugal, with the creation or maintenance of a minimum of five permanent jobs, for a minimum period of three years.[137]

The Portuguese Securities Market Commission (CMVM) does not provide a list of eligible entities for golden visa investments but a lawyer working in the field, Vanessa Lima, estimates around forty entities, although some funds may not be available for investment.[138]

Examples of these funds are sustainable agriculture investment fund Pela Terra,[139] which regenerates farmland, and Sharing Education,[140] a fund for

---

137 ARI – Autorização de Residência para Atividade de Investimento, 2024, SEF Serviço de Estrangeiros e Fronteiras, available on: https://www.sef.pt/pt/pages/conteudo-detalhe.aspx?nID=62, Access on: 28.05.2024

138 Demoy, Catarina; Vicente Rua, Patricia, REUTERS, Portugal's revamped golden visa scheme to boost investment funds, 9 January, 2024, available on: https://www.reuters.com/markets/europe/portugals-revamped-golden-visa-scheme-boost-investment-funds-2024-01-09/, Access on: 16.04.2024

139 Pela Terra, available on: https://pelaterra.com/welcome/, Access on: 16.04.2024

140 Sharing Education, Welcome to Sharing Education Funds, available on: https://sharingeducation.fund/, Access on: 16.04.2024

investment in international schools in Portugal.[141] Estimates put investment funds to be around 80–90 % of all golden visa investment destinations since the legislative changes in 2023.

Due to the backlog from the pandemic and the immigration office restructuring, it has been possible to renew investment visas online.[142] Although online renewal was already a reality for other residence permits in Portugal,[143] the immigration office only announced the possibility of renewing visas by investment online in January 2023.[144] At the end of a tumultuous 2023, Portuguese Prime Minister Antonio Costa resigned[145] from his post, and the president called new parliamentary elections for March 2024. After the election, the new Portuguese Prime Minister Luis Montenegro, announced a new Action Plan for Migration,[146] including possible changes to the golden visas.[147] The new "solidarity" golden visa aims to offer residence permits in exchange for EUR 250,000, invested in equipment and infrastructure to support immigrants in difficulty. This would take advantage of the existing scheme (ARI-golden visa) to enable investment for solidarity purposes and

---

141 Demoy, Catarina; Vicente Rua, Patricia, REUTERS, Portugal's revamped golden visa scheme to boost investment funds, 9 January, 2024, available on: https://www.reuters.com/markets/europe/portugals-revamped-golden-visa-scheme-boost-investment-funds-2024-01-09/, Access on: 16.04.2024

142 ARIs (Golden Visas) need to be renewed every two years

143 Portugal, Novo Serviço de renovação automática do título de residencia, 27.07.2020, available on: https://eportugal.gov.pt/noticias/novo-servico-de-renovacao-automatica-do-titulo-de-residencia, Access on: 28.05.2024

144 Henriques, Ana. Vistos de residência para imigrantes: renovação online voltou e abrange os gold, Público, available on: https://www.publico.pt/2023/01/15/sociedade/noticia/vistos-residencia-imigrantes-renovacao-online-voltou-abrange-gold-2035132, Access on: 28.05.2024

145 SIC notícias, Marcelo formaliza demissão do governo, 07.12.2023, available on: https://sicnoticias.pt/pais/2023-12-07-Marcelo-formaliza-demissao-do-Governo-6b1ce3d6, Access on: 06.06.2024

146 Portugal, Plano de Ação para as Migrações, conheça as principais medidas, 03.06.2024, available on: https://www.portugal.gov.pt/pt/gc24/comunicacao/noticia?i=plano-de-acao-para-as-migracoes-conheca-as-principais-medidas, Access on: 06.06.2024

147 Idealista, Governo cria novo visto gold "solidário" para apoiar imigrantes, 04.06.2024, available on: https://www.idealista.pt/news/financas/investimentos/2024/06/04/64269-governo-cria-novo-visto-gold-solidario-para-apoiar-imigrantes, Access on: 06.06.2024

a redistributive logic.[148] The press release for the new changes confirmed the end of expressions of interest (*Manifestação de Interesse*), a mechanism that made it possible to enter Portugal and apply for residence by simply expressing interest, without previously needing a visa. Portugal has a backlog of 400,000 residence applications.[149]

1.2.8 Conclusion: Residence by Investment in Portugal

Since its inception in 2012, the Portuguese golden visa (residence by investment), which grants affluent non-EU citizens the right to reside in Portugal in exchange for investment, has garnered EUR 7.3 billion in funding. The majority of participants originate from China, Brazil, and the United States. Approximately 90 % of these funds were allocated to real estate, leading to accusations about the inflation of property prices in a country with lower salaries and high living costs.

Although the European Commission has not filed infringement procedures against Portugal and the other 22 Member States that allow residence by investment, debates about risks such as corruption, lack of transparency, money laundering, and increased rental costs in Portugal are problems hindering acceptance of this scheme, despite the fact that it is completely legal in terms of Portugal's competence to decide on the admission of third-country nationals. The legality of this programme is then addressed in the second chapter on EU law (Section 2.11).

1.3 The Case of Malta (Citizenship by Investment)

Investor citizenship has existed for a long time. St Kitts and Nevis, a federation of two islands in the West Indies, has the oldest citizenship by investment programme in the world. This was adopted in 1984 in the Constitution and

148 Portugal, Conselho de Ministros – Plano de Ação para as Migrações, Minute: 57:00, 03.06.2024, available on: https://www.youtube.com/watch?v=wKZeFodMryo&ab_channel=Rep%C3%BAblicaPortuguesa, Access on: 06.06.2024

149 Portugal, Conselho de Ministros – Plano de Ação para as Migrações, 03.06.2024, available on: https://www.youtube.com/watch?v=wKZeFodMryo&ab_channel=Rep%C3%BAblicaPortuguesa, Access on: 06.06.2024

Citizenship Act, one year after independence from United Kingdom.[150] The programme emerged as a result of geographical location, low GDP per capita, and lack of competitiveness in global markets for goods and services.[151] In Europe, the years 2013/2014 saw the introduction of the first citizenship by investment schemes in Malta and Cyprus. In 2023, different rules on acquiring citizenship by investment are found around the world:

Table 5. Countries with Citizenship by Investment

Country	Inception Year	Minimum Investment	Residency Requirement	Citizenship Qualifying Period	Number of countries with visa-free for passport holders
Antigua and Barbuda	2013	US$250,000	5 days within a 5-year period	Immediate	140
Dominica	1993	US$100,000	No	Immediate	131
Grenada[152]	2014	US$250,000	12 months	Immediate	134
Jordan[153]	2019	US$750,000	No	Three months	50
Malta	2013	US$738,000	36 months or 12 months by exception	36 months or 12 months by exception	170
Montenegro	2018 (ended in 2022)	US$250,000	No	Eight to ten months	126
St Kitts and Nevis	1984	US$250,000	No	Immediate	142

150 Džankić, J., The Global Market for Investor Citizenship. 1 ed. Politics of Citizenship and Migration. 2019: Palgrave Macmillan

151 Džankić, J., The Global Market for Investor Citizenship. 1 ed. Politics of Citizenship and Migration. 2019: Palgrave Macmillan

152 Belton, Kristy A., *Comparative regional report on citizenship law: Anglophone Caribbean*, [Global Governance Programme], GLOBALCIT, Comparative Reports, 2020/03, [Global Citizenship] – https://hdl.handle.net/1814/66909, page 20

153 Frost, Lillian. Report on Citizenship Law: Jordan. Country Report 2022/2, Global Citizenship Observatory, available on: https://cadmus.eui.eu/bitstream/handle/1814/74189/RSC_GLOBALCIT_CR_2022_2.pdf?sequence=1, Access on: 29.05.2024

Country	Inception Year	Minimum Investment	Residency Requirement	Citizenship Qualifying Period	Number of countries with visa-free for passport holders
St Lucia[154]	2015	US$100,000	No	Three to four months	135
Turkey	2017	US$400,00	No	Three to four months	128

Sources: Henley & Partners, Arton Capital, Passport Index, national authorities.

As of 1 November 2020, the Cyprus investment programme was suspended for new applicants. Bulgaria did likewise on 24 March 2022. Malta, the only active case in the European Union, has transformed its programme numerous times and keeps processing new applicants. Its main argument is that naturalisation is a competence of Member States and therefore in accordance with the law. As an in-depth example of the only active case of citizenship by investment in the European Union, this section will present the context in which Maltese legislation was enacted and details of the application requirements. The previously presented Portuguese golden visa scheme – residency by investment – grants far fewer rights than the second case presented here: citizenship by investment. For this reason, the case of Portugal was presented first.

This section presents the only remaining citizenship by investment scheme in the European Union: Maltese Citizenship Naturalization for Exceptional Services (formerly the Individual Investor Programme).[155]

154 Belton, Kristy A., *Comparative regional report on citizenship law: Anglophone Caribbean*, [Global Governance Programme], GLOBALCIT, Comparative Reports, 2020/03, [Global Citizenship] – https://hdl.handle.net/1814/66909, Access on: 29.05.2024

155 In this Dissertation when referring to the Maltese Citizenship by Investment Programme I will use the word Programme instead of Program as the law uses the term "Programme," see Legal Notice 27 of 2014.

1.3.1 Not Investment but Exceptional Service: The Second Version of the Scheme and its Changes in 2020 (2020–2024)

The Individual Investor Programme received applications until 14 August 2020 with the rules on requirements and fees of the previously presented Legal Notice 47 of 2014. From 2020 on, Robert Abela – also of the Labour Party – continued the citizenship by investment programme. The programme was close to reaching the pre-established quota of 1,800 successful main applications. Consequently, on 31 July 2020, amendments were carried out to the Malta Citizenship Act, Cap 188, repealing the IPP Regulations, and the Malta Individual Investor Programme Agency was wound up.

The Individual Investor Programme (IPP) was repealed by Legal Notice 437/2020, which was replaced by Maltese Citizenship by Naturalization for Exceptional Services by Direct Investment. This scheme is currently in place. The changes also tried to incorporate recommendations from the Regulator and a response to the European institutions (mainly the European Commission and European Parliament) because of the pressure from these institutions. The number of naturalisation certificates from 2020 will not exceed 400 main applicants annually and will be capped at a total accumulated amount of 1,500 main applicants (excluding dependents).

The Legal Notice n. 435 of 2020 – Agents (Licences) amending the Maltese Citizenship Act (Chapter 188 of the Laws of Malta) transferred all functions and duties in matters relating to Maltese citizenship from Identity Malta to the Community Malta Agency. The new agency is responsible for processing applications for the acquisition of Maltese citizenship by descent, merit, long-term residence, and exceptional service by merit and exceptional service by investment.[156] It is also responsible for carrying out in-depth due diligence for every application submitted.

The Agency published *The Maltese Citizenship by Naturalization for Exceptional Services by Direct Investment Handbook*, considered the principal policy and guideline on how applications under the regulations should be submitted to the minister for citizenship through the Agency. Among the documents required for the application of citizenship by investment in Malta,

---

156 Identity Malta, Citizenship has moved to a new agency. 11/12/2020, Available in: https://www.identitymalta.com/citizenship-moved-to-new-agency/, Access on: 29/03/2023

the manual asks for an *Introduction Letter* in which the applicants "showcase commitments that evidence personal, commercial or financial ties to the country."[157] In this instance, the usage of "or" in lieu of "and" indicates that the applicant is not obligated to have personal ties to Malta – something defended by the European Commission, although it never defined what these personal ties should be – but rather may only possess commercial or financial ties. This represents an official assertion that the Maltese Citizenship by Investment programme does not seek to mandate emotional attachments from the applicant to the country.

The "new" 2020 programme presents two options for investment: a EUR 750,000.00 investment and 12-month residency; or EUR 650,000.00 and 36-month residency. These investments must be presented as evidence to fulfil the citizenship by investment requirement. How is residence proven? The policy manual explains that boarding passes must be attached to the evidence documentation sent to the agency. When travelling by private jet, a manifest from the applicant is enough.[158] Besides the exceptional investment (direct investment), the applicant must donate EUR 10,000 to a philanthropic organisation[159] and prove a property investment, which can be a purchase of a property with a minimum value of EUR 700,000.00. Or a lease can be taken out for an immovable residential property in Malta for a minimum annual rent of EUR 16,000. Both cases need to be retained for a minimum period of five years from the date of issue of the certificate of citizenship.

Each applicant can also bring their family, and they will also be awarded citizenship. Each dependent costs EUR 50,000. By "dependent," the law defines (a) the spouse of the main applicant in a monogamous marriage or another relationship having the same or a similar status to marriage, unless the minister authorises otherwise on a case-by-case basis; (b) a child,

---

157 Government of Malta, *The Maltese Citizenship by Naturalization for Exceptional Services by Direct Investment Handbook*. 2021

158 Government of Malta, *The Maltese Citizenship by Naturalization for Exceptional Services by Direct Investment Handbook*. 2021, p. 15

159 A warning in the handbook states that agents involved in the citizenship procedure should refrain from suggesting to clients' philanthropic organisations in which the agents are involved (such as shareholders, for example). Government of Malta, *The Maltese Citizenship by Naturalization for Exceptional Services by Direct Investment Handbook*. 2021, p. 7

including an adopted child; (c) a child older than eighteen and younger than 29 years old, as long as they are not married and wholly maintained by the main applicant; (d) a parent or grandparent of the main applicant, or of their spouse, above the age of 55, who proves to the satisfaction of the minister that they are wholly maintained or supported by the main applicant and forms part of the household of the main applicant; (e) a child of the main applicant or of the spouse of the main applicant who is at least 18 years old, is physically or mentally challenged, and who is living with and fully supported by the main applicant.[160] Two aspects draw attention regarding dependents. First, the definition of a monogamous relationship excludes the possibility of polygamous relationships. Some fifty-eight countries (of a total of 200) allow polygamous relationships, including many countries listed as countries of origin of applicants for citizenship by investment. How the agency has handled this detail or whether there have been cases is not public knowledge. Second, the unlimited power of discretion given to the minister in defining what a family is can create a lack of transparency in the process.

1.3.2 General Immigration Policies in Malta

The immigration regulation in Malta was established by the Immigration Act of 1970. As a transitory migratory route, Malta was never a final destination until 2002. For example, in 2000, there were only twenty-four irregular migration arrivals in Malta, and the topic never received much attention from the government, the public, or the newspaper headlines.[161] This number changed in 2002 when 1,686 migrants and refugees arrived without authorisation,[162] and the increase is attributed, at least in part, to a rerouting of migratory movements due to enhanced patrols along the West African route to Spain and the Canary Islands.[163]

Malta's asylum law was established by the Refugees Act of 2001, and the country also has a Refugee Commissioner's Office. With accession to the

160 Malta. Subsidiary Legislation 188.06 Granting of Citizenship for Exceptional Services Regulations, 20/11/2020

161 Mainwaring, C. (2012), Constructing a Crisis: the Role of Immigration Detention in Malta. Popul. Space Place, 18: 687–700. https://doi.org/10.1002/psp.1721

162 National Statistics Office, 2006

163 Lutterbeck, D. 2006, Policing migration in the Mediterranean. Mediterranean Politics 11(1): 59–82

European Union in 2004, several legislative changes accompanied the pre-accession process and followed after as well. One of the main features of the Maltese refugee system is detention. In 2002, Malta opened its first detention centre, the Lyster Barracks Closed Centre in Hal Far, and over the years, the country has opened two more detention centres (the Safi Closed Centre and the Ta'Kandja Closed Centre). NGOs have regularly criticised immigration detention conditions for "being overcrowded, unhygienic, and inhumane."[164] Since it does not have the military and economic power to influence migration policy at the EU level, the government has used a migration crisis strategy to justify its policy of detaining asylum seekers.[165]

Migrants who arrive irregularly in Malta are met with an expulsion order and can be detained for a maximum of 18 months. Previously, under the 1970 legislation, this period was unlimited.[166] The rhetoric of crisis, despite the low numbers of irregular migrants arriving, has been successful for the government. For example, a survey in 2009 showed that 84 % of respondents saw migration to the island as a "national crisis."[167]

On the other hand, highly skilled migrants can find less restrictive rules on admission to Maltese territory. Although EU nationals make up the majority of foreign migrants, compared to third-country nationals, the stay of these skilled migrants is short.[168] For highly skilled workers, EU citizens can make use of their freedom of movement to take up positions in Malta. For third-country nationals, a residence permit is available as a highly qualified worker under the Key Employee Initiative, which provides a fast-track service to highly specialised third-country nationals. The scheme is applicable to managerial or highly skilled positions which require relevant qualifications

164 Mainwaring, C. (2012), Constructing a Crisis: the Role of Immigration Detention in Malta. Popul. Space Place, 18: 687–700, page 690

165 Mainwaring, C. (2012), Constructing a Crisis: the Role of Immigration Detention in Malta. Popul. Space Place, 18: 687–700, page

166 Mainwaring, C. (2012), Constructing a Crisis: the Role of Immigration Detention in Malta. Popul. Space Place, 18: 687–700, page 689

167 Malta Today, "Immigration is 'national crisis', 84 % say," available on: http://archive.maltatoday.com.mt/2009/04/05/t1.html 05.04.2009

168 Borg, Ian. 219. "The length of stay of foreign workers in Malta," CBM Policy Papers PP/01/2019, Central Bank of Malta.

or adequate experience related to the position offered. An annual gross salary of at least EUR 30,000 per annum is among the requirements.[169]

Malta also has a residence-by-investment scheme (Malta Permanent Residence Programme), which requires an investment or purchased property of a minimum value of EUR 300,000 in the South of Malta/Gozo or EUR 350,000 in the rest of Malta, or the rental of a property for a minimum of EUR 10,000 in the South of Malta/Gozo or EUR 12,000 in the rest of Malta, among other fees. The scheme grants the right to settle, stay, and reside permanently in Malta, as well as visa-free travel across the Schengen zone, for 90 days in 180-day period.[170] In comparison to new citizenship by investment scheme, long-term residents were excluded from electoral rights, whereas investors who naturalise via citizenship by investment – (see 1.3.1) – enjoy all the rights of Maltese citizenship, including electoral rights[171] and EU citizen rights.

1.3.3 The Legal System in Malta and Citizenship Law

The Maltese legal system is a synthesis of the various legal cultures that influenced it during the long years of colonial rule. Malta became independent from British colonial rule in 1964, and the Maltese independence constitution of 1964 expresses many British constitutional principles.[172] The citizenship regime, therefore, is also young. It emerged together with Maltese independence. The first provisions prohibited dual/multiple citizenship, expressed gender inequality in rules for transmission of citizenship, and combined the principles of *ius soli*[173]

---

169 Malta. Highly qualified worker, 2024, available on: https://immigration-portal.ec.europa.eu/malta-highly-qualified-worker_en, Access on: 22.05.2024

170 Malta. Malta Permanent Residence Programme, Residency Malta Agency, available on: https://residencymalta.gov.mt/the-mprp-programme/ Access on: 22.05.2024

171 DeBono, Daniela, Access to Electoral Rights, EUDO Citizenship Observatory, Robert Schuman Centre for Advanced Studies, Florence, June 2013

172 Chamber of Advocates, Malta. The Maltese Legal System. Available on: https://www.avukati.org/public/law-system-in-malta/ Access on: 03.07.2023

173 *Ius soli* is "the principle that the nationality of a person is determined on the basis of their country of birth" while *ius sanguinis* is the determination of a person's nationality on the basis of the nationality of their parents (or one parent or one particular parent) at the time of the target person's birth and at the time of acquisition of nationality by the target person (the two points in time are different in cases of acquisition after birth). Available on: https://home-affairs.ec.europa.eu/networks/

and *ius sanguinis*.[174] Maltese legislation is organised by chapters, and citizenship is placed in Chapter 188 (Citizenship Act). Subsidiary Legislation (S.L.) is enacted via Legal Notices (L.N.) and Acts. Three reforms to the Citizenship Act marked important changes in 1989, 2000, and 2007. In 1989, the principle of *ius sanguinis* remained as guiding the path to citizenship in Malta. Before, people in Maltese territory were Maltese. From 1989, if a child had only one Maltese parent, they would be Maltese too.

In 2000, all restrictions on multiple citizenship were lifted. This meant an increase in citizenship acquisition from 2007, after the Dual Citizenship Act was enacted that year. The change in the law allowing dual citizenship was extended to those who had been Maltese citizens at birth and lost their Maltese citizenship by emigrating. Moreover, it was extended to first, second, and subsequent generations of Maltese born outside Malta and living abroad, whose Maltese citizenship derived from descent rather than birth in Malta.[175] In 2004, Malta acceded to the European Union together with Cyprus, the Czech Republic, Estonia, Hungary, Latvia, Lithuania, Poland, Slovakia, and Slovenia. As members of the Union, Maltese citizens also enjoy Union citizenship (Article 20 (1), Treaty on the Functioning of the European Union)[176] and the right to move, work, and reside freely within the territory of other Member States.

1.3.4 General Rules on Naturalisation in Malta

Naturalisation policy in Malta has remained protectionist[177] since the country's independence in 1964. The only exception is citizenship through the

european-migration-network-emn/emn-asylum-and-migration-glossary_en, Access on: 03.07.2023

174 De Bono, Daniela; Buttieg, Eugène. Country Report on Citizenship Law: Malta, EUDO Citizenship Observatory (2015)

175 De Bono, Daniela; Buttieg, Eugène. Country Report on Citizenship Law: Malta, EUDO Citizenship Observatory (2015), page 09

176 Article 20 TFEU 1. Citizenship of the Union is hereby established. Every person holding the nationality of a Member State shall be a citizen of the Union. Citizenship of the Union shall be additional to and not replace national citizenship

177 By protectionist policy in the context of migration I mean that the government has adopted policies emphasising border control, rather than migration facilitation or migrant protection. In Boynton, E. 2015. Protectionism and national migration policy in South Africa. University of Cape Town.

investment programme. This is mainly due to the fact that naturalisation in Malta is a discretionary act by the Ministry for Home Affairs and has very broad and vague requirements.[178] These requirements are set out in Article 10 of the Maltese Citizenship Act, which states that an alien or statelessness person, being a person of full age and capacity, may (discretionarily) be granted citizenship by naturalisation on the basis of residence if they satisfy the Minister of the Interior:

> that he has resided in Malta throughout the period of twelve months immediately preceding the date of application and (*b*) that, during the six years immediately preceding the said period of twelve months, he has resided in Malta for periods amounting in the aggregate to not less than four years; and (*c*) that he has an adequate knowledge of the Maltese or the English language; and (*d*) that he is of good character; and (*e*) that he would be a suitable citizen of Malta.
>
> Provided that the Minister may, if he so thinks fit in the special circumstances of any particular case, allow periods of residence earlier than seven years before the date of application to be reckoned in computing the aggregate mentioned in paragraph (*b*).

All these requirements do not guarantee naturalisation, since the minister has discretionary power at the end of the procedure. Regarding the requirements, three features deserve attention. The first is related to language. In practice, there is no systematic assessment of its fulfilment, such as through a language test. There have never been any publicly run or subsidised language courses for naturalisation applicants.[179] The second issue is being of "good character" and a "suitable citizen of Malta," both essential requirements. There are no available policy guidelines or definitions for those two terms, leaving them to the discretion of the minister. MIPEX's (Migration Integration Policy Index) conclusions highlight that "its bureaucratic and discretionary path to citizenship is the main factor depressing naturalisation rates."[180] Lastly, people applying for naturalisation in Malta also need two sponsors, one of whom must be a member of parliament, a judge, a magistrate, a parish priest,

---

178 De Bono, Daniela; Buttieg, Eugène. Country Report on Citizenship Law: Malta, EUDO Citizenship Observatory (2015), page 1

179 DeBono, Daniela. Naturalization Procedures for Immigrants Malta, EUDO Citizenship Observatory, Robert Schuman Centre for Advanced Studies, March 2013

180 MIPEX, Key Findings Malta 2019, Available on: https://www.mipex.eu/malta, Access on: March 2023

a doctor, a lawyer, a public notary, or an officer in the army or civil service.[181] The second sponsor may be any citizen of Malta as long as they have not acquired Maltese citizenship by naturalisation and are at least 18 years old.

As can be seen, several points in Malta's discretionary naturalisation legislation are vaguely defined. Considering this background, the introduction of the Individual Investor Programme (IPP) represented a significant shift in naturalisation policy. The next section introduces the Citizenship by Investment scheme, tracing a historical line of legislative changes from its inception to changes in 2020.

1.3.5 The First Version of the Scheme: From its Inception to its Changes – Individual Investor Programme (2013–2019)

The Maltese Citizenship programme was created during the government of Joseph Muscat (Labour Party). This mode of acquiring citizenship represented a major change in citizenship policy from the previously large list of requirements for naturalisation in Malta. One of the major programmes of the new government was the IPP (Individual Investor Programme). Amendments to the Maltese Citizenship Act in 2013 provided the legal basis for the creation of the IPP.

The law was passed first by approval of the House of Representatives on 12 November 2013 and subsequently by Legal Notice 450 of 2013. The initial regulation had a price for naturalisation by investment of EUR 650,000, of which a non-refundable payment of EUR 10,000 needed to be remitted as a non-refundable deposit prior to submission of the application.[182] An additional EUR 25,000 was applicable in the case of the addition of a spouse, as well as EUR 25,000 for every child below 18 years old of age, EUR 50,000

---

181 DeBono, Daniela. Naturalization Procedures for Immigrants Malta, EUDO Citizenship Observatory, Robert Schuman Centre for Advanced Studies, March 2013, p. 6

182 Maltese Citizenship Act (Cap. 188), Individual Investor Programme of the Republic of Malta Regulations, 2013, L.N. 450 of 2013, Contribution Requirements and Schedule of Fees

for every unmarried child between 18 years of age and 26 years of age, and EUR 50,000 for every dependent parent above 55 years of age.[183]

The amended Citizenship Act that allowed citizenship by Investment initially had no clear information on how residence should be effectively proved. It stated that the applicant "(d) commits himself to provide proof of a residential address in Malta as provided in these regulations."[184] On 13 January 2014, the opposition in the Maltese parliament presented motion ninety-three to the parliament in order to repeal, revoke, and annul Legal Notice 450 of 2013, which brought into force the regulations of 2013 regarding the Individual Investor Programme. Among their reasons, the Opposition argued that: (a) it was not in the national interest that Maltese citizenship should be for sale; (b) that the Legal Notice undermined the national interest, not only in terms of economic and social interest, but also as a threat to Malta's identity as a Member of the European Union; (c) that the regulation transformed Maltese citizenship into an object that could be sold and bought by persons who did not have and would not have any connection with Malta; (d) that the regulation destroys the respect and good reputation that Malta has managed to acquire at international level, particularly with foreign investors; that it attracted strong criticism, not only among the Opposition and among the Maltese and Gozitan[185] people, but also among international media; (e) that the scheme did not offer any real economic solution for the development of Malta; (f) and that it undermined and distorted, to the detriment of the national interest, the principle of loyal cooperation between Malta and the Member States of the European Union.[186]

---

183 Malta. Legal Notice 450/2013, Maltese Citizenship Act Chapter 188, Individual Investor Programme of the Republic of Malta Regulations, Contribution Requirements and Fees

184 Maltese Citizenship Act (Cap. 188), Individual Investor Programme of the Republic of Malta Regulations, 2013, L.N. 450 of 2013.

185 Gozitan people are the inhabitants of the island of Gozo, which is part of the Maltese archipelago. In Mamo, Suzanne, "Maltese and Gozitans: a social identity approach," (Dissertation, University of Malta 2012)

186 Parliament of Malta, Motion 93 for the Repeal of Legal Notice 450 of 2013, available on: https://parlament.mt/en/12th-leg/motions-12th/motion-no-093/?page=1&numItems=10&text=&number=93&totalItems=1&isPrivate=0&isFirst=0 Access on: 21.05.2024

As referred to in the motion, this critique had the effect of replacing the initial Legal Notice 450 of 2013 with Legal Notice 47 of 2014. A clause was added for applicants to provide proof of residence before being granted a certificate of naturalisation, as follows: "No certificate of naturalisation under these regulations shall be issued unless the main applicant provides proof that he has been a resident of Malta for a period of at least 12 months preceding the day of the issuing of the certificate of naturalization."[187] The change came as a result of negotiations with the European Commission, since the Commission raised concerns about the programme, arguing that EU law should be considered and that the granting of citizenship should be based upon genuine links with the country. As the Commission accepted the residence requirement, this also showed that the European Commission would give its seal of approval to the scheme.[188]

The new legislation, Legal Notice 47 of 2014, stated that applicants must invest a sum of EUR 650,000. The same rules and prices applied for spouses and dependents as in the preceding Legal Notice 450 of 2013. In exchange, applicants received Maltese citizenship and, consequently, European citizenship. The initial motion 93, presented before the inclusion of the 12-month period of residence, was superseded by motion 115, which defended the repeal of Legal Notice 47, 2014.[189] The motion criticised the fact that the new regulation did not mention that the 12-month residence period must be effective; nor did it provide a definition of evidence the Maltese government was willing to accept in order for an applicant to prove the requirement to have resided in Malta for 12 months, which also applied to all dependents of the applicant.[190] The motion was not passed in Session 113 of Tuesday 25 March 2014.

---

187 Maltese Citizenship Act (Chap 188) L.N. 47 of 2014

188 De Bono, Daniela; Buttigied, Eugène. Country Report on Citizenship Law: Malta EUDO Citizenship Observatory, European University Institute, 2015

189 Parliament of Malta, Motion 115 for the Repeal of Legal Notice 47 of 2014, available on: https://parlament.mt/en/12th-leg/motions-12th/motion-no-115/?page=1&numItems=10&text=&number=115&totalItems=1&isPrivate=0&isFirst=0, Access on: 21.05.2024

190 Parliament of Malta, Motion 115 for the Repeal of Legal Notice 47 of 2014, available on: https://parlament.mt/en/12th-leg/motions-12th/motion-no-115/?page=1&numItems=10&text=&number=115&totalItems=1&isPrivate=0&isFirst=0, Access on: 21.05.2024

The main aim of these regulations implementing citizenship by investment in Malta (Legal Notice 450 of 2013 and 47 of 2014) was "to allow for the grant of citizenship by a certificate of naturalization to foreign individuals and their families who contribute to the economic development of Malta."[191] For the programme to start working, three bodies were created: the agency *Identity Malta* (later renamed MIIPA, Malta Individual Investor Programme Agency), responsible for the naturalisation processes; a concessionaire, which carried out the design, implementation, administration, operation, and promotion of the programme; and finally, agents qualified as intermediaries for the regulation's goals.

Moreover, Malta also created a way to regulate the citizenship by investment scheme in the form of a person named "the Regulator." Starting in 2014 with Dr Godwin Grima, the regulator produced seven reports releasing data and legislative changes to the scheme. Article 25A of the Citizenship Act explains that the Regulator shall ensure that the process of granting Maltese citizenship by naturalisation for exceptional services or in terms of the Individual Investor Programme is duly followed. A complaints system was been established regarding the eligibility process of the applicants. Moreover, the Regulator was given the authority to "act in his individual judgment" and "not be subject to the direction or control of any other person or authority."[192] Furthermore, provisions of Article 25B of the Maltese Citizenship Act (Cap 188) set up a Monitoring Committee for the Individual Investor Programme. The Committee is composed of the prime minister (who presides), the minister responsible for matters relating to Maltese citizenship, and the leader of the opposition.

The Citizenship by Investment regulation also had a list of ineligible applicants, which are listed in Article 6 of the Regulation as persons: (a) providing false information on their application; (b) with a criminal record; (c) subject to a criminal investigation; (d) potential national security threats to Malta; (e) who are, or who are likely to be, involved in any activity likely to cause disrepute to Malta; or (f) who have been denied a visa to a country

---

191 Legal Notice 47, 2014, 3 (1), Individual Investor Programme of the Republic of Malta Regulations

192 Maltese Citizenship Act, Chap. 188

with which Malta has visa-free travel arrangements and have not subsequently obtained a visa to the country that issued the denial.

The programme was capped by law at 1,800 main applicants, excluding dependents. The names of applicants who were granted nationality would not initially be disclosed. This provision has since been removed, and naturalised persons are published in the official list of naturalised persons. However, there is no information in the publication about the reason for naturalisation (marriage or IPP), making it impossible to know who has been naturalised through the citizenship-by-investment programme or for other reasons. The "publicity requirement" can be seen as a demand for transparency. Indeed, ever since the Maltese Citizenship Act (1965), it has been policy (as a legal requirement) to publish the names of persons who acquire Maltese citizenship through naturalisation and registration. This was done with the argument that doing so is in the public interest.[193]

Among the beneficiaries of the scheme, the first Regulator's report on the Individual Investor Programme showed that it "may be easily inferred that most of the applications (54.3 %) were submitted from Russia."[194] Among the benefits of the purchase are the right to travel, work and reside in the European Union, the right to free movement within the Schengen area and the right to visa-free travel to more than 160 countries around the world.

Regulation 13 of LN 47 (2014) created a National Development and Social Fund into which 70 % of contributions received by Identity Malta under the programme should be paid. The funds received were to be used in the public interest for the advancement of education, research, innovation, social purposes, justice and the rule of law, employment initiatives, the environment, and public health. A total of 1,532 people (the figure does not include relatives and dependents) assumed Maltese citizenship under the scheme.[195] Including relatives and dependents, this number rises to 6,163 new Maltese

---

[193] Office of the Regulator Individual Investor Programme (ORiip), Second Annual Report on the IPP Programme of the Government of Malta, October 2015.

[194] Grima, Dr Godwin, First Annual Report on the IPP Programme of the Government of Malta, October 2014.

[195] Malta, Times of. Over 1.500 people became Maltese citizens through golden passports scheme. Available in: https://timesofmalta.com/articles/view/1500-people-maltese-citizens-golden-passport-scheme.1013883 Access on: 27/03/2023

citizens. These numbers count naturalised applicants and dependents only until 30 December 2021, when the latest data was published.

Table 6. Number of Applicants for Maltese Citizenship by Investment Programme Per Year

Year	Number of Main Applicants	Dependents	Approved Applications (Letters of Approval sent)	Naturalised	Naturalised Dependents	Rejected applicants
From 2013 to 06/2014	173[196]	197	none	none	none	x
01/07/2015 to 30/06/2015	245	Not informed	75	137	95	11
01/07/2015 to 30/06/2016	450	1186	241	134	477	52
01/07/2016 to 30/06/2017	377	962	422	386	1409	83
01/07/2017 to 30/06/2018	330	818	223	266	914	75
01/07/2018 to 30/06/2019	311	758	237	221	768	115
01/07/2019 to 31/12/2020[197]	317	742	185	134	443	103
01/01/2021 to 30/12/2021	23	54	109	160	525	112

Source: Annual Reports of the Individual Investor Programme of the Government of Malta

196 The first report of the Regulator informs that from the 173 applications, only seven had progressed to the second stage. No information is stated about rejected applications and whether any of the applications reached the certificate of naturalisation at this year. First Annual Report on the IPP Programme of the Government of Malta, October 2014.

197 As from the year 2021 the yearly Report should be covering a full calendar year, i.e. from the 1st of January till the 31st of December, both dates included. This is the reason the last report on data from the IPP covers 18 months in order to adjust for the future reports.

1.3.6 Discussion of the Scheme in the Literature

The preceding sections presented the citizenship scheme implemented in Malta from its inception in 2013 to its current state of development. Three points stand out and deserve to be highlighted for discussion and analysis: transparency; the value of citizenship; and the concept of residence. The following paragraphs are presented in context with the literature and reports from the scheme's regulator in Malta.

The Maltese scheme could prove much more transparent if it adopted measures that put the public interest first, rather than individual interests. In the first case, the system has evolved over the years but still needs more transparency. For example, one section of the Maltese regulation[198] allows that applicants with one of the ineligible requirements can still be approved if "Identity Malta is satisfied that the applicant is still worthy of being considered for approval due to special circumstances to be demonstrated by the applicant. In such cases, Identity Malta shall issue a reasoned opinion as to why such applicants should still be considered for approval and shall refer such applications to the minister, who will have the sole authority to grant such approval."[199] In fact, this regulation is extremely discretionary. However, according to the Regulator, this provision has never been used. The Regulator's sixth report (2019)[200] suggested amending this provision to end this possibility and avoid criticism, because the loophole could be abused. The suggestion was taken up, and in the new regulation of 2020,[201] the clause that allowed the agency to recommend ineligible applicants was removed.

A second point regarding transparency regards publishing the names of naturalised people and whether the reason for naturalisation should be published together with the name as well. Ever since the introduction of the Maltese Citizenship Act, the policy (a legal requirement) has been that the names of naturalised citizens must be published. The practice has been in place for 40 years, and the argument is that doing so it is in the public

---

198 Malta. Legal Notice 47 of 2014, Article 6

199 Malta. Legal Notice 47 (2014) Individual Investor Programme Regulation

200 Office of the Regulator Individual Investor Programme (ORiip), Sixth Annual Report on the IPP Programme of the Government of Malta, November 2019.

201 Malta. Legal Notice 437 (2020) Granting of Citizenship for Exceptional Services Regulation

interest.[202] The controversy is that it may expose applicants from some regions of the world, particularly those from the Middle East and the Gulf states.[203] For instance, the Regulator, in the second annual report,[204] highlighted that many applicants are from "particular regions," which it later refers to as "regimes," and that disclosing applicant names could put applicants and their dependents at risk. It is indeed a relevant consideration that could be challenged in court due to data protection regulation in both the EU and Malta, but the public interest principle is, in this specific case of citizenship by investment, more important than the protection of an individual and their family, especially since there are international protection mechanisms for vulnerable people (if this was the case), such as refugee law. Although this is a particularity of the Maltese system, it seems odd that is no action against this practice due to regulations on data protection. However, if this is the practice, there is no doubt that excluding investors from the publication of the list would be incompatible, since all other people naturalised through other avenues are published.

Disclosure of the naturalised applicants enables greater control by society over who becomes Maltese and gives greater transparency about who will also become European – as a consequence of the derivative aspect of EU citizenship. If investors have the privilege of not publishing their names on the naturalisation list, unlike other people naturalised for other reasons, this could be a clear problem not only in terms of transparency but also as a difference in the treatment of citizens. In other words, publishing names is something that has already happened, and if it is a standard procedure for all new Maltese citizens, it should continue to happen in the Maltese Gazette.[205]

---

202 Office of the Regulator Individual Investor Programme (ORiip), Second Annual Report on the IPP Programme of the Government of Malta, October 2015, page iii

203 Office of the Regulator Individual Investor Programme (ORiip), Second Annual Report on the IPP Programme of the Government of Malta, October 2015, page 22

204 Office of the Regulator Individual Investor Programme (ORiip), Second Annual Report on the IPP Programme of the Government of Malta, October 2015.

205 The Malta Government Gazette is a government gazette published by the Department of Information of the Government of Malta. An example of the list of persons naturalised as citizens of Malta can be seen here: https://www.gov.mt/en/Government/DOI/Government%20Gazette/Government%20Notices/Documents/naturalised%20persons.pdf Access on: 22.05.2024

The second point about possible issues of Maltese Citizenship by Investment is the question of how great the required investment is. When the scheme was launched, the prime minister of Malta said that "we are not into selling this right cheap,"[206] in reference to the EUR 650,000 figure. The figure had already been the subject of discussion in the literature. For example, Raul Berton's[207] argument that the problem is not the price charged for the passport but the lack of other options for naturalisation has some basis. As exemplified earlier, the "natural" way of naturalisation through length of residence in Malta is full of vague terms and discretion. Asylum seekers would also buy citizenship if they had the financial means, but the normal pathway for naturalisation in Malta is extremely long and beholden to requirements that do not confer a right but offer discretionary power to the minister. Research already demonstrates that the lack of pathways for regular migration makes people take more risks and routes that are unsafe or illegal.[208] So, regarding the perspective of the price, as Raul Berton states, it is not the price that is the problem but the general system, which presents no other opportunities to migrate and acquire rights that people would take if offered. On the other hand, it is also right to affirm that if an investor has the desire to live and work in Malta, the person could find a suitable position as a highly skilled worker and benefit from fast and privileged access that already exists for highly skilled workers. This would make Berton's argument that the price is not important contestable. But even if we think about the case of an asylum seeker, they would not have the opportunity to buy a Maltese passport or seek regularisation that could allow them to work and receive a highly skilled visa. In both cases, in fact, the biggest problem is the lack of residence permits that allow people greater opportunity to choose where they want to

---

206 Times Malta. PM defends Citizenship-on-sale scheme. 9 October 2013. Available on: https://timesofmalta.com/articles/view/20131009/local/Citizenship-on-sale-in-scheme-to-net-30m.489548#.UlZ44Ba8KWd, Access on: 30 March, 2023

207 Berton, Raul. Citizenship for those who invest into the future of the state is not wrong, the price is the problem. In Should Citizenship be For Sale? EUI Working Papers, Robert Schuman Centre for Advanced Studies, 2014

208 Andersson, R. (2016). Europe's failed "fight" against irregular migration: ethnographic notes on a counterproductive industry. *Journal of Ethnic and Migration Studies*, *42*(7), 1055–1075. https://doi.org/10.1080/1369183X.2016.1139446

work or build their lives. Citizenship by investment is an alternative to this lack of options, but it comes with a high price.

Peter Spiro's argument of 2014[209] was that as long as the price stayed high (and with it the numbers of applicants), there would be no critique or actions by European institutions against the practice of selling passports. The actions against the scheme came earlier than expected, because since the launch of the programme, critique emerged from European institutions and other Member States.[210] Spiro's prediction has a point, given that the number of applicants is negligible (around 1,800 in the first version of the programme), in addition to their dependents. But the argument is weak, since the point is not about numbers or price, but about the way in which the naturalisation process takes place. Regardless of whether there were fewer or more than 1,800 applicants, the reactions of the European institutions and other Member States were the same. Even with a low number (1,800), the citizenship-by-investment scheme has been contested from its implementation to the present day.

The third layer of discussion relates to the concept of residence. What would then be the definition of residence? The definition of this concept of citizenship is subject to debate and over its conceptualisation. According to the Regulator report from 2015, Identity Malta consulted Professor Dimitry Kochenov on the meaning of residence, which he summarised in five key observations: (a) residence is not physical presence; (b) the essence of residence, legally speaking, consists in the status established by law and the rights connected to such a status; (c) the status is usually acquired based on a residence permit issued by the competent authority; (d) the conditions to which such issuance is subject are established by law and only mention physical presence in overwhelmingly exceptional cases; (e) the EU legal context, with the Free Travel Area and the Schengen Zone, made the connection between residence in law and physical presence, in fact, more elusive.[211] This opinion

---

209 Spiro, Peter. Cash-for-passports and the end of citizenship (2014), in Should Citizenship be for Sale? Robert Schuman Centre for Advanced Studies, EUDO Citizenship Observatory.

210 For a general overview of the Institutions actions against the scheme in Malta, please refer to the section "What the Institutions want to protect?" in Chapter 2 of this Dissertation.

211 Office of the Regulator Individual Investor Programme (ORiip), Second Annual Report on the IPP Programme of the Government of Malta, October 2015, p. 14

represents a completely different position from Ayelet Shachar, for whom, in the context of investor citizenship, the only way to establish a genuine link in the EU context is with real residence (physical residence).[212] The argument of Ayelet Shachar is a normative one. In practice, residence just means holding a residence permit, and, I would add, having an address with your name on it. Could it include penalties in the case of longer absences? For example, in all the major immigration countries such as the United States, Canada, Australia, and in the European case, Germany, residence for naturalisation means physical presence, not simply having an address. Even in the case of absences, there are penalties. In Germany, for example, a master's student with a residence permit for two years cannot be absent for more than six months, otherwise the residence permit is simply cancelled.[213] If we take into consideration the practice of other Member States, a minimum requirement of physical presence would be important to be in line with other Member States. Creating a privileged path constructed by money gives the wrong impression that the investor does not care about being Maltese, but only about the benefits of holding a Maltese passport.

The lack of a clear indication regarding how many days the applicant should stay on the island is a concern for some of the agents offering the citizenship scheme. However, the lack of clear policy on that has also helped applicants to have the chance to experience the country they are joining, as described by the Regulator report: "applicants tend to become so enamoured with the island and what it has to offer, that they immediately feel a sense of belonging and demonstrate a willingness to be active citizens."[214] Ayelet Shachar argues that money cannot buy membership: "We must resist, with even greater force, the notion that money can buy 'love of country' – or secure membership in it." The concept of "love of a country,"[215] as Shachar puts it, is a difficult argument in legal terms.

212 GLOBALCIT, Webinar Investor Citizenship: a challenge for Citizenship or a Sign of its transformation, 2021, 20:13.

213 AufenthalhG, Section 51, 7

214 Office of the Regulator Individual Investor Programme (ORiip), Second Annual Report on the IPP Programme of the Government of Malta, October 2015, p. 17

215 Shachar, Ayelet, Dangerous Liasons: Money and Citizenship in Should be Citizenship be for Sale?, Robert Schumann Centre for Advanced Studies, EUDO Citizenship Observatory, (2014).

As much as someone loves a country, this will not grant them a residence permit or citizenship. The rules establishing the granting of a residence permit and citizenship are clear in the naturalisation legislation of Member States. Some require language certificates, proof of income, citizenship tests, time of residence, proof of contribution to the pension system, and so one. Love of a country is not on the list of any country, although the closest possible thing to it in naturalisation law is the case of an argument that a candidate for naturalisation in Switzerland did not love Switzerland enough, as proved by previous actions; she had her citizenship denied twice for being too annoying.[216]

In summary, money can buy many things in the world, but whether it can buy citizenship is maybe something the creators of the Union did not even imagine could exist during the drafting of the Treaties. In the next chapter, the competence for naturalisation in the European Treaties (principle of conferral – Chapter 2) and the differences in these rules in the Member States as well as the rules in international law (Chapter 3) are analysed in relation to the Maltese case.

1.3.7 National Case Law Related to the IPP

Two applicants entered a case against Identity Malta in 2016 related to the fact they felt aggrieved by the negative concession of the citizenship decision without being given any explanatory details. Case No. 144/2016 (Mifsud Cedric L-Avukat Dr Noe Vs L-Agenzija Identity Malta Et) was registered on 23 February 2016. Case No. 834/2016 (Schembri Alexander L-Avukat Dottor Noe Vs L-Agenzija Identity Malta Et) was registered on 23 September 2016. Both were concluded and judged in favour of the defendant (the Agency) on 25 June 2020 and 20 October 2020, respectively. Appeals were lodged by the complainants on 13 July 2020 (Ref. No. 144/2016/1, Ref. No. 834/2016/2) and await judgement. An email to the Maltese Judicial System on 27 April 2023 requesting the decisions was never answered.

---

216 BBC, 2017, Cowbell campaigner denied Swiss passport by locals for being too annoying, Available on: https://www.bbc.com/news/newsbeat-38595807, Access on: 23.05.2024

1.3.8 Welcoming and Non-Welcoming: Comparing Policy for Asylum Seekers and Investors

One point that creates debate about the difference in a country's treatment of different categories of migrants is the fact that, on one hand, the country has a welcoming policy for highly skilled migrants or investors, and on the other hand, a different migration policy for economic migrants and refugees.[217] That is why a description of the situation of this second category of migrants was given at the beginning of this section.

The welcoming policy visible for investors is completely different for asylum seekers. In May 2021, the Maltese Ministry of Home Affairs introduced a new policy denying asylum seekers from "safe countries" (including those awaiting asylum decisions, appealing decisions, or who had had their request for asylum rejected) the right to work for nine months after arrival in Malta.[218] Malta is also the gateway for many migrant boats arriving through the Mediterranean, and its search policies are also a subject of criticism and analysis from both the literature and NGOs.[219] In the Mediterranean, 27,629 have people lost their lives on routes to Europe, according to data from the IOM Missing Migrants Project.[220]

1.3.9 The National Environment Against/In Favour of the Citizenship by Investment Scheme

At the time the law was enacted, 53 % of the Maltese population was against citizenship by investment, and only 10 % supported the measure on the

217 For more on the inclusive-exclusive aspects of Maltese migrant integration programme see: Sonne, Kirstin (2021) Learning to "belong": processes of inclusion and exclusion in Malta's migrant integration programme.

218 European Commission, Malta: New policy denies asylum seekers from safe countries the right to work, 11/06/2021, Available on: https://ec.europa.eu/migrant-integration/news/malta-new-policy-denies-asylum-seekers-safe-countries-right-work_en, Access on: 03/04/2023 .

219 Malta is ramping up "despicable and illegal" migrant pushbacks – new report by Amnesty International. Available on: https://www.amnesty.org.uk/press-releases/malta-ramping-despicable-and-illegal-migrant-pushbacks-new-report Access on: 03.07.2023

220 Missing Migrants Project, IOM, 2023. Available on: https://missingmigrants.iom.int/ Access on: 03.07.2023

condition that applicants would make a significant investment in the country.[221] Would citizenship by investment be less problematic if the majority were in favour? Political theorist Chris Armstrong asked the same question back in 2014,[222] but did not answer it. Since it is not the purpose of this dissertation to check whether a referendum consulting the population would be in agreement with the sale of citizenship, I will just offer some thoughts on the question. First, the idea of direct democracy over naturalisation has already been practiced. For example, in Switzerland, referenda on naturalisation are a common practice.[223] In the case of Malta, only seven referendums have been held in its entire history. Perhaps the most important for this topic is the 2003 referendum, where the population was asked, "Do you agree that Malta becomes a member of the European Union, which will take place on 1 May 2004?" Malta applied for EU membership in 1990, and in 1996, the application was suspended because the Labour Party took power. In 1998, a new change of government resumed negotiations until a referendum confirmed Malta's membership in 2004. Interestingly, 48.04 % were in favour, but 41.50 % voted against.[224] This means that Malta's membership in the European Union is extremely contested. There would have been even more direct participation by the Maltese population if, during the establishment of the citizenship by investment scheme, Malta had consulted its population via referendum.[225] At least in this case, the government would also have been endorsed by the Maltese population, and it would have offered more transparency on the elaboration of requirements, applicants excluded, and time of expected effective residence from applicants in the country. A larger

---

[221] Malta Today, Malta says yes to budget, no to sale of citizenship. 11/11/2013, Available on: https://www.maltatoday.com.mt/news/data_and_surveys/31360/maltatoday-survey-budget-citizenship-20131111#.ZCWTB-xBzpA, Access on: 30/03/2023

[222] Armstrong, Chris. The Price of Selling Citizenship. EUI Working Papers, Robert Schuman Centre for Advanced Studies: Should Citizenship be for Sale?, 2014

[223] Oltermann, Philip. Switzerland votes to ease citizenship process. Available on: https://www.theguardian.com/world/2017/feb/12/switzerland-votes-immigrants-citizenship-rights-islamophobia Access on: 26/04/2023

[224] University of Malta. Referenda in Malta, referenda questions and voting results. Available on: https://www.um.edu.mt/r/projects/maltaelections/referenda Access on: 26/04/2023

[225] The current legislation that regulates the conduct of referenda is the Referenda Act of 1973.

period of debate would have allowed a more participatory and democratic elaboration of the legislation. The Labour Party campaigned for Malta not to join the European Union. That same party launched the citizenship by investment programme in 2013.[226]

1.3.10 Conclusion: Maltese Citizenship by Investment

This chapter presented two case studies that will be used throughout the dissertation. One example is residence by investment (Portugal), and one example is citizenship by investment (Malta). The next chapter presents the possible breaches of European law in the Maltese and Portuguese schemes, as well as the reactions of the European institutions regarding the two types of programmes.

1.4 Conclusion of Chapter 1

Chapter one of this dissertation presented two investment migration models to exemplify how they work in their respective countries, something that is a gap in the literature. We chose to have a case of residence by investment (Portugal) and a case of citizenship by investment (Malta). The Portuguese case was chosen to represent an investment visa that lasts for more than a decade and is one of the visas with the highest number of applicants. The Maltese case was chosen because it is the only investment citizenship programme that still exists in the European Union and because it is a case that the European Commission has opposed with infringements, alleging a violation of European law and the lack of a genuine link between the investor and the country granting nationality.

The Portuguese case, called ARI (*Autorização de Residência por Investimento* – Residence Permit for Investment), came into being in 2012 and remained in force until 2024. It granted a residence permit in Portugal for an initial period of two years, which had to be renewed every two years. In return, the investor had to choose one of five investment possibilities among the categories of capital transfer or business: (a) EUR 500,000 for the acquisition of investment funds or venture capital fund units committed to the

---

226 Pace, Roderick. A Small State and the European Union: Malta's EU Accession Experience. (2009) South European Society & Politics

capitalisation of companies incorporated under Portuguese law; (b) EUR 500,000 for research activities of public or private entities that are part of the national scientific and technological system or EUR 400,000 in a low population density area;[227] (c) EUR 250,000 in support of artistic production or in the recovery or maintenance of national cultural heritage, or EUR 200,000 in a low population density area. In terms of business options, one of the following must be applied: (d) creation of a minimum of ten new jobs, or eight new jobs in a low population density area; or (e) EUR 500,000 for the incorporation of a commercial company that is registered and headquartered in Portugal, creating a minimum of five permanent jobs or maintaining at least ten jobs for three years.

The benefits of holding the Portuguese golden visa are that you can live, work, and study in Portugal, as well as have the right to move around the Schengen area for 90 days within a period of 180 days. The visa also allows you to apply for Portuguese citizenship after five years. Among the main criticisms from the European Parliament and NGOs are the risks of corruption, the lack of transparency, and a possible increase in the cost of housing in Portugal.

The second case, Malta, illustrates the only case of citizenship by investment still in force in the European Union. The scheme (Citizenship for Exceptional Services by Direct Investment; S.L 188.06 – Maltese Citizenship Act, Cap. 188, LN 437 of 2020) grants Maltese nationality to an investor and their dependents in exchange for an investment. This investment must be a contribution of at least EUR 600,000 for a minimum residence period of 36 months or EUR 750,000 for a minimum of 12 months. Additionally, the applicant must purchase a residential property in Malta worth at least EUR 700,000, which must be held for five years, or lease a residential property with a rental value of at least EUR 16,000 per annum. An additional donation of EUR 10,000 must be made to a sporting, cultural, scientific, philanthropic, animal welfare or artistic non-governmental organisation or society.

The benefits of the Maltese passport are numerous. It provides access to over 190 visa-free countries and the right to live, work, and study in Malta. As the country is part of the European Union, the holder and their family members also acquire European citizenship as a result of the Maltese passport

---

227 A low population density area is defined as less than 100 inhabitants per km or with a GDP per capita below 75 % of the national average.

(Article 9 TEU and Article 20 TFEU). This entitles the holder to live, work, and study in any member state of the European Union, and to political and diplomatic rights.

Criticism of the investment naturalisation model led the European Commission to file a case with the European Court of Justice. Among the criticisms, which also refer to a lack of transparency, corruption, and money laundering risks, the violation of the principle of sincere cooperation (Article 4, TEU) and international law stemming from the genuine link theory (*Nottebohm* case – ICJ) stand out among the European Commission's arguments.

The chapter, therefore, provides a detailed description of the schemes' historical evolution, from their implementation to subsequent changes and present status. It prepares the reader to understand the criticisms of these programmes, which are presented in the second chapter, specifically on European law.

EU Citizenship & EU Competence: The Reactions from European Institutions

In an unprecedented move, since the area of citizenship is generally seen as the exclusive competence of each Member State[228], the European institutions have raised a number of concerns regarding citizenship and residence by investment[229]. The legal argument put forward by the European institutions is that citizenship by investment violates the principle of sincere cooperation. This principle, enshrined in Article 4(3) of the Treaty on European Union (TEU), requires both the EU and its Member States to assist each other in fulfilling their obligations under the EU Treaties. This chapter initially introduces several concepts that will be important to understand the arguments of European institutions against investment migration. Citizenship, EU citizenship, and the principle of conferral are part of the introductory part of the chapter. Later, the chapter explains what has been claimed in the past by the

228 In the context of the European Union (EU), the process of naturalisation, which entails the acquisition of citizenship by individuals, is regulated at the level of Member States rather than by the EU as a collective entity. This decentralised approach is underpinned by the principle of conferral (Articles 4 and 5 TEU), which asserts that the EU possesses only those competencies that have been explicitly conferred upon it by the Member States.

229 European Parliament Resolution of 16 January 2014 on EU citizenship for sale (2013/2995(RSP)), European Commission, Report on Investor Residence and Citizenship of 23 January 2019

European Parliament,[230] European Commission,[231] and wider scholarship[232] as contrary to European law on naturalisation and residence by investment. The chapter then presents the current allegations of breaches of European law regarding citizenship and residence by investment. My assessment uses the case law of the Court of Justice of the European Union and the literature to argue that there is no breach of European Union law regarding both residence and citizenship by investment. In the case of citizenship by investment, the principle of conferral gives the competence on matters of nationality to Member States, and this principle cannot be challenged by the principle of sincere cooperation unless the rules on the acquisition of nationality change, via a Treaty change, in the future to place this competence in the hands of the European Union. On matters of residence by investment, the granting of residence permits is temporary, and only after five years can they be converted into permanent residence permits (as in the case of Portugal). The tension here is the fact that the long-term Directive, which establishes the requirements for permanent residence, states that periods of absence from the territory of the Member State concerned shall not interrupt the five-year period of continuous and legal residence, when they are shorter than six consecutive months and do not exceed 10 months in total.[233]

The same Directive gives discretion to Member States in cases of "specific or exceptional reasons of a temporary nature and in accordance with their national law" to accept that a longer period of absence [...] "shall not interrupt the period"[234] of five years of legal and continuous residence. Applying this

---

230 European Parliament Resolution of 16 January 2014 on EU citizenship for sale (2013/2995(RSP))

231 European Commission, Report on Investor Residence and Citizenship of 23 January 2019

232 Young, Alexia. The duty of sincere cooperation and its implications on the acquisition of citizenship by investment, 2022, University of Malta; Carrera, Sergio. The Price of EU Citizenship The Maltese Citizenship-for-Sale Affair and the Principle of Sincere Cooperation in Nationality Matters (2014) Maastrich Journal of European and Comparative Law No. 2014-3; Prats, E. Are Citizenship by Investment Programs Legitimate? Suggesting Some Assessment Methods, in Money Matters in Migration, W. M. Tesseltje de Lange, Annette Schrauwen, Editor 2021, Cambridge University Press: Cambridge

233 Article 4 (3) Directive 2003/109/EC

234 Article 4 (3) Directive 2003/109/EC

to the case of an investor who has retained a temporary residence permit by investment for five years, but remains outside the territory longer than six months, this would still – if the Member State allows – count toward the time of the five years of residence, as per the long-term Directive. In that sense, I also do not see a breach of European Union law, since this is in compliance with the long-term Directive, and the Directive allows discretion for Member States. Finally, the second part of the chapter goes through what the European institutions are attempting to protect and how they are doing so. This second part of the chapter represents the other concerns connected to investment migration, which are not part of the scope of analysis of this dissertation but are important to mention and distinguish from the legal arguments central to the dissertation. This chapter attempts to clarify whether there is any violation of European law through citizenship and residence by investment. Regarding the principle of sincere cooperation, I argue that there is no violation of the principle, since naturalisation and the granting of residence permits are the competence of the Member States, established by the European Treaties (TFEU, TEU). In an assessment of the principle of conferral and the principle of sincere cooperation, along with the case law of the Court of Justice of the European Union, I do not see how the principle of sincere cooperation and the current state of interpretation of the CJEU can change a competence that was established by the principle of conferral as resting with the Member States. What I see is an ideal of a regularisation of investment migration within the European Union that is not yet in place, but could become a reality in the future of the Union if the Member States decide to implement requirements for naturalisation at the European Union level.

2.1 The Concept of Citizenship

As this chapter is dedicated to Europe and the responses of its institutions to citizenship and residence by investment, it first requires a definition of what citizenship is and which contributions are required for the acquisition of citizenship. Requirements to acquire citizenship have been historically contested and the chapter will provide some examples accordingly. Nationality is the legal status between a citizen and a state. It confers rights and duties to the holder. It is a legal bond created by law and the regulations on the acquisition of nationality defined by a State. It is a *domaine réservé* and competence of states. I will use and defend this definition of nationality. The definition is developed on the basis of what the European Convention on Nationality[235] defines in Article 2 (a) as a "legal bond between a person and a State and does not indicate the person's ethnic origin" and the Convention on Certain Questions Relating to the Conflict of Nationality Law, where Article 1 states that "it is for each State to determine under its own law who are its nationals. This shall be recognised by other States in so far as it is consistent with international conventions, international custom, and the principles of law generally recognised with regard to nationality."

Chapter three of my research will delve into international law and one of the most frequently cited concepts of nationality, which originates from the International Court of Justice's ruling in the *Nottebohm* case.[236] In this landmark case, the Court defined nationality as a legal bond grounded in a social fact of attachment, which involves a genuine connection of existence, interest, and sentiments, along with the presence of reciprocal rights and duties. This definition is widely recognised and has become a cornerstone in discussions around nationality and citizenship.

The emergence of the modern concept of nationality can be traced back to the Peace of Westphalia in 1648, which marked the beginning of the rise of separate sovereign states.[237] The creation of the nation-state served to define whether a person owed allegiance to a country or not. Back then, nationality was a matter of domestic legislation, just as it is today. Each country defines its nationality laws. However, despite being a domestic issue, it has international consequences. Nationality is essentially a matter of domestic law, but one with international consequences.[238]

---

235 European Convention on Nationality 1997, 6 November 1997, in force 3 January 2000, ETC No. 166, Article 2(a)

236 *Nottebohm Case (Liechtenstein* v. *Guatemala); Second Phase*, International Court of Justice (ICJ), 6 April 1955, ICJ Reports 1955, p. 4; General List, No. 18

237 For a comprehensive overview on the history of the concept of nationality: Ivan Shearer and Brian Opeskin, "Nationality and Statelessness" in Brian Opeskin, Richard Perruchoud and Jillyanne Redpath-Cross (eds.), *Foundations of International Migration Law* (Cambridge University Press, 2012), page 93

238 Ivan Shearer and Brian Opeskin, "Nationality and Statelessness" in Brian Opeskin, Richard Perruchoud and Jillyanne Redpath-Cross (eds.), *Foundations of International Migration Law* (Cambridge University Press, 2012)

Throughout this chapter and the next, I will show that although nationality and the rules on acquisition have varied throughout history, they were always contested. Whether money can be a requirement for nationality is just one more example of tension arising over whether this is a requirement supported by or in accordance with European Union law and international law.

On the rules of acquisition of nationality, most people acquire their nationality because (a) they were born in the territory of a State – *ius soli*; (b) their ancestors transmitted nationality via 0 (*ius sanguinis*); or (c) they naturalise in a State. In the third case, naturalisation rules have different requirements: time of residence, whether the person speaks the language at some level, and what contribution to the State the person offers (e.g. a highly skilled residence permit, as well as money, can be requirements for citizenship). Furthermore, participation in society is something that has always been contested. Examples include the time that residents are required to fulfil in order to apply for citizenship, and the knowledge of cultural and legal rules most prominent in the integration or citizenship tests required by many countries.[239]

Another example of contested requirements and rules regarding nationality is whether women can transmit nationality to their children. In twenty-eight countries, women are prevented from passing their nationality onto children on an equal basis with men. In forty-six countries, women do not transmit their nationality to their spouses on an equal basis either. In many countries, being extremely talented in sports can provide a fast-track citizenship without any other requirement besides talent; this is described as Olympic citizenship.[240] On the talent requirement, examples can also come from extraordinary contributions, such as the Malian immigrant who scaled a building in Paris and saved a child, and was afterward awarded French citizenship due to this act.[241] These are examples of what counts for States

---

239 Van Oers, Ricky. "Deserving citizenship: Citizenship tests in Germany, the Netherlands and the United Kingdom." *Deserving Citizenship*. Brill Nijhoff, 2013

240 SHACHAR, AYELET. "Picking Winners: Olympic Citizenship and the Global Race for Talent." *The Yale Law Journal*, vol. 120, no. 8, 2011, pp. 2088–139. *JSTOR*, http://www.jstor.org/stable/41149587. Accessed 18 Dec. 2023.

241 REUTERS, France offers citizenship to Malaian immigrant who scaled Building to save child, 28th May, 2018. Available on: https://www.reuters.com/article/us-france-hero/france-offers-citizenship-to-malian-immigrant-who-scaled-building-to-save-child-idUSKCN1IS0UF/#:~:text=France%20offers%20citizenship%20to%20Malian%20immigrant%20who%20scaled%20building%20to%20save%20

as requirements for acquisition of nationality. The question of whether this should be the case or not is not the focus of this thesis; this question has a large normative literature surrounding it. However, my question is to what extent the contributions to the State based on money in order to receive a residence permit or citizenship are in accordance with international law and European Union law.

In order to answer this question, it is also necessary to understand that the possibility of having two nationalities has allowed states to be creative in the contributions they require. While processes of naturalisation have been part of State responsibility for centuries, dual citizenship, citizenship by investment, and deprivation (revocation) of nationality represent challenges to the concept of citizenship.[242] This is a challenge because it influences the concept of citizenship by including new requirements that raise questions about whether they are in accordance with the law or not.

2.2 The Phenomenon of Dual Citizenship

One needs also to add that the phenomenon of dual citizenship (which consequently has an important impact on the topics of CBI and RBI) can be explained historically. Harpaz revealed that dual citizenship became a global asset with global growth of dual citizenship with instrumental motivations.[243] Currently, 75 % of states in the world accept dual citizenship and allow their nationals to acquire destination country citizenship while maintaining their home country nationality. Maarten Vink et al. showed that in 1960, only one-third of countries accepted dual citizenship, while in 2017, three-quarters of countries allowed dual citizenship.[244] This progressive change can

---

child,-Reuters&text=PARIS%20(Reuters)%20%2D%20France%20on,balcony%2C%20President%20Emmanuel%20Macron%20said. Access on: 18. December 2023

242 Bauböck, Rainer; Paskalev, Vesco. Citizenship Deprivation: A Normative Analysis, ÇEPS Paper in Liberty and Security in Europe no. 82 (2015), available on: https://www.ceps.eu/ceps-publications/citizenship-deprivation-normative-analysis/, Access on: 11/07/2023

243 Harpaz, Yossi. Citizenship 2.0: Dual Nationality as a Global Asset. (2019) Princeton University Press

244 Maarten Vink and others, The international diffusion of expatriate dual citizenship, *Migration Studies*, Volume 7, Issue 3, September 2019, page 363

be explained by several reasons. One of the historical explanations is the neighbour effect. For example, in Scandinavia, the reform to allow dual citizenship in Sweden was influenced by diaspora communities.[245] Sweden allowed dual citizenship in 2001, followed by Norway (only materialised in 2018), which influenced Finland to reform its citizenship law in 2003.[246] Also, looking from the perspective of countries sending and receiving migrants, there is a phenomenon that Maarten Vink calls "emulation." As more states accept dual-citizen status without too many negative consequences, it becomes harder for countries of origin to reject the more open policy shift to dual citizenship.[247] As Peter Spiro puts it, "dual citizenship has been normalized as an incident of globalization."[248]

But why does this movement to acquire a second nationality occur? Although the ideals of equality related to citizenship are related to citizens who already have the same citizenship, citizenship is a tool of inclusion and exclusion. As Yossi Harpaz explains, "Richer countries tend to be more stable and democratic, and their citizens enjoy extensive travel freedom. The opposite holds for poorer countries."[249] Various rankings have emerged to show how many countries a citizen can travel to with a passport from a particular country. The Yossi Harpaz model includes internal and external values (internal for the worth of citizenship for someone living in the country based on economic development, security, and democracy, and external for

---

245 Bernitz, H. Country Report: Sweden. Robert Schuman Centre for Advanced Studies: EUDO Citizenship Observatory, 2012, Available on: https://ec.europa.eu/migrant-integration/library-document/eudo-citizenship-observatory-country-report-sweden-0_en, Access on: 15.06.2023

246 Fagerlund, Jessica, Brander, Sampo, Country report: Finland, [GLOBALCIT], EUDO Citizenship Observatory, 2010/12, Country Reports – https://hdl.handle.net/1814/19612 Access on: 15.06.2023

247 Vink, Maarten; Schakel, Arjan; Reichel, David; Chun Luk, Ngo; de Groot, Gerard-René; The international diffusion of expatriate dual citizenship, *Migration Studies*, Volume 7, Issue 3, September 2019, Pages 362–383, https://doi.org/10.1093/migration/mnz011

248 Spiro, Peter, At home in two countries, New York University Press, New York, 2016, page 129

249 Harpaz, Yossi. Citizenship and Residence Rights as Vehicles of Global Inequality in Citizenship and Residence Sales Rethinking the Boundaries of Belonging Edited by Dimitry Kochenov and Kristin Surak, 2023, Cambridge, page 288

the degree of travel freedom).[250] They all show that the highest categories of passports are dominated by Western European countries, the United States, and Australia. Following these come some Latin American and Eastern European countries, and the bottom categories mostly consist of Asian and African countries. With globalisation and the world of multiple citizenships in mind, a new phenomenon started. As Peter J. Spiro defined it, "citizenship planning"[251] became a reality, in which the wealthy plan their business and their citizenship/residence affiliation according to their best interests.

The phenomenon of globalisation, coupled with the varying benefits of different passports and a rise in the number of millionaires in developing nations, has led to an increasing demand from individuals from third-world countries for secondary citizenship. While residency and citizenship programmes are available in various regions, Europe offers a unique opportunity: acquiring citizenship in a Member State automatically grants European citizenship, along with the privileges of residing, working, and establishing oneself in any of the other 26 Member States. To fully comprehend the implications of this regional citizenship, it is imperative to delve into its historical development. This understanding will provide a foundation for examining the reactions of the European institutions and their efforts to protect European citizenship.

2.3 Citizenship of the European Union

Introduced in 1992, the Maastricht Treaty introduced the legal concept of EU citizenship as part of the attempt to advance from a mainly economic community to a political union.[252] The aim was to facilitate free circulation in a Europe with no internal borders.[253] There were three reasons for adopting

---

[250] Harpaz, Yossi. Compensatory Citizenship: Dual Nationality as a Strategy of Global Upward Mobility, 2019, 45(6) Journal of Ethnic and Migration Studies 897

[251] Spiro, Peter. Investment Citizenship and the Long Leash of International Law. In Citizenship and Residence Sales Rethinking the Boundaries of Belonging Edited by Dimitry Kochenov and Kristin Surak. Cambridge: Cambridge University Press, 2023, page 137

[252] Craig, Paul; de Búrca, Gráinne. EU Law Text, Cases, and Materials, Seventh Edition (2020) Oxford, Oxford University Press.

[253] Rotaeche, Cristina. Identity, Member States Nationality and EU Citizenship. In The Reconceptualization of European Union Citizenship Edited by Elspeth Guild, Cristina Rotaeche and Dora Kostakopoulou. Brill/Nijhoff, Leiden: 2014, page 16

EU citizenship. First, the idea of EU citizenship was circulating even in the European Economy Community (ECC) and was inscribed in the rhetoric of a "People's Europe," or the idea of a European federation.[254] The second reason is that the Maastricht Treaty reinforced the idea that citizenship need not be exclusively connected to the nation-state.[255] Why would that be the case? The concept aimed to redefine citizenship in a post-national context, with the intention of eliminating the nationalistic connotations that were extolled by the fascist regimes of the interwar era.[256] The third reason was the desire for a greater democratisation within the ECC.[257] In the words of J. Weiler, the concept of European citizenship is distinguished by its radical innovation, as it is based on the notion that the Union is comprised of citizens who do not share a common nationality.[258] Articles 20–25 of the Treaty of the Foundations of the European Union contain provisions on EU citizenship. Article 20 of the TFEU is the foundational provision and summarises the main elements of EU citizenship:

1. Citizenship of the Union is hereby established. Every person holding the nationality of a Member State shall be a citizen of the Union. Citizenship of the Union shall be additional to and not replace national citizenship.
2. Citizens of the Union shall enjoy the rights and be subject to the duties provided for in the Treaties. They shall have, inter alia:
   (a) the right to move and reside freely within the territory of the Member States;
   (b) the right to vote and to stand as candidates in elections to the European Parliament and in municipal elections in their Member State of residence, under the same conditions as nationals of that State; C 326/56 EN Official Journal of the European Union 26.10.2012;

---

254 Craig, Paul; de Búrca, Gráinne. EU Law Text, Cases, and Materials, Seventh Edition (2020) Oxford, Oxford University Press, page 890

255 A Menezes, "Which Citizenship? Whose Europe? The Many Paradoxes of European Citizenship" (2014) 15 German Law Journal 907, 913

256 A Menezes, "Which Citizenship? Whose Europe? The Many Paradoxes of European Citizenship" (2014) 15 German Law Journal 907, 912

257 A Menezes, "Which Citizenship? Whose Europe? The Many Paradoxes of European Citizenship" (2014) 15 German Law Journal 014-915

258 Weiler, J. The Constitution of Europe, Cambridge University Press, 1999, p. 344

(c) the right to enjoy, in the territory of a third country in which the Member State of which they are nationals is not represented, the protection of the diplomatic and consular authorities of any Member State on the same conditions as the nationals of that State;
(d) the right to petition the European Parliament, to apply to the European Ombudsman, and to address the institutions and advisory bodies of the Union in any of the Treaty languages and to obtain a reply in the same language.
(e) These rights shall be exercised in accordance with the conditions and limits defined by the Treaties and by the measures adopted thereunder.

As the Treaty states, it "shall be additional" which means that EU citizenship is dependent upon the possession of Member State nationality. Therefore, someone who obtains Portuguese or Maltese nationality will also have EU citizenship. As EU law does not regulate the conditions for naturalisation, the granting of citizenship is, as Ayelet Shachar puts it, the last bastion of sovereignty.[259] One of the main EU citizenship rights under discussion when commenting on residence or citizenship by investment is the right of free movement and residence. This right is prescribed in Article 21 of the TFEU, which states as follows:

> Article 21 1. Every citizen of the Union shall have the right to move and reside freely within the territory of the Member States, subject to the limitations and conditions laid down in the Treaties and by the measures adopted to give them effect.
>
> 2. If action by the Union should prove necessary to attain this objective and the Treaties have not provided the necessary powers, the European Parliament and the Council, acting in accordance with the ordinary legislative procedure, may adopt provisions with a view to facilitating the exercise of the rights referred to in paragraph 3. For the same purposes as those referred to in paragraph 1 and if the Treaties have not provided the necessary powers, the Council, acting in accordance with a special legislative procedure, may adopt measures concerning social security or social protection. The Council shall act unanimously after consulting the European Parliament.

---

[259] Ayelet Shachar, Coda, EUI Working Papers, Robert Schuman Centre for Advanced Studies: Should Citizenship be for Sale?, 2014

Despite many rights, EU citizenship mentions the word "duties" in the Treaties only once, with some scholars arguing that there are no empirically observable duties of EU citizenship.[260] It is important to say that since the Maastricht Treaty in 1993, the European Union has changed in many ways. Notably, the 2004 enlargement (which included Malta) was one of the major changes due to the addition of ten new members, going from 18 to 28 Member States (now 27).

EU citizenship is paradoxical because it depends on the naturalisation policies of its members and not on itself. As Jo Shaw puts it, "formally constitutionalized in the Union's Treaty framework, yet dependent upon national citizenship to provide the gateway to membership."[261] In this paradox also lies the question of the influence of EU law in Portugal and Malta regarding residency and citizenship by investment. While these countries are responsible for deciding who will be their citizens, the European Union feels aggrieved since, due to automatic EU citizenship, these citizens will also be able to live, work, and study in the other 26 countries of the Union.

It is important to say that conferring European citizenship to the nationals of Member States was not an attempt to reduce the power of the Member States on matters of acquisition and loss of nationality. Daniel Sarmiento explains that this conferral "was originally conceived as a symbolic act of empowerment on the grounds of new EU rights, but it did not weaken, nor was it intended to weaken, the rights or status of Member State nationality."[262] It should be noted that despite the current absence of comprehensive regulations, there have been endeavours within the European Parliament to establish guidelines for the acquisition and loss of citizenship at the EU level. In 1991, the European Parliament resolved that the European "Union may establish certain uniform conditions governing the acquisition or loss of the citizenship of the Member States." Nonetheless, this resolution failed to be included in the Maastricht Treaty.[263]

---

260 Kochenov, Dimitry EU Citizenship without Duties, European Law Journal, Vol. 20, No 4, July 2014, pp. 482–498

261 Shaw, Jo. EU Citizenship: Still a fundamental status? In Debating European Citizenship, Rainer Bauböck (Editor), IMISCOE Springer Open, 2018

262 Sarmiento, D., EU Competence and the Attribution of Nationality in Member States. IMC Working Papers, 2019/2 (Investment Migration Working Papers), page 11

263 European Parliament "Resolution on Union Citizenship," 14 June 1991

Discussions about whether European Union citizenship should be autonomous are also present in the literature.[264] Dora Kostakopoulou is in favour of an autonomous EU citizenship. The proposal put forward by the individual in question is to make EU citizenship conditional on domicile for a minimum of five years within the Union. This approach is viewed as a viable means of establishing community membership as a true determinant of belonging, while also addressing the longstanding issue of excluding 20 million long-term resident third-country nationals. Additionally, it would remedy the lack of uniformity in the application of EU law due to varying naturalisation requirements in different Member States. This approach could also serve as an alternative for UK nationals impacted by Brexit, allowing them to opt for autonomous "Eurozenship," as well as highly skilled third-country nationals who seek citizenship through investment.[265] Overall, this proposal presents a potential solution to several longstanding issues within the EU, while also promoting greater inclusivity and uniformity across Member States.

Contrary to this idea, Richard Bellamy argues against an idea of autonomous Eurozenship. Regarding the example of British citizens keeping their EU citizenship after Brexit, he argues that there is no argument to be made in favour of this idea. Once the state has withdrawn from the EU and relinquished the rights associated with membership, British citizens should no longer possess EU citizenship. He believes that allowing people to benefit from the social and legal systems of Member States without taking on the responsibilities of national citizenship would have a detrimental effect on "civility and solidarity" among Europeans. This erosion could occur within their respective states, between the Member States, or towards non-Europeans.[266]

---

264 Orgad, Liav and Lepoutre, Jules (2019). Should EU Citizenship Be Disentangled from Member State Nationality? Robert Schuman Centre for Advanced Studies Research Paper No. RSCAS 2019/24

265 Kostakopoulou, Dora. Who Should Be a Citizen of the Union? Toward an Autonomous European Union Citizenship in Orgad, Liav and Lepoutre, Jules (2019). Should EU Citizenship Be Disentangled from Member State Nationality? Robert Schuman Centre for Advanced Studies Research Paper No. RSCAS 2019/24, page 4

266 Bellamy, Richard. On Mushroom Reasoning and Kostakopoulou's Argument for Eurozenship in Orgad, Liav and Lepoutre, Jules (2019). Should EU Citizenship Be Disentangled from Member State Nationality? Robert Schuman Centre for Advanced Studies Research Paper No. RSCAS 2019/24, page 5

2.4 The Principle of Conferral and the Allocation of Powers Between the EU and its Member States

It is important to explain the differences between competence in matters of naturalisation and competence in matters of immigration, because while the former is the exclusive competence of Member States (naturalisation), the latter is also the competence of the European Union. This is relevant since residence by investment relates to granting residence permits, and therefore, the competence to decide who is granted a residence permit is from the Member States but has consequences for the European Union as well. A broad number of directives on immigration have been agreed between the Union and Member States in recent decades.[267] Hence, the significance of immigration competence in this thesis is noteworthy, as residence by investment may fall within the purview of the European Union's competencies related to immigration, given its implications for immigration matters. With this overview of the conferral principle, it will be possible to delve more deeply into the principle of sincere cooperation. In the debate that follows, there is tension between the two principles: conferral and sincere cooperation. The literature has already explained that this tension between the two principles has resulted in various legal developments. For example, loyalty (sincere cooperation) was instrumental in expanding the competences of the Union in cases such as ERTA,[268] among others. As a rival principle, conferral is an instrument that preserves Member State prerogatives.

2.5 Competence on Matters of Naturalisation

2.5.1 Is the EU Competent for Naturalisation Matters? Article 5 (1) TEU

The principle of conferral is a fundamental principle of EU law. For many years, it was an implicit but unanimously recognised limit on the powers of the European Communities.[269] It emerged in the late 1980s and was

---

267 Family Reunification Directive 2003/86/EC, the Long-term Directive 2003/109/EC and the Students and Researchers Directive 2016/801

268 Commission of the European Communities v Council of the European Communities. European Agreement on Road Transport, Case 22-70 European Court of Justice, 1971

269 Iglesias, Gil Carlos Rodríguez. Reflections on the General Principles of Community Law, 1998 Cambridge Yearbook of European Legal Studies, 1, 13–14

introduced by the Maastricht Treaty, as a consensus on the need to codify the principle.[270] This was done on the text enshrined in Article 5 (1) TEU: "the limits of Union competences are governed by the principle of conferral."

The principle means that the EU is a union of its Member States, and all its competences are voluntarily conferred by its Member States. The Treaty on European Union refers to Article 4: "1. In accordance with Article 5, competences not conferred upon the Union in the Treaties remain with the Member States."[271] From these provisions, the Union cannot confer powers on itself. For example, the Union cannot confer to itself the power to legislate on matters of acquisition and loss of nationality. As a result, if the Union acts beyond its powers, the act in question will be invalid. Deciding whether an act is invalid is the responsibility of the European Court of Justice (ECJ).

Article 5 (2) of the Treaty on European Union states that "Under the principle of conferral, the Union shall act only within the limits of the competences conferred upon it by the Member States in the Treaties to attain the objectives set out therein. Competences not conferred upon the Union in the Treaties remain with the Member States."[272] However, the formulation of Article 5 (2) can be misleading if one believes that the Union enjoys only those – limited – competences expressly conferred by the Treaties, whereas Member States retain those competences not conferred upon the Union. Why would that be? Robert Schütze explains that there are two reasons. Throughout its history, the Union has been able to expand its competences beyond what was originally specified in the Treaties. This has been possible due to teleological interpretation and the broad application of general competences, which have allowed the Union to enjoy a certain level of competence expansion. Additionally, it is not accurate to assume that the Member States only retain competences not conferred in the Treaties. In fact, the Union and the Member States share their competences in such a way that they may both

270 Sarmiento, Daniel; Van den Brink, Martijn. EU Competence and Investor Migration in Citizenship and Residence Sales Rethinking the Boundaries of Belonging Edited by Dimitry Kochenov and Kristin Surak, Cambridge, 2023, page 185

271 European Union, Treaty on European Union. 1993.

272 Treaty on European Union, Article 5 (2)

act in a field where the Union is competent to act, aside from one limited category of Union competence.[273]

The European Court of Justice has developed a long-established jurisprudence on annex-competence. For example, the European Union lacks the authority to legislate in the field of public health, as per its granted competences. However, in the Tobacco Advertising II Case,[274] the ECJ confirmed the validity of an EU directive on the advertising and sponsorship of tobacco products. The case aimed to demonstrate that the European Union engaged in complementary participation with Member States, despite its lack of initial competence in certain areas. This participation was driven by a shared interest or willingness to pursue a given objective.

Each area of policy is subject to a type of competence that can be exclusive, shared, or coordinated.[275] The EU has the exclusive competence enshrined in Article 3 of the Treaty of the Functioning of the European Union, and in these areas, the EU alone is able to legislate and adopt binding acts. Member States have competence in these areas only if given the powers by the EU to implement these acts. Examples of areas in which the EU has exclusive competence are the customs union, the establishing of competition rules necessary for the functioning of the internal market, monetary policy for Euro-area countries, conservation of marine biological resources under the common fisheries policy, and common commercial policy.[276]

Article 4 of the TFEU enumerates the shared competences between the Member States and the EU. Both the EU and the Member States are able to enact legally binding acts in the following areas: internal market; social policy (but only for aspects specifically defined in the Treaty); economic, social, and

---

273 Schütze, Robert, EU Competences Existence and Exercise in The Oxford Handbook of European Union Law, Edited by Anthony Arnull and Damian Chalmers Oxford, 2015, page 77

274 Case C-380/03, Federal Republic of Germany v European Parliament and Council of the European Union

275 See Articles 2–8 TFEU. For a broad description of the typology of competences and its effects, see Hartley, TC. The Foundations of European Union Law: an introduction to the constitutional and administrative law of the European Union. Eighth Edition, Oxford: Oxford University Press, 2014, page, 119

276 EUR-Lex, Division of competences within the European Union, Available on: https://eur-lex.europa.eu/EN/legal-content/summary/division-of-competences-within-the-european-union.html, Access on: 29.08.2023

territorial cohesion (regional policy); agriculture and fisheries (except conservation of marine biological resources); environment; consumer protection; transport; trans-European networks; energy; area of freedom, security and justice; common safety concerns in public health matters (limited to the aspects defined in the TFEU); research, technological development and space; and development cooperation and humanitarian aid.[277] In the shared competence, the Member States will exercise their own competence in these areas when the EU does not exercise or has decided not to exercise competence.

Finally, coordinated or supporting competences are established in Article 6 of the TFEU. In the following areas, the EU can only intervene to support, coordinate, or complement the actions of its Member States. These are industry, culture, tourism, education, vocational training, youth and sport, civil protection, and administrative cooperation. As visible in the previously mentioned areas, naturalisation is not listed in any of the Treaties as a competence of the European Union. Moreover, Article 5 of the Treaty on European Union states that "The limits of Union competences are governed by the principle of conferral. The use of Union competences is governed by the principles of subsidiarity and proportionality."[278] Some authors argue that although naturalisation is indeed the competence of Member States, Brussels "decided to test this clear division of competences using investment migration as a starting point."[279]

The limitations of the principle of conferral are established in Article 352 TFEU:

> If action by the Union should prove necessary, within the framework of the policies defined in the Treaties, to attain one of the objectives set out in the Treaties, and the Treaties have not provided the necessary powers, the Council, acting unanimously on a proposal from the Commission and after obtaining the consent of the European Parliament, shall adopt the appropriate measures. Where the measures

---

277 EUR-Lex, Division of competences within the European Union, Available on: https://eur-lex.europa.eu/EN/legal-content/summary/division-of-competences-within-the-european-union.html, Access on: 29.08.2023

278 European Union, Treaty on European Union. 1993

279 Kochenov, D. B., Elena, It's All about Blood, Baby! The European Commission's Ongoing Attack against Investment Migration in the Context of EU Law and International Law. Working Paper no. 161 The Centre on Migration, Policy & Society, 2022.

> in question are adopted by the Council in accordance with a special legislative procedure, it shall also act unanimously on a proposal from the Commission and after obtaining the consent of the European Parliament.

This provision allows the EU to take measures beyond the principle of conferral but must be read together with Opinion 2/94 from the Court, which states that this provision "cannot serve as a basis for widening the scope of Community powers beyond the general framework created by the provisions of the Treaty." However, some would view that as it allows for flexible adjustments of EU competences and has been used to that end.[280]

Daniel Sarmiento argues that at present, the European Union does not possess the authority to intervene in the nationality policies of its Member States by imposing conditions for the acquisition of nationality, unless there are objective challenges that necessitate such intervention. In such cases, the EU must provide substantiated arguments under Article 352 TFEU to take appropriate measures. This would be a long way for the Commission to go to seek an end to investment migration programmes and imply the risk and difficulty of being able to adopt measures unanimously, as the article requires.

Furthermore, one could think that Article 114 TFEU[281] would be a legal basis for action by the European Union in matters of naturalisation. That is not viable, as the Article gives competence to the EU to enact measures for the approximation of laws, with the objective of "the establishment and functioning of the internal market." There is no reference to naturalisation law. Therefore, the EU would not have competence to intervene in CBI programmes because conditions for acquiring nationality are a competence of Member States.[282]

---

280 Schütze, Robert. EU Competences: Existence and Exercise in Antony Arnull and Damien Chalmers (eds) The Oxford Handbook of EU Law, Oxford University Press 2015, pages 79–80

281 TFEU, Article 114-1. Save where otherwise provided in the Treaties, the following provisions shall apply for the achievement of the objectives set out in Article 26. The European Parliament and the Council shall, acting in accordance with the ordinary legislative procedure and after consulting the Economic and Social Committee, adopt the measures for the approximation of the provisions laid down by law, regulation or administrative action in Member States which have as their object the establishment and functioning of the internal market.

282 Sarmiento, D., EU Competence and the Attribution of Nationality in Member States. IMC Working Papers, 2019/2 (Investment Migration Working Papers)

Member States are competent regarding naturalisation due to the conferral principle. However, the CJEU and European institutions have attempted to prevent deviations from the EU's legal principles on matters of acquisition and loss of nationality. The EU normally only interferes in nationality issues when Member States have enacted policies that restrict the rights of EU citizens, instead of when the rights are to be enjoyed by new citizens. For example, the *Rottmann* case[283] was the first time the CJEU directly interfered in the field of citizenship law. The case concerns an Austrian national who acquired German citizenship after moving to Germany. However, the applicant did not inform the German authorities at the time of the naturalisation application that he was subject to criminal proceedings in Austria. As the case was treated as fraud, Germany had to withdraw German nationality. However, as the applicant had to renounce his Austrian nationality when applying for German nationality, he became stateless.

Against this background, the Luxembourg Court ruled that to comply with EU law, measures to withdraw and deprive a person of EU citizenship needed to be amenable to judicial review at the national level and needed to be proportionate. However, the Court also noted that withdrawing nationality would be a legitimate state interest in fraud. Especially when it comes to competence, when a Member State strips its citizen of their citizenship, the situation "falls by reason of its nature and its consequences, within the ambit of EU law."[284]

Naturalisation is a competence of Member States. That is the mantra Malta has mentioned many times regarding citizenship by investment. The Investment Migration Council, in their statement against the European Commission, argued that the European Union is acting "in the absence of competence; based on flawed legal reasoning; and potentially capable of undermining the core principles of the internal market."[285] One of these principles is constitutional democracy. As Joseph Weiler has argued, "it is not for the Commission on its own to address these complexities and, respectfully, neither is it for the Court. If there are to be Union norms setting

283 European Court of Justice. Janko Rottmann v Freistaat of Bayern (2010) C-135/08
284 ECJ. Janko Rottmann v Freistaat of Bayern (2010) C-135/08
285 Investment Migration Council, Statement by the Investment Migration Council concerning the European Commission's case against Malta. 2022

out conditions for granting citizenship or residence, these delicate political issues should be thrashed out and decided by the appropriate democratic political procedures, inconvenient as this might be."[286] This path of respecting constitutional democracy and competence on naturalisation matters seems more persuasive. Especially because, as seen in the last chapter, the scheme in Malta was put into force via democratic constitutional deliberation in the Maltese parliament, where the opposition party had the same arguments that are now being argued by the Commission. It is not that the whole of Malta – the country and all its citizens and politicians – was in favour of the scheme. There was resistance and arguments for the end of the Legal Notices that brought the scheme to force.

In summary, the exercise of EU competence relies on the existence of a legal basis in the Treaties defining the powers of the legislative and executive EU institutions.[287] I do not see any possibility for the EU to act on matters of acquisition of nationality. First, due to the established competence that naturalisation is a competence of Member State. Second, even if the European Union identified arguments to act according to Article 352 of the Treaty on the Functioning of the European Union, the action requires a unanimous vote in the Council, in which every Member State has a right of veto. As some Member States have CBI programmes, it is unlikely that they would vote in favour of action against their own policy. Therefore, the action requires broad agreement among all Member States.

2.6 Competence in Matters of Immigration

In contrast to matters of nationality, the EU enjoys competence to create a "common policy on asylum, immigration and external border control" as part of the Area of Freedom, Security, and Justice.[288] Article 79 of the TFEU establishes that the Union "shall develop a common immigration policy aimed at ensuring, at all stages, the efficient management of migration flows,

---

286 Weiler, Joseph H. H.: Citizenship for Sale (Commission v Malta): Who of the Two is Selling European Values?, VerfBlog, 2024/4/14, https://verfassungsblog.de/citizenship-for-sale/, DOI: 10.59704/f3c2e8cfd7fcbbe7

287 Sarmiento, D., EU Competence and the Attribution of Nationality in Member States. IMC Working Papers, 2019/2 (Investment Migration Working Papers), page 05

288 Article 67 (2) of TFEU

fair treatment of third-country nationals residing legally in Member States, and the prevention of, and enhanced measures to combat, illegal immigration and trafficking in human beings."

Therefore, the EU can legislate in four fields: (a) the conditions of entry and residence, and standards on the issue by Member State of long-term visas and residence permits; (b) the definition of the rights of third-country nationals residing legally in a Member State, including the conditions governing freedom of movement and of residence in other Member States; (c) illegal immigration and unauthorised residence; (d) and combating trafficking in persons. Does this mean the EU is in a position to take action against investor residence schemes? The European Union would have some competence over investor residency schemes, but this competence would be very limited. While the details of these schemes are primarily controlled by individual Member States, the EU has the power to develop regulations that may establish stricter basic criteria, harmonise procedural aspects or impose additional requirements in relation to the granting of long-term visas and residence permits. However, the EU's capacity in this area is limited to the formulation of common standards, as ultimate sovereignty over the granting of residence permits based on investment remains with the Member States. At the level of naturalisation, this is not on this list of competences of the EU and therefore, action from the EU in the case of naturalisation by investment is not allowed. Moreover, in the field of residence by investment it is not only Portugal that has a golden visa scheme (residence by investment), but nineteen other Member States also have residence by investment schemes. This means there is almost zero possibility that the Council will authorise a restriction of power by EU regarding these residence by investment programmes. This is controversial, as the same EU Member States are mostly against Citizenship by Investment. This would make more sense if there were some kind of convergence on whether money can be a criterion of admission both for residence by investment and citizenship by investment.

Another form of convergence on immigration and residence can be seen in the issue of highly skilled migration. For example, several European countries have adopted measures to attract professionals in specific fields since the 2000s. This policy has been shaped by the scarcity of local labour and the European Commission's emphasis on welcoming highly skilled immigrants to open the markets.[289] The practice of attracting highly skilled professionals stands in stark contrast to that of investment residency programmes. While the former seeks to acquire human capital, the latter is primarily concerned with economic capital. Furthermore, it is worth noting that several investment residency programmes grant permanent residence status without the need for physical presence during the acquisition period, a requirement that is not applicable in the case of highly skilled migration residence.

Despite the limitations on competence in matters of residence present in Article 79 TFEU, paragraph 5[290] of the same article reinforces the competence of Member States to decide on the volume of admission of third-country nationals for work. That is, Member States can decide whether to restrict or increase the number of third-country nationals admitted to their territory for work, without interference from the European Union.

If the EU is not competent in matters of naturalisation but has some competence in matters of immigration, would it be possible to argue that there is a breach of EU law in CBI or RBI due to the case law of the Court of Justice of the European Union? This will be answered in the next section, an analysis of five cases involving mostly EU citizenship, in order to argue that at the current stage of EU reasoning on citizenship, RBI and CBI remain competences of Member States, as established in the Treaties. The analysis also encompasses the possibility of action from the EU against CBI and RBI using Articles 114 and 352 of the TFEU as a legal basis. These articles do not seem to have a reasonable possibility of action here without interfering with Member State competence.

---

289 Enríquez, Carmen et al., The EU performance in the global competition for highly skilled migrants. Available on: https://www.realinstitutoelcano.org/en/analyses/the-eu-performance-in-the-global-competition-for-highly-skilled-migrants/, Access on 14 August, 2023

290 5. This Article shall not affect the right of Member States to determine volumes of admission of third-country nationals coming from third countries to their territory in order to seek work, whether employed or self-employed.

2.7 Accessing the Legality of RBI and CBI by Analysing the European Court of Justice's Decisions on Citizenship

As seen in the previous section, naturalisation is enshrined as a competence of Member States due to the conferral principle. Immigration has already been regulated within the European Union, but decisions on the volume of entries for third-country nationals remain the competence of Member States. If in this area of competence, there is no breach of European law in the field of CBI and RBI, since residence and citizenship by investment are ways of granting either residence or citizenship, and this is a guarantee that Member States have, a second question raises: in the case law of the Court of Justice of the European Union, are there elements in the decisions to argue otherwise? The next section explores five cases that deal with the Court's decisions on EU citizenship or have been used in respect to other themes for arguments by scholars in the field of citizenship to help answer this question: *Micheletti; Rottmann; Tjebbes*; *Syndicat interprofessionnel de défense du fromage Morbier contra Société Fromagère du Livradois SAS; JY v Wiener Landesregierung*. The answer is negative. The case law of the CJEU does not allow an interpretation that argues the European Union has power to impose rules on acquisition of nationality. Most of the cases deal with guaranteeing the rights of European citizens and revocation of citizenship. Nothing is said about the acquisition of nationality, and arguments about the violation of the principle of sincere cooperation are not convincing if read in comparison with other naturalisation programmes all over the European Union, which could also be argued to violate the principle of sincere cooperation in a more aggravated manner. First, I conceptualise and explain the principle of sincere cooperation, since it is the European Commission's main argument in terms of a violation of European law. The chapter is then divided into an analysis of Court decisions that have already touched on the subject of EU citizenship, and then I explore an analysis of current possible violations of European law regarding citizenship by investment.

The following section is devoted to residence by investment. It can be seen that there is little criticism of European institutions in terms of competence, since half the Member States have residence through investment programmes. The analysis is therefore based on other allegations by the

European Commission against residence programmes and then on the possible incompatibility of residence by investment and European law.

2.7.1 The Principle of Sincere Cooperation

When interpreting EU law (e.g. TFEU, TEU), principles of European law have become part of the work of judges and academics. Two traditions fight an interpretative duel: positivist and non-positivist. Positivists approach the law as a set of rules derived from authoritative sources and recognised by particular legal systems, and they view legal interpretation as the appropriate application of these rules. In contrast, non-positivists hold that the law, and its interpretation, extends beyond the established materials of a legal system to encompass underlying principles or other independent moral or ethical considerations.[291] Especially for the case of citizenship and residence by investment, non-positivist theories offer a rich possibility of analysis for the phenomenon of investment migration and the use of EU legal principles and moral and ethical considerations. In the field of European law, particular attention is given to the distinction between structural and substantial principles. Structural principles refer to the organisation and operation of institutions and encompass concepts such as primacy, attribution of competences, institutional balance, subsidiarity, and sincere cooperation.[292] These principles are essential to the effective functioning of the European legal system and have a significant impact on the decision-making process of EU institutions.

The principle of sincere cooperation is enshrined in Article 4 (3) of the Treaty on European Union:

> 3. Pursuant to the principle of sincere cooperation, the Union and the Member States shall, in full mutual respect, assist each other in carrying out tasks which flow from the Treaties. The Member States shall take any appropriate measure, general or particular, to ensure fulfilment of the obligations arising out of the Treaties or resulting from the acts of the institutions of the Union. The Member States shall

291 Walker, Neil; The Philosophy of European Union Law, in The Oxford Handbook of European Union Law, Oxford, Oxford University Press, page 17

292 Walker, Neil; The Philosophy of European Union Law, in The Oxford Handbook of European Union Law, Oxford, Oxford University Press, page 17

> facilitate the achievement of the Union's tasks and refrain from any measure which could jeopardise the attainment of the Union's objectives.

As Article 4 is a core provision to understand the "federal" nature of the European Union, one must understand that this provision contains three paragraphs. The first paragraph entails the "principle of presumed Member States competences," meaning that competencies not conferred to the EU remain with the Member States. The second paragraph commands the EU to respect Member States' national identities. The third paragraph consecrates the principle of sincere cooperation. As explained by Barbara Guastaferro, Article 4 (1) TEU focuses on the vertical division of competencies and strengthens the respect of the principle of conferral; Article 4 (2) TEU presents the idea that protecting diversities in the composite legal order of EU is a goal; and lastly, Article 4 (3) blesses the principle of loyalty, which should inform cooperation among levels of government.[293]

This particular provision encompasses two overarching duties or affirmative obligations that are incumbent upon Member States with regard to their relations both among themselves and with the European Union. First, a mutual duty to provide support to one another, and second, a responsibility to undertake any measures that would aid in the fulfilment of obligations arising from either primary or secondary EU law. This further encompasses a specific prohibition or negative obligation, which mandates Member States to refrain from implementing any measures that may potentially undermine the objectives of the Union.[294]

Article 4(3) TEU is reinforced by Article 24 (3) TEU, in which Member States have the duty to support the EU's external and security policy "actively and unreservedly in a spirit of loyalty and mutual solidarity." The CJEU has used the provision on Article 4(3) to put pressure on the EU institutions and

---

293 Guastaferro, Barbara. Sincere Cooperation and Respect for National Identities. In Oxford Principles of European Union Law Volume I: The European Union Legal Order Edited by Robert Schütze and Takis Tridimas Oxford, Oxford University Press, 2018, page, 351

294 Carrera, Sergio. The Price of EU Citizenship The Maltese Citizenship-for-Sale Affair and the Principle of Sincere Cooperation in Nationality Matters (2014) Maastricht Journal of European and Comparative Law No. 2014-3, page 420

Member States to act in defence of the EU's common interests.[295] Also, as Craig and de Búrca have explained, this duty of genuine cooperation is of general application and does not depend either on whether the Community [now EU] competence is exclusive, or on any right of the Member State to enter into obligations towards non-member countries.[296]

Is there any violation of the principle of sincere cooperation in the context of Citizenship by Investment? For the European Commission, there is a violation of the principle of sincere cooperation in the case of citizenship by investment because there is no genuine link established with the Member State, and this undermines the essence of EU citizenship.[297] This argument, as brought from public international law in the *Nottebohm* case, is explained and deliberated in the next chapter. As this chapter is devoted to EU law and its possible breaches, the analysis of the case law of the Court of Justice of the European Union, aligned with the current literature, will present three arguments that argue there is no violation of EU law: the mass naturalisation argument; the procedural argument on the sincere cooperation argument; and the free riders argument.

2.7.2 The Court of Justice of the European Union

The main role of the Court is to "ensure that in the interpretation and application of the Treaties the law is observed."[298] I think it is important to explain the role of the Court before going into the case law, for two reasons: First, several EU legal cases will be mentioned and the role they play within the context of citizenship and residence by investment is a central part of the argument about the validity of these programmes under EU law. Second,

---

295 De Búrca, Gráinne; Craig Paul; EU Law Text, Cases, and Materials Seventh Edition, Oxford University Press, 2020, page 411

296 De Búrca, Gráinne; Craig Paul; EU Law Text, Cases, and Materials Seventh Edition, Oxford University Press, 2020, page 411

297 European Commission Press Release, "Investor Citizenship Schemes: European Commission opens infringements against Cyprus and Malta for 'selling' EU citizenship" (20 October 2020) available at: <https://ec.europa.eu/commission/presscorner/detail/en/ip_20_1925>

298 Treaty on European Union, Article 19 (1)

the European Commission has referred Malta[299] to the Court of Justice of the European Union, and a decision on the issue is expected soon.

The Court of Justice is based in Luxembourg and has one judge per EU Member State (27 judges). The Court is helped by eleven Advocates General (AGs) whose job is "to present opinions on the cases brought before the Court."[300] They are required to act "with complete impartiality and independence" in delivering "reasoned submissions on cases" with which the Court is involved (Article 252 (2) TFEU). An AG opinion is not required in every case.[301] The Advocates General are members of the Court, but "their Opinions reflect their personal views on how a case should be decided and the freedom that they enjoy stands in contrast with the constraints to achieve consensus under which the judges operate."[302] There appears to be some inconsistency within the Court's approach towards addressing parties' arguments, as some are given full analysis while others are overlooked. Furthermore, dissenting opinions are not published, leaving the opinions of Luxembourg's Advocates General as the only alternative sources of perspective.[303]

The CJEU may sit as a full Court, a Grand Chamber composed of fifteen judges, or in Chambers, in accordance with rules laid down by the Statute.[304] Although there is no system of binding precedent in the Treaty on the European Union, the rulings of the Court of Justice are generally considered a source of law.[305]

---

299 Investment Migration Council, Malta: European Commission refers Malta to the European Court of Justice against all legal advice. 2022; Available from: https://investmentmigration.org/news/malta-european-commission-refers-malta-to-the-european-court-of-justice-against-all-legal-advice/

300 Horspool, Margot; Humphreys Matthew; Wells-Greco Michael. European Union Law 11th edition (2021) Oxford, Oxford University Press.

301 Protocol (No 3) On the Statute of the Court of Justice of the European Union, Consolidated Version, 5 May 2019

302 Barnard, Catherine; Peers, Steve. European Union Law Third Edition (2020) Oxford, Oxford University Press, page 284–285

303 Komárek, Jan, Legal Reasoning in EU Law, in The Oxford Handbook of European Union Law, Oxford, Oxford University Press, 2015, page 49

304 Article 251 TFEU

305 Horspool, Margot; Humphreys Matthew; Wells-Greco Michael. European Union Law 11th edition (2021) Oxford, Oxford University Press, page 122

2.8 Previous Allegations on Matters of EU Law and Incompatibility with EU Citizenship

This section provides examples of past allegations concerning the incompatibility of EU law with regard to EU citizenship. For this discussion, EU law is defined as the principles of EU law derived from the Treaties, with a specific emphasis on the principle of sincere cooperation. As Armin von Bogdandy puts it, "The word 'principle' not only denotes a term of positive EU law but also of jurisprudential analysis, and it is indispensable for the fulfilment of the tasks of legal scholarship."[306] As the principle of sincere cooperation is laid down in Article 4 of Title I TEU, it would be understood as a founding principle (loyal cooperation).[307] The principle can be classified into obligations of the Member States and obligations of the Union.[308] The national legislators of Member States are one of the prime targets of the obligations (sincere cooperation) under Article 4 (3) TEU.[309]

2.8.1 Prohibition of Additional Conditions for Recognition of Naturalisation by Other Member States and Due Regard to EU Law (Micheletti)

The Court has had an important role in matters of nationality. The first decision of the Court in the field of nationality is the *Micheletti* case[310] (1992), in which the Court ruled that within the EU, any Member State nationality legislation must also have "due regard to Community law."[311] This means following any principle held by the EU, for example, proportionality. But why would the Court stress the necessity of respect for Community law? At the time of the decision, 7 July 1992, the European Union had not enacted any

306 Von Bogdandy, Armin, Founding Principles of EU law A Theoretical and Doctrinal Sketch, Revus 12 (2010), 35–56

307 Von Bogdandy, Armin, Founding Principles of EU law A Theoretical and Doctrinal Sketch, Revus 12 (2010), 35–56, page 49

308 Von Bogdandy, Armin and Schill, S. Art 4EUV, in E. Grabitz, M. Hilf, and M. Nettescheim (eds), Das Recht der Europäische Union, Kommentar, Vol. II (Munich: Beck, 2011)

309 Klamert, Marcus, The Principle of Loyalty in EU Law, Oxford: Oxford University Press, 2014, page 26

310 Case C-369/90 Micheletti [1992] ECR I-4239, para. 10

311 Since the entry into force of the Treaty of Lisbon in 2009, the term "Community Law" should now be read as EU law.

regulation or directive in the field of nationality law. In Dora Kostakopoulou's view, "when it became apparent that EU citizens were facing impediments in the exercise of the fundamental freedoms of free movement and residence, the Court of Justice of the EU ruled in 1992 that while the determination of nationality falls within the exclusive competence of the Member States, this competence must be exercised with due regard to the requirements of Community Law."[312]

Mr Micheletti had dual Argentine and Italian nationality, having acquired Italian nationality in accordance with Article 1 of Law No 555 of 13 June 1912 (*Gazzetta Ufficiale della Repubblica Italiana* of 30 June 1912), which, as amended by Article 5 of Law No 123 of 21 April 1983 (*Gazzetta Ufficiale della Repubblica Italiana* of 26 April 1983), stated that the child of an Italian mother or father is an Italian citizen. Mr Micheletti applied to the Spanish authorities for a permanent residence card as a Community national in order to set up a dentistry practice in Spain. That application and a subsequent administrative appeal were dismissed, based on Article 9 of the Spanish Civil Code, which established that in cases of dual nationality where neither nationality is Spanish, the nationality corresponding to the habitual residence of the person concerned before their arrival in Spain was to take precedence, that being Argentine nationality in the case of the plaintiff in the main proceedings. The Court ruled that the provisions of Community Law on freedom of establishment preclude a Member State from denying a national of another Member State, who possesses at the same time the nationality of a non-member country, entitlement to that freedom on the grounds that the law of the host State deems them a national of the non-member country.

In the same Case, the Court reasoned that it was not permissible for the legislation of a Member State to restrict the effects of the nationality granted by another Member State. Paragraph 10 of the decision stated that "Under international law, it is for each Member State, having due regard to Community Law, to lay down the conditions for the acquisition and loss of nationality. However, it is not permissible for the legislation of a Member

312 Kostakopoulou, Dora. Who Should Be a Citizen of the Union? Toward an Autonomous European Union Citizenship, in Should EU Citizenship Be Disentangled from Member State Nationality? Edited by Liav Orgad and Jules Lepoutre European University Institute Robert Schuman Centre for Advanced Studies Global Citizenship Governance

State to restrict the effects of the grant of the nationality of another Member State by imposing an additional condition for recognition of that nationality with a view to the exercise of the fundamental freedoms provided for in the Treaty."[313]

2.8.2 Mass Naturalisation (Rottmann)

In the *Rottmann* case, the European Court of Justice became a "reviewer of the regulatory choices" of the Member States.[314] The Court acknowledged that matters of nationality fall within the competence of national law,[315] and that the exercise of withdrawing the nationality of an EU citizen is due in light of EU law.[316] The Court referred to Declaration No 2, which is annexed by the Member States to the final act of the TEU and was mostly intended to provide Denmark an assurance that matters of nationality remain with the Member States. According to the Declaration,

> The provisions of Part Two of the Treaty establishing the European Community relating to citizenship of the Union give nationals of the Member States additional rights and protection as specified in that Part. They do not in any way take the place of national citizenship. The question whether an individual possesses the nationality of a Member State will be settled solely by reference to the national law of the Member State concerned.[317]

Mr Rottmann was born in Austria and therefore had Austrian nationality. In the 1990s, he was prosecuted in Austria and accused of fraud. In 1995, he moved to Germany. While in Germany, he applied for German nationality but did not reveal to the authorities that he was facing prosecution in Austria. As a result of naturalisation, he lost his Austrian nationality through the operation of law. In the same year of naturalisation, the Austrian authorities

---

313 Case C-369/90 Micheletti [1992] ECR I-4239, para. 10

314 Kostakopoulou, Dora, Who Should Be a Citizen of the Union? Toward an Autonomous European Union Citizenship in Should EU Citizenship Be Disentangled from Member State Nationality? Edited by Liav Orgad and Jules Lepoutre European University Institute Robert Schuman Centre for Advanced Studies Global Citizenship Governance

315 Case C-135/08, Rottmann [2010] EU:C:2020:104, para. 40–41

316 Case C-135/08, Rottmann [2010] EU:C:2020:104, para. 48

317 Declaration No 2, TEU

informed Germany about the criminal proceedings against *Rottmann*, and this led to the revocation of his German nationality. Losing his two nationalities, *Rottmann* became stateless. Furthermore, he was stripped of his EU citizenship and all the privileges and entitlements that came with it, such as free movement, non-discrimination, participation in elections at the European Parliament as well as local elections, and diplomatic protection, among other things.

Rottmann entered an appeal at the German Supreme Federal Administrative Court to challenge the decision of revocation of his German nationality. The Court referred to the European Court of Justice, seeking advice on two questions: (a) Does the loss of Union citizenship in the event of withdrawal of naturalisation, obtained through intentional deception, violate EU law? Such a withdrawal, while lawful under national law, may result in the individual becoming stateless, particularly if they are unable to regain the nationality of another Member State that they previously held, due to the relevant provisions of that state's law. If so, (b) does a Member State which has naturalised a citizen of the Union and now intends to withdraw the naturalisation (obtained by deception) have to pay due regard to EU law, and refrain altogether or temporarily from withdrawing the naturalisation if or so long as the withdrawal would have the legal consequence of loss of citizenship of the Union? Or is the Member State of the former nationality obliged, with due regard to EU law, to interpret and apply, or even adjust, its national law so as to avoid that legal consequence?

The Court of Justice's Grand Chamber determined that the national decision in question must undergo examination under EU law through the application of a proportionality standard. The concept of proportionality in this particular case refers to the fact that it is the duty of the national court of the Member State to consider all relevant circumstances of the case, to afford appropriate time for the person to recover their nationality of origin. According to observations submitted to the Court by various governments, including the *Freistaat Bayern* and the Commission of the European Communities, regulations pertaining to the acquisition and relinquishment of nationality are under the competence of the respective Member State. The Court upheld that the particular case at hand is a subject matter of EU law. The rationale behind this argument is that when a citizen of the Union, who is in the same position as the applicant in the main proceedings, is confronted with a decision that withdraws their naturalisation and places them in a vulnerable position of losing the nationality of another Member State that they originally possessed, and consequently jeopardising their status under Article 17 EC, and the rights that come with it, this situation inherently falls within the scope and implications of European Union law.[318]

The Court argued that the decision to withdraw nationality acquired by deception is in accordance with EU law, as the reasoning is related to the public interest. In this regard, "it is legitimate for a Member State to wish to protect the special relationship of solidarity and good faith between it and its nationals and also the reciprocity of rights and duties, which form the bedrock of the bond of nationality."[319] The Court cited the European Convention on Nationality, which does not preclude a State party from revoking an individual's nationality, even if it renders them stateless, when that nationality was obtained through fraudulent means, false information, or the withholding of any pertinent information attributable to the individual.[320]

In this case,[321] the Advocate General Poiares Maduro also referred to the possibility of other rules of primary Community legislation and the general principles of Community Law to restrict the legislative power of the Member States in the sphere of nationality. At the time of his opinion – 2009 – citizenship by investment was not a topic in the European Union. But he referred that the literature[322] and Greece, in its observations, already mentioned that the possibility of breach of the principle of sincere cooperation (Article 10 EC) could exist if a Member State were to carry out, without consulting the Commission or its partners, an unjustified mass naturalisation of nationals of non-Member States.

---

318 Case C-135/08, Rottmann [2010] EU:C:2020:104, para 42

319 Case C-135/08, Rottmann [2010] EU:C:2020:104, para 51

320 European Convention on Nationality, Article 7 (1) and (3), 1997

321 Opinion of Mr Poiares Maduro – Case C-1235/08 delivered on 30 September 2009

322 The literature used for the reference in his Opinion were: de Groot, G. R., "The relationship between nationality legislation of the Member States of the European Union and European citizenship," in La Torre, M., (ed.), European citizenship: an institutional challenge, Kluwer Law International 1998, p. 115, specifically pp. 123 and 128 to 135; Zimmermann, A., "Europaïsches Gemeinschaftsrecht und Staatsangehörigkeitsrecht der Mitgliedstaaten unter besonderer Berücksichtigung der Probleme mehrfacher Staatsangehörigkeit," EuR, 1995, No 1/2, p. 54, specifically pp. 62–63.

The opinion did not define mass naturalisation in quantitative terms. Neither did it take a position on whether the literature's reference was correct in affirming a possible breach of EU law (Community Law at the time) in regard to mass naturalisation from one Member State without informing the EU institutions and other Member States. This remained unexplored until the argument of mass naturalisation resurfaced in 2014 through scholars arguing that Citizenship by Investment would not be a case of mass naturalisation, since it concerns a limited number of persons,[323] whereas others affirmed that it would be a violation because although the number of naturalisations via investment were low, the qualitative terms of this type of naturalisation were of great importance.[324] In the next section on current allegations of violations of EU law in Citizenship by Investment, I will explain why I do not think what occurs in Citizenship by Investment is a case of mass naturalisation, and, therefore, that it is not a violation of the principle of sincere cooperation.

2.8.3 Prior Consultation on the Naturalisation of a Large, Disproportionate Number of Non-EU-Citizens (Rottmann)

Also, in the *Rottmann* case[325] at the European Court of Justice, the Advocate General affirmed that when a Member State would, without prior consultation, confer its citizenship to a large, disproportionate number of non-EU citizens, there would be an incompatibility with EU law. The exact wording of the General Opinion is presented in the section "other rules capable of restricting the legislative power of the Member State in the sphere of nationality include the provisions of primary Community legislation and the general principles of Community Law." Following this, the Opinion refers to academic literature and the observations of Greece regarding the Community principle of sincere cooperation laid down by Article 10, the Treaty establishing the European Community.[326] At the time, the argument

---

323 Shaw, J. (2018). Citizenship for Sale: Could and Should the EU Intervene?. In: Bauböck, R. (eds) Debating Transformations of National Citizenship. IMISCOE Research Series. Springer, Cham. https://doi.org/10.1007/978-3-319-92719-0_13

324 Carrera, Sergio, How much does EU citizenship cost?, CEPS Paper in Liberty and Security, No 64, April 2014

325 AG Maduro in Rottmann (2009) EU:C:2009:588

326 Article 10 of the Treaty of European Community: Article 10 Member States shall take all appropriate measures, whether general or particular, to ensure fulfilment of the

was that the principle of sincere cooperation could be affected if a Member State were to carry out, without consulting the Commission or its partners, an unjustified mass naturalisation of nationals of non-Member States.

This thesis was also defended by scholars such as Gerard-René de Groot. For him, the violation would come from the obligation of solidarity (*Gemeninschaftstreue*) enshrined in Article 5 of the Treaty establishing the European Community. According to the Article,

> Member States shall take all general or particular measures which are appropriate for ensuring the carrying out of the obligations arising out of this Treaty or resulting from the acts of the institutions of the Community. They shall facilitate the achievement of the Community's aims. They shall abstain from any measures likely to jeopardise the attainment of the objectives of this Treaty.[327]

A violation of the principle "would be observed if a Member State granted its nationality to an important part of the population of a non-EU country, without any previous consultation with Brussels."[328] One example given by the author was if the Netherlands at the time decided to naturalise all the inhabitants of Suriname. This was not a hypothetical case, as the Dutch prime minister suggested this idea during a speech in 1992. If this had happened without first consulting the European Commission, other Member States could have claimed that the principle of solidarity had been violated.[329]

Interestingly, the literature as early as 1995 referred to this possible violation of the principle of sincere cooperation, with particular emphasis on the

---

obligations arising out of this Treaty or resulting from action taken by the institutions of the Community. They shall facilitate the achievement of the Community's tasks. They shall abstain from any measure which could jeopardise the attainment of the objectives of this Treaty.

327 Treaty establishing the European Economic Community (Rome, 25 March 1957), Article 5

328 De Groot, Geard-René, the relationship between the nationality legislation of the Member States of the European Union and European Citizenship. In European Citizenship: An Institutional Challenge: European Forum (Vol. 3, pp. 115–147). Kluwer Law International, 1998, page 123

329 De Groot, Geard-René, page 135

fact that these new citizens would have access to the labour market of other Member States. According to Andreas Zimmermann,

> Zum Teil wird die Auffassung vertreten, ein Mitgliedstaat verletze die ihm im Rahmen von Art. 5 EGV obliegende Pflicht zur Gemeinschaftstreue, sofern er ohne vorherige Konsultationen mit den Organen der Gemeinschaft und den anderen Mitgliedstaaten einer großen Gruppe von Drittstaatsangehörigen die eigene Staatsangehörigkeit verleihe, wodurch diesen dann der Zugang zum Arbeitsmarket der anderen Mitgliedstaaten ermöglicht würde.[330]

The author said that some authors took the view that if a Member State granted its nationality to a large group of third-country nationals without prior consultation with the institutions of the Community and the other Member States, it would not be fulfilling its duty of loyalty to the Community under Article 5 of the EC Treaty, thereby allowing access to the labour market in other Member States. His reference, however, is from Professor Gerard-René de Groot. The early 1990s marked a significant period with regards to the subject of naturalisation. In particular, the creation of Union citizens by the Maastricht Treaty in February 1992 and the subsequent decision of the European Court of Justice in the *Micheletti* case during the summer of the same year (7 July 1992) played a crucial role. The Court's ruling emphasised the need for Member States to undertake naturalisation in accordance with EU law. It is in this context that de Groot argued,

> Ein Mitgliedstaat verletzt möglicherweise auch Gemeinschaftsrecht, und zwar die aufgrund des Art. 5 EWG-Vertrag bestehende Pflicht zur Gemeinschaftstreue, falls einer sehr großen Gruppe von Personen, die nicht die Staatsangehörigkeit eines Mitgliedstaates der Europäischen Gemeinschaft besitzen, die eigene Staatsangehörigkeit verliehen wird ohne vorherige Beratungen mit der Europäischen Gemeinschaft, bzw. Mit den anderen Mitgliedstaaten der Europäischen Gemeinschaft. So ist vertretbar, daß es eine Verletzung des Gemeinschaftsrechts sein würde, wenn beispielesweise die Niederland der ganzen Bevölkerung der Republik Surinam oder einem großen Teil der Bevölkerung der Republik Surinam oder einem großen Teil der Bevölkerung Surinams die niederländische Staatsangehörigkeit verleihen würden ohne vorherige Beratungen mit Brüssel.

---

330 Zimmermann, A.

The early allegations of violation of the principle of sincere cooperation in the naturalisation of Member States in the early 1990s significantly impacted future legal proceedings. It can be argued that the literature on this subject during that period had a lasting influence, as evidenced by the Advocate General's use of this argument in the *Rottmann* case. The *Micheletti* case, which was brought before the European Court of Justice, highlighted the importance of complying with EU law in matters of naturalisation and citizenship, and demonstrated the relevance of early legal developments in shaping future legal discourse. At the time, the concept of mass naturalisation was open to interpretation, as its definition could vary depending on the response – or lack thereof – from other Member States and the European Commission. This relates to what today is an argument about interpreting citizenship by investment and whether or not, in some countries, a violation of the principle of sincere cooperation occurs due to the "mass naturalisation" of third-country nationals who pay for citizenship. The discussion is developed in section 2.9.1.

2.8.4 Tjebbes and the Court of Justice Challenging Member State Sovereignty in Nationality Law (M. G. Tjebbes and Others v Minister van Buitenlandse Zaken)

Whereas in the previous case of *Rottmann*, who became stateless after losing his German nationality, in the case of *Tjebbes*, several EU citizens lost their status as EU citizens and became third-country nationals. The case was judged by the Grand Chamber on 12 March 2019 and requested for a preliminary ruling concerning interpretations of Articles 20 and 21 TFEU and Article 7 of the Charter of Fundamental Rights of the European Union ("the Charter"). The case concerns legislation in the Netherlands that states that its nationals lose their Dutch nationality if they reside outside the territory of the Netherlands (or any Member State of the Union) for a period of 10 years or more. Paragraph 15 of that law states as follows:

> 1. An adult shall lose his Netherlands nationality: c) if he also holds a foreign nationality and if, after attaining his majority and while holding both nationalities, he has his principal residence for an uninterrupted period of 10 years outside the Netherlands ... and outside the territories to which the [EU Treaty] applies.[331]

---

331 Rijkswet op het Nederlanderschap (Law on Netherlands Nationality), 1985

The period could be interrupted in the case of issuing an identity card, a passport, or a declaration of nationality. Also, returning to the country and residing there for one year would cause the 10-year period to be interrupted. There is also the possibility of regaining nationality after losing it, provided one returns to the Netherlands and resides there for at least one year.

The case concerns four family members who lost their nationality because of the 10-year rule.[332] The first three lost their nationality because they lived outside the country for over 10 years. The fourth applicant, the daughter of one of the applicants, lost her nationality because she was the daughter of a denaturalised person. All the applicants filed a case against the minister of home affairs because of being refused new passports. The inquiry was regarding the compatibility of the deprivation of Dutch nationality by operation

332 Ms. Tjebbes was born on 29 August 1984 in Vancouver (Canada) and has, from birth, Netherlands and Canadian nationalities. Her Dutch passport had expired on 9th May, 2008. It was on 25th April, 2014, that Ms. Tjebbes submitted a new passport application to the Netherlands Consulate located in Calgary, Canada. Ms. Koopman, who was born on 23 March, 1967 in Hoorn (the Netherlands), settled in Switzerland on 21 May, 1985. She entered into matrimony with Mr P. Duboux, a Swiss national, on 7 April, 1988, which led to her acquisition of Swiss nationality. At the time, Ms. Koopman held a Netherlands passport that was issued on 10 July, 2000 and remained valid until 10 July, 2005. To obtain a new passport, Ms. Koopman submitted an application to the Embassy of the Kingdom of the Netherlands in Bern (Switzerland) on 8 September, 2014. Ms. Saleh Abady, an Iranian national by birth, acquired Netherlands nationality by Royal Decree on 3 September, 1999. A Netherlands passport was issued to her on 6 October, 1999, which remained valid until 6 October, 2004. However, on 3 December, 2002, her registration with the Personal Records Database was suspended due to her emigration. Since then, Ms. Saleh Abady has continuously resided in Iran as her principal place of residence. On 29 October, 2014, she submitted a passport application to the Embassy of the Kingdom of the Netherlands in Teheran, Iran. Ms. Duboux was born in Lausanne, Switzerland on 13 April, 1995. Due to the dual nationality of her mother, Ms. Koopman, she acquired Dutch nationality by birth, as well as Swiss nationality through her father, Mr Duboux. Although she was never issued a Netherlands passport, she was entered in her mother's passport as a minor. This passport was issued on 10 July, 2000 and remained valid until 10 July, 2005. Ms. Duboux reached the age of majority on 13 April, 2013. In September 2014, along with her mother, she submitted a passport application to the Embassy of the Kingdom of the Netherlands located in Bern, Switzerland.

of law with the regulations of EU law, specifically with Articles 20 and 21 TFEU, interpreted in the context of the ruling of 2 March 2010, in *Rottmann*.

The General Advocate defended the compatibility of Article 20 TFEU and Article 7 of the Charter of Fundamental Rights of the European Union with the legislative provision on Article 15 (1)(c) and (4) of the Law on Netherlands nationality. According to this provision, an adult who possesses dual nationality, including that of a third country, will lose the nationality of a Member State and consequently their citizenship of the Union if they have their principal residence abroad and outside the European Union for a continuous period of 10 years. The General Advocate argued that this provision does not contravene the aforementioned articles, and thus, may be upheld. However, contrary to the first position, the Advocate General held a divergent viewpoint with regard to the minor in question. Article 20 of the Treaty on the Functioning of the European Union and Article 24 of the Charter of Fundamental Rights would preclude Article 16(1)(d) and (2) of the law on Netherlands nationality.

The Court's decision follows up on the *Rottmann* case (described in the previous section). The Court analysed the matter of loss of nationality and reinforced that when it comes to the loss of nationality of a European citizen, the process must be in accordance with EU law and follow principles such as proportionality. In this case, the Court was able to navigate the grey terrain of competence and not encroach on the competence of the Member States, but at the same time insist that EU law is properly followed in light of EU citizenship. The case does not address the acquisition of nationality but allows one to wonder whether, if questioned in the case of acquisition of nationality, the Court would also use EU law arguments in its decision.

2.8.5 Citizenship of the Union and the Proportionality Principle in Revocation of Nationality (JY v Wiener Landesregierung)

In the *Tjebbes* case, the CJEU clarified that the proportionality assessment on loss of EU status should be conducted by the national authorities to evaluate the impact of this loss on the family and professional life of the individuals.[333] The recent case of *JY v Wiener Landesregierung*,[334] of 18 January 2022, prompted

[333] *Tjebbes* cit. para. 44.

[334] C-118/20 JY v Wiener Landesregierung

the Grand Chamber of the Court of Justice to address a preliminary question requested by the Supreme Administrative Court of Austria relating to the interrelation between EU citizenship and the nationality of a Member State. While in *Rottmann* and *Tjebbes* the Court acknowledged that national rules on nationality may be invalidated by EU law when they entail the revocation of EU citizens' rights, in this case, the Court addressed conditions for the acquisition of nationality and EU citizenship when previously lost.

JY, an Estonian national, moved to Austria and sought to become an Austrian citizen by initiating a naturalisation procedure.[335] The *Staatsbürgerschaftsgesetz* 1985 (Austrian Law on Citizenship) para. 10 requires two conditions for Austrian nationality to be granted: the renouncement of former nationality and that the individual should not pose a threat to public order or security.[336] Another specificity is that the applicant for Austrian nationality cannot have been convicted of more than one serious administrative offence.[337]

Therefore, the *Niederösterreichische Landesregierung* (Government of the Province of Lower Austria) assured JY that she would be granted Austrian nationality if she could prove, within two years, that she had relinquished her citizenship of the Republic of Estonia.[338] JY renounced her Estonian citizenship and became stateless. The Austrian government then decided to revoke her previously granted assurance with the argument that she had committed two serious administrative offences related to road safety. These offences were failure to display a vehicle inspection disc and driving while under the influence of alcohol. It is also important to say that these offences were committed after the assurance was granted, and the applicant had already committed eight administrative offences before the assurance was granted.[339] JY thus became stateless permanently and also lost her status as an EU citizen.

The origin of the preliminary ruling procedure before the Court of Justice can be traced back to an action initiated by JY before the Supreme Administrative Court of Vienna. Prior to this, JY had contested the revocation decision before the Administrative Court of Vienna, which had rejected her

335 JY cit. para. 13.

336 *Staatsbürgerschaftsgesetz* 1985 (Austrian Law on Citizenship) para. 10.

337 *Staatsbürgerschaftsgesetz* 1985 (Austrian Law on Citizenship) para. 10.

338 JY cit. para. 14.

339 JY cit. para. 17.

claim on the basis that European Union law was not applicable to the matter in question.[340] Upon receiving an appeal against the decision, the Supreme Administrative Court referred two preliminary questions to the Court of Justice for consideration. Specifically, the Supreme Administrative Court inquired whether the circumstances of JY's case fell within the purview of European Union law and, in the event of an affirmative response, whether national authorities were obligated to evaluate a revocation decision that restricted the restoration of citizenship from the perspective of proportionality in accordance with EU law.[341]

The Court confirmed that the case fell within the scope of EU law because the rights of an EU citizen (Article 20 TFEU) were lost due to the assurance that she would be granted Austrian nationality.[342] For the Advocate General Szpunar, the situation of someone who renounces their previous nationality and loses citizenship of the Union, with the aim of obtaining the nationality of another Member State, falls within the scope of EU law for several reasons. One is that JY did not have any intention of permanently losing her rights as an EU citizen. Her objective was solely to attain Austrian citizenship, and she had a legitimate expectation of regaining her EU citizenship status after a short period of statelessness.[343] The Court confirmed the AG opinion but had to address, for the first time, the procedure for the acquisition of nationality in another Member State. In this case, whether the national authorities are required to verify that the decision to revoke the assurance of granting citizenship is compatible with the principle of proportionality under EU law.

The Court not only imposed an evaluation of the proportionality of the decision made by national authorities of the Member State but also made, for the first time, a proportionality assessment itself. For the Court it was not proportional for Austrian authorities to revoke the assurance of the citizenship due to the gravity of the offences committed.[344] It is noteworthy that although violations pertaining to road safety did not lead to revocation of the driving licence, they were deemed adequate grounds to reject naturalisation.

---

[340] JY cit. para. 20

[341] JY cit. para. 28

[342] JY cit. para. 40

[343] JY cit., opinion of AG Szpunar, para 38

[344] JY cit. para. 73.

This is disproportionate, as the decision to withdraw the assurance to grant the citizenship led to the irrevocable loss of European Union citizen status.[345]

What deserves attention is the fact that the Court provided a critique of Austrian legal requirements for naturalisation when referring to the fact that these requirements cannot undermine the exercise and effectiveness of the rights attached to EU citizenship.[346] And that the practice of requiring renunciation to acquire a new Member State nationality, at least in cases where the person has been a Union citizen before becoming stateless, was ruled as violating EU law due to the disproportionality of the requirement.[347] However, although the case allowed the Court to protect JY *in casu*, the decision does not declare that the requirement to renounce previous nationality for naturalisation is illegal.[348] The case confirms that the loss of nationality of a Member State as a consequence of provisions of national law is subject to judicial review according to EU law. This means that the principle of proportionality must be followed when withdrawing nationality in the sense that national courts must carry out an individual assessment of the consequences of the loss for the persons concerned.

2.8.6 Notes on the Case Law of the European Court of Justice: From Micheletti to JY

The four cases of *Micheletti*, *Rottmann*, *Tjebbes* and *JY* show that the Court of Justice of the European Union has already decided important cases regarding naturalisation. The lessons learned from these cases are that within the context of the legal case of *Micheletti*, the Court confirmed the discretion of states in the field of citizenship law, noting however that national laws regarding citizenship should take into account and respect Community

---

345 Y cit. para. 70.

346 Case C-118/20 JY v. Wiener Landesregierung, para. 47.

347 Hyltén-Cavallius K. Stateless Union Citizens in a Nationality Conundrum: EU Law Safeguarding Against Broken Promises: ECJ 18 January 2022, Case C-118/20, Wiener Landesregierung (Revocation of an assurance of naturalisation), ECLI:EU:C:2022:34. *European Constitutional Law Review.* 2022;18(3):556–571. doi:10.1017/S1574019622000219, page 570

348 Bellenghi, G. (2023). The Court of Justice in JY v. Wiener Landesregierung: Could we expect more? Maastricht Journal of European and Comparative Law, 30(1), 83–94. https://doi.org/10.1177/1023263X231161017

Law.[349] The *Rottmann* case marked a significant shift in the level of argument, as it elevated the discourse surrounding the relationship between national and Union citizenship to a new and more profound level. The significance of the judgement in the legal case of *Rottmann* lies not in the substantive response provided by the Court to the inquiries posed, but in the principle that enables such a response. This case establishes that certain facets of national citizenship are now encompassed within the realm of EU law and are therefore subject to its jurisdiction and that of the Court of Justice. Here the fact that they result in the loss of EU citizenship defines the connection to EU law. This marks a significant development in the discourse surrounding the relationship between national and Union citizenship. Ruling that the revocation of Mr Rottmann's German citizenship must be tested against the EU principle of proportionality, the Court stated that this revocation, along with the German laws that govern it, fell within the scope of EU law. As a consequence, this means that "where national laws and measures on citizenship or nationality conflict with EU law they will not be applicable, and where there is doubt about whether such conflict exists it will be the Court of Justice, which is the final authority, not national courts."[350]

2.9 Current Allegations on Matters of EU Law and Incompatibility of Naturalisation by Investment (CBI)

2.9.1 The Principle of Sincere Cooperation and Mass Naturalisation (Rottmann)

As previously mentioned, in the *Rottmann* case, AG Poiares Maduro[351] suggested that if a Member State were to carry out, without consulting the Commission or its partners, an unjustified mass naturalisation of nationals of non-Member States, this would affect the principle of sincere cooperation.[352]

---

349 C-369/90, Mario Vicente Micheletti and others v Delegación del Gobierno em Cantabria, 1992.

350 Davies, Gareth. The entirely conventional supremacy of Union citizenship and rights in EUI Working Papers RSCAS 2011/62 Has the European Court of Justice challenged member state sovereignty in nationality law?

351 Janko Rottmann v Freistaat of Bayern (2010) C-135/08

352 Opinion of Advocate General Poiares Maduro – Case C-135/08, para. 30

The context in which he mentioned this was in the section on other rules capable of restricting the legislative power of Member States in the sphere of nationality, using principles of Community Law. The Commission argued that Member States must grant and remove EU citizenship, respecting the principle of sincere cooperation and the limits set out by the Court of Justice.[353] In 2018, the European Parliamentary Research Service also made the argument of sincere cooperation against citizenship rules, referring to the AG opinion.

Would what Malta did be considered a mass naturalisation and therefore a violation of the principle of sincere cooperation? Looking at the Maltese context, Malta has 516,000 inhabitants in a 316 km island archipelago. Through the Citizenship by Investment scheme, Malta naturalised 1,800 main applicants plus 6,431 dependents, without counting the extra 1,500 applicants[354] for the latest version of the scheme in 2020 and the number of dependents naturalised since January 2022. These are 8,231 new Maltese citizens for a 516,000 population, or around 1.3 % of the population. As this is a very small number, it seems odd to argue for the violation of the principle of sincere cooperation using the argument of "mass naturalisation," or for the CJEU to restrict the effects of the naturalisation law of a Member State in Malta or any other Member State that uses citizenship by investment as a criteria for naturalisation.

In case this argument could be of relevance and understood as a rule, many other naturalisation laws could be argued as violating the principle of sincere cooperation because they naturalise a large number of third-country nationals. Take the example of the descendants of Sephardic Jews in Portugal. The legislation that started in 2013 changed the nationality law to enable acquisition of Portuguese nationality through naturalisation for descendants of Sephardic Jews of Portuguese origin who were expelled from Portugal in the late-fifteenth century. The provision waived requirements for residence and proficiency in Portuguese. In seven years, the system naturalised 54,000 people with 63 % of applicants granted citizenship. More than two-thirds of the applicants for citizenship in Portugal are Israeli.

---

353 EU citizenship report 2017, European Commission, 2017, p. 12

354 The new version is capped at 400 certificates annually and 1500 overall.

This is just one example, but it seems odd that the Commission would argue or the CJEU would refer Germany for enacting a mass naturalisation and therefore violating the principle of sincere cooperation because it naturalised over 3 million people, mainly from the former Soviet Union, who could claim a link with Germany.[355] Or the Italian policy of granting citizenship to descendants of Italians without time limits on the transfer of citizenship by descent. In order to acquire Italian citizenship by descent, the 1992 Act does not require residence in the country or language knowledge.[356] All these examples show how weak the "mass naturalisation" argument is when compared with other naturalisation models that do not require the applicant to prove language proficiency or length of residence in the country. Some naturalisation laws do not even require the physical presence of the applicant, and nationality can be granted without the applicant having visited the country.

At another level of comparison, the countries that had the highest numbers of new citizenships in 2022 were Italy (213,700, or 22 % of the EU total), Spain (181,600, or 18 %), Germany (166,600, or 17 %), France (114,500, or 12 %) and Sweden (92,400, or 9%). Malta granted 842 new citizenships. Despite the relatively small size of Malta, the number of citizenships issued per 1000 individuals is not significantly higher than in other EU Member States that do not have citizenship or residence by investment programmes (Italy – 3.6; Spain – 3.8; Germany – 2.0; France – 1.7; Sweden 8.8 and Malta – 1.6).[357] As the figures show, countries that do not have citizenship by investment even have a higher number of naturalisations per 1,000 residents, which reinforces

---

355 Anil, Merih. "No More Foreigners? The Remaking of German Naturalization and Citizenship Law, 1990–2000." *Dialectical Anthropology*, vol. 29, no. 3/4, 2005, pp. 453–70. *JSTOR*, http://www.jstor.org/stable/29790750. Accessed 19 Mar. 2024.

356 ZINCONE, Giovanna, BASILI, Marzia, *Country report: Italy*, [GLOBALCIT], EUDO Citizenship Observatory, 2010/35, Country Reports – https://hdl.handle.net/1814/19619

357 Acquisition of citizenship statistics, available on: https://ec.europa.eu/eurostat/statistics-explained/index.php?title=Acquisition_of_citizenship_statistics#:~:text=Acquisitions%20of%20citizenship%20per%201000%20usual%20residents%2C%202022&text=700%20in%202020.-,Most%20new%20citizenships%20in%202022%20were%20granted%20by%20Italy%20(213,400%2C%20or%209%20%25), Access on 18 March 2024.

the lack of harmful effect on other states due to the low number of naturalised citizens in countries that have citizenship by investment.

Numerically, there is no argument that the principle of sincere cooperation is violated as the impact of less than 10,000 new citizens from Malta has not been a problem for the rights of free travel and settlement, or other reasons notified by other Member States. By reasons notified I mean for example a diplomatic protection request denied by another Member State or a passport not being recognised by other Member States due to being issued by naturalisation by investment.[358] However, the mass naturalisation argument originated in the AG opinion from the *Rottmann* case, in which the second part of the opinion mentioned that the principle of sincere cooperation could be in breach if a Member State does not consult other Member States and the Commission on naturalisation of a large, disproportionate number of non-EU citizens. Therefore, the second possible allegation of violation of the principle of sincere cooperation investigates whether this could be applied to citizenship by investment and, therefore, provides an example of violation of EU law.

2.9.2 The Principle of Sincere Cooperation and Previous Consultation with Other Member States and the Commission on Naturalisation of a Large, Disproportionate Number of Non-EU Citizens (Rottmann)

The last section analysed the term "mass naturalisation" and its possible implications in the case of CBI. This section goes into the procedural component of the possible violation of the principle of sincere cooperation. Could it be argued that countries such as Malta, Cyprus, and Bulgaria, which had previously implemented citizenship by investment programmes, should have sought consultation with other European Union Member States and relevant EU institutions prior to adoption? Taking into account Article 4 (3) of the TEU, which is a duty and not an option, as well as the AG's opinion in the *Rottmann* case that "the principle of sincere cooperation laid down by Article 3(3)

[358] Here, I highlight the Jessup Moot Court case of 2024, in which a fictitious country – Republic of Antrano – does not recognise the passport issued by someone who acquired citizenship by investment in the Kingdom of Remisia. Available on: https://www.ilsa.org/Jessup/Jessup2024/Jessup%202024%20Compromis%20and%20Corrections%20and%20Clarifications.pdf Access on: 18 March 2024

TEU could be affected if a Member State were to carry out, without consulting the Commission or its partners, an unjustified mass naturalisation of nationals of non-Member States," it seems reasonable to argue that it would be necessary to respect this principle when implementing a new policy of naturalisation. However, in the case of Malta, there was communication between the European Commission and Malta. Not only communication but also a press release to announce the agreement between the two.

The Maltese citizenship law was amended following a consultation between the government of Malta and the European Commission on 29 January 2014, where compatibility of the Maltese IPP with EU law was confirmed with the introduction of an "effective residence status in Malta prior to the possibility to acquire Maltese naturalization" and that "no certificate of naturalisation will be issued unless the applicant provides proof that he/she has resided in Malta for a period of at least 12 months immediately preceding the day of issuing of the certificate of naturalization."[359] What is curious in the Citizenship by Investment case is that Cyprus also had a similar investor citizenship programme on 24 May 2013[360] (before Malta implemented its citizenship by investment programme), and that did not breach the principle of sincere cooperation as it did not draw attention from the Commission or neighbouring countries. Neither did the investment residence programmes that were already in place in half the Member States.

It is difficult to see a breach specifically regarding the duty of communication with other Member States and the Commission as when the programme was launched and published, it was reacted to by the European Commission and other Member States. If there was a breach of EU law, first it would be necessary to prove that there was no communication and also prove what is defined as communication by the EU institutions. Publishing the law is already a way to communicate to all interested parties – including the EU and other Member States. To argue the opposite would mean that Austria would have breached EU law when introducing its naturalisation via *außerordentliche*

359 European Commission MEMO, Joint Press Statement by the European Commission and the Maltese Authorities on Malta's Individual Investor Programme (IPP), Brussels, 29 January 2014 (Joint Press Statement), available at https://ec.europa.eu/commission/presscorner/detail/fr/MEMO_14_70, Access on: 19.03.2024

360 Scheme for Naturalization of Investors in Cyprus, Council of Ministers Decision dated 24.05.2013

Leistungen im besonderen Interesse der Republik.[361] The translation would be an exceptional service in the special interest of the Republic. Is this also a kind of naturalisation that could be argued as "an unjustified mass naturalization of nationals of non-Member States"? Probably not, since this is the interest of Austria, and Austria has full competence in its naturalisation law. The same applies to Malta. It is a justified naturalisation that the funds are implemented to the economy of the country, and Malta is also competent to decide on its own naturalisation law as established in the Treaties via the principle of conferral.

If a breach of EU law existed because Malta did not inform other Member States and the European institutions – which does not seem the case as there were dialogue and even agreement between Malta and European Commission – then other naturalisation schemes that have lower requirements or fast-track procedures could be seen as violating the principle of sincere cooperation in the sense that AG Maduro argued in the *Rottmann* case.

2.9.3 The Rottmann Case and the Principle of Proportionality in Deprivation of Citizenship

In the *Rottmann* case, the CJEU stated that the national court must invoke the principle of proportionality in determining whether it is proportionate to revoke citizenship in light of the individual's private and professional life. In order to explore the hypothesis as to whether the principle of proportionality has anything to do with acquisition of nationality and therefore has any impact on citizenship by investment, the principle must be first explained.

The principle of proportionality has its origin in German legal tradition, and at the EU level is provided in Article 5(1) of the Treaty on European Union where it states, "the use of Union competences is governed by the principles of subsidiary and proportionality." In terms of secondary legislation, Article 27 (2) of the Residence Directive states that "measures taken on the grounds of public policy or public security shall comply with the principle of proportionality and shall be based exclusively on the personal conduct of

361 Bundesgesetz über die österreichische Staatsbürgerschaft (Staatsbürgerschaftsgesetz 1985 – StbG), § 10, Absatz 6

the individual concerned."[362] As a principle, it has many interpretations[363] of how it should be "tested," but this section will focus on how the ECJ has used the principle of proportionality in cases of EU citizenship. The Court first mentioned proportionality in the *Rottmann* case, stating that,

> it is not contrary to European Union law, in particular to Article 17 EC, for a Member State to withdraw from a citizen of the Union the nationality of that State acquired by naturalisation when that nationality has been obtained by deception, on condition that the decision to withdraw observes the principle of proportionality.

The use of the principle focused on EU citizens' rights when losing their EU citizenship. There is nothing in the judgement or in the opinion from the AG that would imply that the principle of proportionality should also be used in rules on the acquisition of nationality, as this is a competence of Member States and the focus is not the EU citizen – because they still do not exist – until naturalisation in one of the Member States is completed. On the contrary, the Court specifically notes that this is particularly applicable in the case of a decision to withdraw naturalisation. Therefore, the principle of proportionality does not have any influence in terms of constraining Member States' rules on acquisition of nationality. The case law of the CJEU has demonstrated that is has been used for the withdrawal of nationality regarding the rights of EU citizens, mainly to avoid statelessness.

2.9.4 The Principle of Sincere Cooperation and the Argument of Free Riders (Syndicat interprofessionnel de défense du fromage Morbier contra Société Fromagère du Livradois SAS)

While the first three arguments arose from CJEU cases directly linked to EU citizenship, this section groups together three points of view from the literature that argue that the principle of sincere cooperation is violated

---

362 Directive 2004/38/EC of the European Parliament and of the Council of 29 April 2004 on the right of citizens of the Union and their Family members to move and reside freely within the territory of the Member States

363 The most common view is that the principle comprises only three steps on the proportionality test: (a) suitability, (2) necessity, (3) proportionality (*stricto sensu*) in The Fundamental Principles of EEA Law, Springer, 2017, editor Carl Baudenbacher, p. 175

because Malta is using the fact that it is a Member of the European Union to profit from the granting of nationality by investment and is, therefore, a *free rider*. In other words, this means using the benefits of being part of the Union without contributing to it. The term *free rider* comes from a case that does not concern citizenship,[364] and this is one reason why I believe that it is not a legally persuasive argument. Consequently, it does not seem to be the way to interpret a possible breach of EU law in the case of citizenship by investment. Moreover, this argument contains certain problematic assumptions in the sense of equality between Member States.

Alexia Young[365] defends the idea that by selling citizenship, there is a violation of the principle of sincere cooperation. How would this happen? To explain the connection, it is first necessary to introduce the concept of "free riding." The concept of "free riding" is defined as the act of benefiting from the actions and efforts of others without or sharing the costs.[366] Simply put, the "free riding" ticket, in this case, would be access to all the rights to EU citizenship for someone who acquires citizenship by investment. These rights are in addition to national citizenship. According to Young, in her analysis of the CJEU's expressions on the concept of free riding, the European Court held that the notion of free riding is considered an intrinsically insincere relationship between the parties and that this would be incompatible with the principle of sincere cooperation.

While Young's argument has some relevance in the normative sphere, her argument is based on European Union Court of Justice Case C-490/19. In this case, which concerns the origin of cheese products, *free-riding* is "parasitic competition" and considered to take "unfair advantage of, or be detrimental to, the distinctive character or the repute of the mark."[367] It seems odd to argue with only one case related to agriculture

---

364 C-490/19, 2020, *Syndicat interprofessionnel de défense du fromage Morbier vs Société Fromagère du Livradois SAS*

365 Young, Alexia. The duty of sincere cooperation and its implications on the acquisition of citizenship by investment. Thesis presented in partial fulfilment of the requirements for the degree of Master of Arts in European Legal Studies, Department of European and Comparative Law, Faculty of Law, University of Malta, 2022

366 OECD, "Glossary of Industrial Organisation Economics and Competition Law" (Directorate for Financial, Fiscal and Enterprise Affairs, OECD, 1993)

367 Case C-490/19 Syndicat interprofessionnel de défense du fromage Morbier v Société Fromagère du Livradois *SAS* [2020] ECLI 1043

to justify the violation of the principle of sincere cooperation in matters of nationality. It does not have the legal force to be convincing that it is possible to transpose an argument used by the Court in matters of agriculture to the rules on acquisition of nationality, especially because one deals with goods (cheese) while the other with freedom of mobility and rights (people).

Also, this logic would imply that Malta would not be contributing to the European Union but only using the fact that it is in the European Union to acquire revenues via citizenship. I believe it is difficult to measure how much each Member State contributes to the Union. What kind of contribution are we talking about? This could be a breeding ground for ideas of inequality between Member States. There are, however, authors who believe that Malta has not contributed to this, such as Rainer Bauböck when he says that "Malta behaves like a member of a cooperative that sells membership to outsiders at a price that in no way reflects her own contributions."[368] This is a political argument, not a legal argument, which does not resonate with the clear competence of Member States in matters of nationality established in the conferral principle (Article 4 and 5 of TEU).

Sergio Carreira has affirmed that if programmes in the EU where citizenship is sold are used by people to live elsewhere in the EU, these Member States may be classified as free riders and to "unjustly benefit from the attractiveness of life in other Member States they have not paid for or participated in creating. By instrumentalising the granting of their citizenship, they are selling something they do not own (or pay for) – life in other Member States."[369] The instrumentalisation of citizenship is a phenomenon that occurs not only in citizenship by investment but also in many other naturalisation policies, as demonstrated by Yossi Yarpaz[370] in his analysis of how globalisation has changed the concept of citizenship. First there is the legitimacy and prevalence

---

368 Bauböck, Rainer. What is wrong with selling citizenship? It corrupts democracy! In Should be Citizenship be for Sale? EUI Working Papers. Robert Schuman Centre for Advanced Studies EUDO Citizenship Observatory, 2014

369 Carrera, Sergio. The Price of EU Citizenship The Maltese Citizenship-for-Sale Affair and the Principle of Sincere Cooperation in Nationality Matters (2014) Maastricht Journal of European and Comparative Law No. 2014-3, page 411

370 Harpaz, Yossi. Citizenship 2.0 Dual Nationality as a Global Asset. Princeton: Princeton University Press, 2019

of dual citizenship. Second, he demonstrates how Serbians, Israelis, and Mexicans aim to gain second, compensatory citizenship that provides them with travel freedom, broader opportunities, and an insurance policy in case of political turmoil in their home countries. Therefore, the fact that someone acquires a second citizenship for strategic reasons does not correspond to a legal argument and it merely represents a political opinion about dual citizenship. Again, whether a country prohibits dual citizenship or allows it is a national competence according to Article 4 and 5 of the Treaty on European Union.

Therefore, it is not persuasive to argue that there is a violation of the principle of sincere cooperation by Malta or any other country that adopts citizenship by investment, in the sense of free riding, for two reasons: First, the case law used has nothing to do with EU citizenship and disregards the cases that have actually dealt with the issue (*Micheletti, Tjebbes, Rottmann, JY*). Second, it seems fertile ground for ideas of discrimination against Member States who would argue that they are contributing more to the European Union than others; this would leave legal arguments and move into political claims.

2.10 Previous Allegation of Violation of EU Law in Matters of Residence Permits for Third-Country Nationals

The initial part of this chapter addressed the previous and current allegations regarding EU citizenship and citizenship by investment. Subsequently, the following section examines the discourse surrounding the grant of residence permits to third-country nationals and residence by investment. In the case of Portugal, one previous allegation of violation of EU law in matters of residence permits to third-country nationals is related to the CPLP, explained in the following sub-section.

2.10.1 Community of Portuguese Language Countries (CPLP) Mobility Agreement With EU Law

On 17 July 2021, in Luanda, Angola, a mobility agreement between the Community of Portuguese Language Countries (CPLP) was signed between its members.[371] In Portugal, the agreement was transposed into domestic law via Decree No. 4/2022,[372] which amended the law on entry, stay, exit, and removal of foreigners from the national territory. It created temporary stay visas for job searches and residence to nationals from Member States of the CPLP. The legislation also excepts applicants from several requirements: (a) valid travel insurance; (b) proof of existence of means of subsistence; (c) copy of a return ticket.

On 13 March 2023, Portugal launched the CPLP Portal,[373] provided by the Portuguese immigration and borders service, *Serviço de Estrangeiros e Fronteiras (SEF)*, which gives CPLP immigrants with pending cases until 31 December 2022 to obtain residence permits automatically. According to SEF, over 154,000 immigrants from Portuguese-speaking countries, with the majority being Brazilians, have submitted applications for residence permits through the CPLP portal, and more than 140,000 were granted the document within a period of six months.

In November 2023, the European Commission opened an infringement procedure (INFR(2023)4012)[374] against Portugal concerning the provisions of the CPLP Mobility Agreement. The Commission argued that Portugal failed to fulfil its obligations under Council Regulation (EC) 1030/2002 of June 2002, laying down a uniform format for residence permits for third-country nationals and, under the Convention, implementing the Schengen Agreement of June 1985, as amended by Regulation (EU) 265/2010.

---

371 Nine Portuguese-speaking countries are part of the Agreement: Angola, Brazil, Cape Verde, Guinea-Bissau, Equatorial Guinea, Mozambique, Portugal, São Tomé and Príncipe, and East Timor.

372 Portugal, Decree 4/2022, Available on: https://diariodarepublica.pt/dr/en/detail/regulatory-decree/4-2022-201699171 Access on: 20 March 2024

373 Portugal, Cidadão da Comunidade dos Países de Língua Portuguesa: solicite a sua autorização de residência (Citizen of the Community of Portuguese-Speaking Countries: apply for your residence permit). Available on: https://cplp.sef.pt/, Access on: 8 November 2023

374 European Commission, Infringement Procedure 2023-4012) Document Security and Schengen Convention: Commission calls on Portugal to align the provisions of their Community of Portuguese Language Countries (CPLP) Mobility Agreement with EU law, Available on: https://ec.europa.eu/commission/presscorner/detail/en/inf_23_4367, Access on: 8 November, 2023

For the Commission, there are two main issues with the agreement: one regarding the format of the residence permit and the other regarding the rights entitled to holders of the CPLP residence permit. First, the CPLP residence permit would not be compliant with the uniform format laid down in Regulation (EC) 1030/2002. The Regulation establishes the following format:

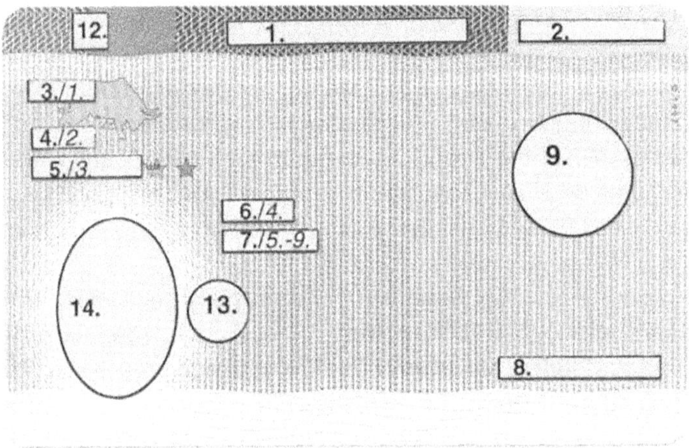

Figure 1. Residence Permit for Third-Country Nationals in Card Form

Source: Council Regulation (EC) No 1030/2002 of 13 June 2002 laying down a uniform format for residence permits for third-country nationals

The new portal for a CPLP residence permit issued a digital residence permit to the applicants valid for one year, renewable for two successive two-year periods. A fee of EUR 15 is charged to CPLP immigrants who wish to obtain a residence permit. It must be available in electronic format within an average period of 72 hours. The *Portaria* n. 97/2023 from 28 February 2023 established the model of the residence permit to be emitted by paper as shown in Figure 2.

CERTIFICADO DE CONCESSÃO DE AUTORIZAÇÃO DE RESIDÊNCIA PARA CIDADÃOS DA COMUNIDADE DOS PAÍSES DE LINGUA PORTUGUESA

23/C09000015 | Válido até **20/03/2024**

O Serviço de Estrangeiros e Fronteiras, em conformidade com o disposto no artigo 87.º - A, da Lei n.º 23/2007, de 04 de julho, na sua atual redação, certifica que foi concedida autorização de residência ao abrigo do Acordo sobre a Mobilidade entre os Estados Membros da Comunidade dos Países de Língua Portuguesa (CPLP), nos termos do mesmo diploma, a favor de:

APELIDOS: **SILVA**

NOMES: **MIGUEL ANTÓNIO**

DATA DE NASCIMENTO: **13/10/1965**

NACIONALIDADE: **BRASIL**

Nº PASSAPORTE: **AB0345097**

Emitido em **20/03/2023**

Este documento deverá ser acompanhado do documento de identificação do titular

Código de autenticação e acesso

A354C843-5786-4D9E-8E7C-7C9BC8B0E91B

Para validar este código aceda a https://##########.pt ou leia o código QR impresso nesta página

Figure 2. Residence Permit Certificate for Citizens of the Community of Portuguese-Speaking Countries

Source: Portaria n. 97/2023 of 28th February 2023[375]

---

375 Diário da República, 28 de fevereiro de 2023, Portaria n. 97/2023, Available on: https://files.diariodarepublica.pt/2s/2023/02/042000000/0009200094.pdf Access on: 20 March 2024.

Here, the Commission urges Portugal to harmonise the residence permit; instead of it being paper-based, the residence permit card should be in accordance with the Council Regulation n. 1030/2002.

The second issue was regarding the rights granted to the holder of the CPLP residence permit. As the residence permit was not in accordance with Council Regulation No 1030/2002, the holder would not be allowed to travel for the maximum of 90 days in the Schengen area. While in the case of citizenship by investment, the holder of an EU passport can settle in any of the twenty-seven Member States, that is not so in the case of residence by CPLP, as the title only allows the bearer to reside and work in the issuing country (Portugal, in this case). Despite the possibility of staying up to 90 days in another Schengen country within the 180-day period, this does not extend the right to live and work in these other countries.

In terms of preliminary reactions by the Portuguese government, the Secretary of State for European Issues said the CPLP would continue and that they were surprised with the infringement procedure by the European Commission.[376] The Council decision requires, for example, the document number, validity, place of issue, and date of beginning of validity, among other things.[377]

What is curious here again is the action of the European Commission to enter infringement proceedings against Portugal in the CPLP case, whereas for Ukrainians this has not been the case, nor for British citizens. Both groups have received residence permits by paper in Portugal. European citizens that register in the *Câmara Municial* also receive a paper after registration as EU citizens. However, Portugal did not notify the European Commission about the inclusion of this legal regime for CPLP.

On possible solutions is that the Portuguese government will start to offer the residence permits in plastic according to the Council Regulation. As the first CPLP residence permit were offered in March 2023, the renewal should be

---

376 Lusa, Governo diz que vistos CPLP vão continuar e rejeita incompatibilidade com Schengen, 2nd October, 2023. Available on: https://www.publico.pt/2023/10/02/politica/noticia/governo-vistos-cplp-vao-continuar-rejeita-incompatibilidade-schengen-2065359?utm_source=copy_paste Access on: 20 March 2024

377 Council Regulation No 1030/2022 of 13 June 2002 laying down a uniform format for residence permit for third-country nationals. Available on: https://eur-lex.europa.eu/legal-content/en/ALL/?uri=CELEX%3A32002R1030 Access on: 20 March, 2024

done in March 2024. The new migration agency, which replaced the police-immigration service SEF, has already said that all residence permits from CPLP will continue to be accepted and remain valid until 30 June 2024 within the framework of the decree-law that regulates the "Exceptional and temporary measures relating to the epidemiological situation of the new Coronavirus – COVID 19."[378] The infringement procedure is awaiting a response from Portugal and, after that, will depend on the next steps from the European Commission. At the launch of the new Action Plan for Migration in Portugal on 3 June 2024, the minister for the presidency reported that the benevolent idea of the CPLP agreement should be preserved but that its implementation leaves citizens of CPLP countries in an undignified situation. He explained that since these people do not have a residence card, they are unable to leave Portuguese territory and cannot travel within the Schengen area.[379]

2.11 Current Allegations on Matters of EU Law and Incompatibility of Residence by Investment (RBI)

Eleven Member States have residence by investment schemes (Cyprus, Estonia, Greece, Spain, Hungary, Ireland, Latvia, Luxembourg, Malta, the Netherlands, and Portugal).[380] They allow third-country nationals to be granted a temporary residence permit to live, work and study in the EU country where they receive the residence permit, in exchange for an investment. One of the key differences with Citizenship by investment is that while the acquisition of a Member State nationality provides the individual with all rights and privileges of EU citizenship, the acquisition of EU Member State visas provides fewer rights. For example, with a residence permit it is not possible to establish oneself in any Member State but only in the Member

---

378 Portugal News, Expired visas valid until 30 June, Available on: https://www.theportugalnews.com/news/2024-03-13/expired-visas-valid-until-30-june/86907 Access on: 20th March, 2024

379 Portugal, Conselho de Ministros – Plano de Ação para as Migrações, 03.06.2024, available on: https://www.youtube.com/watch?v=wKZeFodMryo&ab_channel=Rep%C3%BAblicaPortuguesa, Access on: 06.06.2024

380 European Parliament, Citizenship and Residence by Investment schemes, 2022. Available on: https://www.europarl.europa.eu/RegData/etudes/ATAG/2022/729268/EPRS_ATA(2022)729268_EN.pdf Access on: 20 March, 2024

State that grants the temporary residence permit. Political rights are also not part of the rights conferred, which in the case of citizenship are part of the benefits of EU citizenship. Is residence by investment be in accordance with EU law? To address this question, the Long-Term Directive scheme will be analysed.

2.11.1 Residence by Investment and Compatibility with the Long-Term Directive

The European Union adopted the Council Directive 2003/109/EC in order to help long-term residents "to have a stable and secure residence status, granting full access to work, education, and social security" as this is important for the integration of non-EU nationals into the society where they live.[381] It is a status granted after a person has lived legally in an EU country for an uninterrupted period of five years as long as the person provides documentation on having a stable and regular source of income, health insurance and, when required by the EU country, integration measures such as language certificates or integration tests. Also, the person must not constitute a threat to public security or public policy.[382] An inquiry that emerges is whether individuals who have obtained residence through investment also could benefit from the long-term Directive. Or, following the main research question of this dissertation, whether residence by investment would be in accordance with EU law, specifically with the Long-Term Directive.

As I will argue in what follows, I do not see a breach of EU law here or see how residents who receive a residence permit via investment could also be recipients of the long-term residence permit after five years of legal residence, as long as some rules are followed. However, there is legal confusion about the fact that Member States can grant permanent residence permits before the five-year period of the Directive is fulfilled. In this case, the individual

---

381 European Commission, Migration and Home Affairs, Long-term residentes, Available on: https://home-affairs.ec.europa.eu/policies/migration-and-asylum/legal-migration-and-integration/long-term-residents_en Access on: 21.04.2023

382 Council Directive 2003/109/EC of 25 November 2003 concerning the status of third-country nationals who are long-term residents

does not have the right to reside in another Member State. This is a clear reading of Article 13 of the Directive:

> Member States may issue residence permits of permanent or unlimited validity on terms that are more favourable than those laid down by this Directive. Such residence permits shall not confer the right of residence in the other Member States as provided by [...] this Directive.

This means an individual who acquires residence by investment does not automatically have the right to reside in other Member States, besides the country granting the residence permit. Only when the requirement of five years is fulfilled, along with the other requirements of the Directive, would the person have the right to reside in another Member State. In the case that one Member State would apply a more favourable long-term residence permit that requires less than five years legal residence, as the Directive is a secondary EU legislation, the European Court of Justice would be responsible for verifying the interpretation of the Directive. Here, the Court would declare it is in breach of EU law, as it undermines EU law by not following the established time period in the Directive.

Nonetheless, residence by investment, although a mercantilist[383] practice, would enable acquisition of long-term residence as long as the five-year period of legal residence is fulfilled and the other requirements too. Only then is the individual able to reside in another Member state.[384] Another important question is whether possession of a national residence permit for a period of five years corresponds to the requirement of the Directive as follows: "*have*

---

383 By mercantilist practice I mean the reference to mercantilism, a nationalist school of economics that promoted trade as the best method of increasing the wealth of a nation that had no gold or silver mines. The comparison fits the context in which Malta is embedded, as a small island without gold or silver (could be replaced by industry or other economic activity), the government found the practice of trade (in this case citizenship) to improve the wealth of the nation. In LaHaye, L. (2008). Mercantilism. In: The New Palgrave Dictionary of Economics. Palgrave Macmillan, London. https://doi.org/10.1057/978-1-349-95121-5_838-2

384 As Ireland and Denmark are not part of the Long-term Directive, in case these countries would have a residence by investment programme, even after the five years, They would not acquire EU long-term residency status. However, Denmark does not have a residence by investment and Ireland abolished its IPP Programme (Residency by Investment) in 2023.

resided legally and continuously within its territory for five years immediately prior to the submission of the relevant application."[385]

Carrera answers this question negatively. For him, this requirement of living five years "cannot be manipulated so that wealthy third-country nationals do not have the inconvenience of having to actually live in the host member state for five years."[386] Carrera is supported by Van den Brink in the sense that residence would be "to actually live in the host member state for five years."[387] This interpretation, however, is not what the Luxembourg Court understands:

> Directive 2003/109 does not lay down the conditions which the residence of those nationals must satisfy for them to be regarded as legally resident in the territory of a Member State. It follows that those conditions are governed by national law alone[388].

As the Directive does not specify the rules on the meaning of residence but leaves it at the discretion of Member States, even periods of absence may count towards the five-year requirement. The grey area lies with Article 4(3) of the Directive in which is stated that "periods of absence from the territory of the Member State concerned shall not interrupt the five-year period of continuous and legal residence, where they are shorter than six consecutive months or ten months in total, or whether this also mandates them to deny this status to those who have not been physically present for longer periods."[389]

In a literal reading of the provision, "*shall not*" would mean that Member States would not be able to deny the long-term resident status to those who

---

385 Council Directive 2003/109/EC of 25 November 2003 concerning the status of third-country nationals who are long-term residentes, Article 4, I

386 How Much does EU citizenship cost? The Maltese citizenship-for-sale affair: a breakthrough for sincere cooperation in citizenship of the union? CEPS Paper in Liberty and Security in Europe, No. 64/April 2014, page 18.

387 How Much does EU citizenship cost? The Maltese citizenship-for-sale affair: a breakthrough for sincere cooperation in citizenship of the union? CEPS Paper in Liberty and Security in Europe, No. 64/April 2014, page 18; van den Brink, Martijn. Investment Residence and the Concept of Residence in EU Law Interactions, Tensions, and Opportunities, Investment Migration Working Papers 2017/1, page 16.

388 Case C-40/11 Iida, ECLI:EU:C:2012:691, para 36

389 Council Directive 2003/109/EC of 25 November 2003 concerning the status of third-country nationals who are long-term residentes, Article 4 (3)

have been absent for periods shorter than six consecutive months or ten months in total. A second interpretation would mean that Member States are obliged to deny the status to those who have not been physically present for longer periods.

The first interpretation would allow holders of golden visas to acquire long-term EU residence after the period of five years even with periods of absence. For example, an EUR 200,000 investment in support of artistic production or in the recovery or maintenance of national cultural heritage in Portugal would require the applicant to be present for seven days in the first year in Portugal and fourteen days in the two subsequent years. After five years, the individual would be able to apply for EU long-term residence status. This interpretation is the current practice in Portugal.

The second interpretation, which is supported by van den Brink, would require Member States to deny long-term residence for people who have been not present for longer periods than six months or ten months in total. His argument derives from the wording of the Directive which states that the Directive's purpose is to promote the "mutual confidence between Member States."[390] In his view, this purpose would be undermined if left completely to national law to decide the meaning of physical presence as per the five-year requirement to apply for EU long-term residence status.

On another note, I see that this provision on mutual confidence is undermined by another exception that the Directive allows. In Article 4 (3), it is mentioned that in "cases of exceptional reasons of temporary nature and in accordance with their national law, Member States may accept that a longer period of absence than that which is referred to in the first subparagraph shall not interrupt the period referred to in paragraph 1. In such cases, Member States shall not take into account the relevant period of absence in the calculation of the period referred to in paragraph 1."[391] This provision would allow that, for instance, the Portuguese golden visa would require only seven days in the first years and fourteen days in the two subsequent years, as this could be decided *in accordance with their national law.*

---

[390] Article 17 Directive 2003/109/EC

[391] Directive 2003/109/EC

Finally, on 9 March 2022 the European Parliament sent to the Commission a proposal to revise the Long-Term Residence Directive.[392] The first proposal is to limit the possibility of third-country nationals who have obtained residence under an RBI scheme benefiting from more favourable treatment under that Directive. In order to do that, Article 13 of the Long-Term Residence Directive would expressly exclude beneficiaries of RBI schemes. The second proposal it to ensure that the legal and continuous residence of five years, required by Article 4 (1) of the Long-Term Residence Directive, is not circumvented through RBI schemes, including by ensuring that Member States enforce stronger controls and reporting obligations on applicants under RBI schemes.

In view of the various provisions of the Directive, which are often confused, I believe that the period for counting residence time by investment activity authorises Member States to count the time for the purposes of long-term residence EU status, even with periods longer than six months consecutively or ten months in total. This, however, does not prevent the courts of countries where residence visas exist from questioning the interpretation of the Directive in the CJEU to clarify whether the principle of sincere cooperation is being violated when Member States establish a shorter period or exceptions that do not stop the five-year period counting.

2.12 Concerns of European Institutions: Money Laundering, Corruption, Lack of Transparency, and Due Diligence

The European Commission report launched on 23 January 2019 begins its first paragraph by highlighting that investor citizenship and investor residence have raised "concerns about certain inherent risks, in particular as regards security, money laundry, tax evasion, and corruption."[393] At the time, three Member States (Bulgaria, Malta, and Cyprus) had programmes in which citizenship was granted without prior residence in the country. The Commission also displayed concern about the fact that these programmes

392 Proposal 5, European Parliament, Resolution of 9 March 2022 with proposal to the Commission on citizenship and residence by investment schemes (2021/2026(INL)).

393 European Commission, Report on Investor Residence and Citizenship of 23 January 2019.

are "explicitly advertised as a means of acquiring Union citizenship."[394] What risks are the Commission referring to?

Regarding security, for instance, Kirstin Surak has highlighted that there were no reported cases worldwide of terrorist activities "carried out by individuals travelling on investor visas or passports acquired through investment migration programmes."[395] In her opinion, alternative routes to residence and citizenship that have been made easier could be preferable for those who pose a security threat.[396]

Regarding money laundering, a positive point of change in European legislation is that the 2018 5th Anti-Money Laundering Directive obliges everyone involved in economic transactions to perform enhanced due diligence on third-country nationals applying for some form of investment migration (residency or citizenship by investment). It should be noted that the European Parliament has expressed criticism regarding the exclusion of public entities that handle Citizenship by Investment (CBI) and Residency by Investment (RBI) applications from the list of obligated entities.[397] Therefore, gaps will remain.

This rule on actors involved in residence and citizenship by investment was due by 10 January 2020, and since then, Member States have also had to ensure that the application of the EU rules on anti-money laundering

---

394 European Commission, Report on Investor Residence and Citizenship of 23 January 2019.

395 Surak, Kristin. Citizenship and Residence by investment schemes – State of play and avenues for EU action. Anex II in Avenues for EU action on citizenship and residence by investment schemes: European added value assessment. Meenakshi Fernandes, Cecilia Navarra, and David de Groot with María García Muñoz, 2021

396 Surak, Kristin. Citizenship and Residence by Investment schemes – State of play and avenues for EU action. Anex II in Avenues for EU action on citizenship and residence by investment schemes: European added value assessment. Meenakshi Fernandes, Cecilia Navarra, and David de Groot with María García Muñoz, 2021, page 30 How Much does EU citizenship cost? The Maltese citizenship-for-sale affair: a breakthrough for sincere cooperation in citizenship of the union? CEPS Paper in Liberty and Security in Europe, No. 64/April 2014, page 18; van den Brink, Martijn. Investment Residence and the Concept of Residence in EU Law Interactions, Tensions, and Opportunities, Investment Migration Working Papers 2017/1, page 18

397 European Parliament Resolution of 9 March 2022 with proposals to the Commission on citizenship and residence by investment schemes (2021/2026(INL)), Point 15

are not circumvented under investor citizenship or residence schemes.[398] Kristin Surak also highlights that if states have not made these reforms and do not aggregate their Financial Intelligence Units (FIU) in the assessment of Residence and Citizenship by Investment, they may be in breach of the implementation of the anti-money laundering checks.[399]

In the Portuguese context, much has been said about the link of residence by investment and money laundering, especially by Transparency International[400] and the OCCRP, the Organized Crime and Corruption Reporting Project.[401] They propose suggestions on how to prevent money laundering, which are important regarding the due diligence process. However, there is no evidence that proves a direct link between investment migration programmes and money laundering. What is problematic is weak due diligence checks, which could allow individuals to hide the origins of their wealth and use other sources for direct investment. It remains to be seen whether, in the future, financial intelligence investigations will prove a direct link between investment migration and money laundering.

Regarding tax evasion, it is first important to say that an individual's tax residence is determined by physical presence and not citizenship or legal residence (most of the time). As a basic rule, individuals become tax residents in any country where they spend more than 183 days annually.[402] It is correct to say that many investment migration programmes have more attractive tax regimes and are even developed to attract investors, but qualitative research

---

398 European Commission, Questions and Answers on the Report on Investor Citizenship and Residence Schemes in the European Union, 2019, Available on: https://ec.europa.eu/commission/presscorner/detail/ro/MEMO_19_527 Access on: 04.07.2023

399 Surak, Kristin. Annex: Citizenship and residence by investment schemes – State of play and avenues for EU action in Avenues for EU action on citizenship and residence by investment schemes, European Parliamentary Research Service, October 2021, page 134

400 Transparency International, European Getaway: Inside the Murky World of Golden Visas, 2018, p. 31

401 OCCPR A Portuguese Crusader Seeks to Tap the Brakes on Golden Visas, 5 March 2018, Available on: https://www.occrp.org/en/goldforvisas/a-portuguese-crusader-seeks-to-tap-the-brakes-on-golden-visas Access on: 04.07.2023

402 Surak, Kristin. Annex: Citizenship and residence by investment schemes – State of play and avenues for EU action in Avenues for EU action on citizenship and residence by investment schemes, European Parliamentary Research Service, October 202, page 38

shows that tax avoidance is not the driving motive in acquiring citizenship or residence by investment.[403]

Regarding corruption, if we look at the reported cases of corruption and the acquisition of citizenship[404] or residency[405] by investment, there is a connection between corruption and the acquisition process. For example, in Cyprus, an investigation of the citizenship by investment scheme showed that lawmakers helped to arrange a passport for a businessman despite the fact that he was a convicted criminal.[406] In Portugal, leaked documents showed that corrupt Brazilians were among applicants for the golden visas, as well as Angolan politicians accused of bribery.[407] For citizenship and residence by investment schemes, corruption should hold significant weight: if it occurs, it should receive exemplary punishment and investigation.

Regarding the importance of due diligence, several points can be made. Thorough customer due diligence (CDD) is crucial for EU countries with investment migration programmes, such as Malta and Portugal, to ensure compliance with international standards for preventing money laundering and terrorist financing. This requirement applies to all Member States that offer such programmes. Currently, there is a lack of uniform standards for

---

403 Surak, Kristin. Annex: Citizenship and residence by investment schemes – State of play and avenues for EU action in Avenues for EU action on citizenship and residence by investment schemes, European Parliamentary Research Service, October 202, page 38

404 Kwai, Isabella. Cyprus Ends "Golden Passport" Program After Corruption Accusations. The New York Times, 2020, Available on: https://www.nytimes.com/2020/10/15/world/europe/cyprus-golden-passports-corruption.html, Access on: 24.05.2024

405 Pegg, David et al. Corrupt Brazilian tycoon among applicants for Portugal's Golden Visas, The Guardian, 2018. Available on: https://www.theguardian.com/world/2017/sep/18/portugal-golden-visas-corrupt-brazilian-tycoon-among-applicants Access on: 24.05.2023

406 Kwai, Isabella. Cyprus Ends "Golden Passport" Program After Corruption Accusations. The New York Times, 2020, Available on: https://www.nytimes.com/2020/10/15/world/europe/cyprus-golden-passports-corruption.html, Access on: 25.03.2024

407 Pegg, David et al. Corrupt Brazilian tycoon among applicants for Portugal's Golden Visas, The Guardian, 2018. Available on: https://www.theguardian.com/world/2017/sep/18/portugal-golden-visas-corrupt-brazilian-tycoon-among-applicants Access on: 24.05.2023

due diligence and an oversight body similar to the FATF[408] for citizenship by investment and residence by investment programmes.[409] In Malta, the due diligence check system includes (a) standard Know Your Customer (KYC) checks; (b) criminal background checks in multiple closed source police databases; (c) documentation validation checks, and open-source due diligence checks on the applicant and their family; (d) checks for Politically Exposed Persons (PEP) and sanctioned individuals, and companies of the applicant and their family, as well as significant business associates.[410]

It was a failure from the Commission not to address the topic or the differences between citizenship and residence by investment with the discretionary naturalisation procedures used in individual cases to grant citizenship in exchange for investment. By discretionary naturalisation procedures, I mean cases in which Member States grant naturalisation without any requirement besides an economic contribution. One example is Austrian naturalisation[411] due to exceptional contributions to the economy. As they are similar because they give the possibility of acquiring residence or citizenship via money, it would have had a possibility to the Commission to develop more on the difference as they both give access to the citizenship of Member States via money. The Commission only states that "Such discretionary naturalisation procedures are highly individualised and used on a limited basis. They are, therefore, not the object of this report."[412]

---

408 The Financial Action Task Force was founded in 1989 and has its headquarters in Paris. It has the goal to "set standards and promote effective implementation of legal, regulatory, and operational measures for combating money laundering, terrorist financing and other related threats to the integrity of the international financial system." In "Who We Are," Financial Action Task Force 2019, available on: https://www.fatf-gafi.org/en/the-fatf/who-we-are.html, accessed 8 August, 2023.

409 Corrado, Mark, Marsh, Kim. Investment Migration and the Importance of Due Diligence. Examples of Canada, Saint-Kitts and Nevis, and the EU in Citizenship and Residence Sales Rethinking the Boundaries of Belonging Edited by Dimitry Kochenov and Kristin Surak. Cambridge: Cambridge University Press, 2023, page 488

410 Malta, "Due Diligence," website Acquisition of Citizenship for Exceptional Services by Direct Investment 2023, https://komunita.gov.mt/en/services/acquisition-of-citizenship/#ForExceptionalServices, accessed 8 August, 2023

411 Bundesgesetz über die österreichische Staatsbürgerschaft (Staatsbürgerschaftsgesetz 1985 – StbG), § 10, Absatz 6

412 European Commission, Report on Investor Residence and Citizenship of 23 January 2019.

2.12.1 Protecting EU Citizenship: The Commission Referral of Malta to the European Court of Justice

In October 2020, the European Commission initiated infringement procedures[413] (number 20202301) against Malta and Cyprus over the operation of citizenship by investment programmes. Article 258 TFEU provides as follows:

> If the Commission considers that a Member State has failed to fulfil an obligation under the Treaties, it shall deliver a reasoned opinion on the matter after giving the State concerned the opportunity to submit its observations. If the State concerned does not comply with the opinion within the period laid down by the Commission, the latter may bring the matter before the Court of Justice of the European Union[414].

There are two possibilities to initiate an infringement procedure: the Commission acts in response to a complaint or on its own initiative. In the case of Infringement 20202301 (against Malta and Cyprus), this was initiated by the Commission. The infringement procedure can be divided into four distinct stages, which were all carried out in the case of Malta. Initially, the Commission gives the Member State the opportunity to explain its position and the opportunity to reach an agreement with the Commission.[415]

The Cypriot and Maltese government had two months[416] to answer the letters of formal notice. Cyprus repealed its scheme less than two weeks later. The Commission asked for explanations and argued that this type of naturalisation and, consequently, granting of citizenship was not compatible with the principle of sincere cooperation enshrined in Article 4 (3) of the Treaty on European Union. The Commission also claimed that the programme could undermine the integrity of the status of EU citizenship provided in Article 20 of the Treaty on the Functioning of the European Union. The infringement procedure led to changes in the programme and requirements

---

413 Infringement procedure: According to the EU Treaties, the Commission may take legal action – an infringement procedure – against an EU country that fails to implement EU law. The Commission may refer the issue to the Court of Justice, which in certain cases, can impose financial penalties (European Commission, 2021).

414 Article 258 TFEU

415 Craig, Paul; de Búrca, Gráinne. EU Law Text, Cases, and Materials, Seventh Edition (2020) Oxford, Oxford University Press, page 466

416 The state is usually given two months to reply, except in cases of urgency. Craig, Paul; de Búrca, Gráinne. EU Law Text, Cases, and Materials, Seventh Edition (2020) Oxford, Oxford University Press, page 466

in Malta. Malta added two more years to its one-year residence requirement, although there remains a fast-track of one year if the investor decides to add EUR 150,000 to the original amount of EUR 650,000.

It can happen that the Commission is not satisfied with the outcome, which was the case. The European Commission sent a *Reasoned Opinion* to Malta and invoked two arguments in breach of EU law that the Maltese Investment Programme was violating. The Commission used Article 4(3) of the Treaty on European Union to argue that these schemes are not compatible with the principle of sincere cooperation, as well as arguing that they undermined the integrity of the status of EU citizenship, using Article 20 of the Treaty on the Functioning of the European Union as a legal basis.[417] This is firstly because the Treaty on Functioning of the European Union states that citizenship of any country within the EU also confers EU citizenship rights: freedom of movement, the right to stand in elections of the European Parliament and vote in those elections, and in local elections, and the right to petition the EU Commission and expect a reply (Article 20 TFEU). Second, an EU citizen has the right to diplomatic and consular protection by the embassy of any EU country in any third country where the country that awarded their citizenship does not have an embassy (Article 20, 2, (c) TFEU). In the Maltese case, this is relevant because the country has only seventeen Embassies and ninety-seven Consulates around the world.

Malta reaffirmed in Press Release 220440 that "the granting of citizenship falls within the national competence of a Member State, and it should remain as such. That being said, the government reiterates that only worthy individuals benefit from an important right as citizenship on such basis, and that it will be keeping an open dialogue with the Commission."[418] This answer led to the last stage of the infringement procedure: referral of the matter by the Commission to the Court of Justice.

---

417 European Commission, Investor citizenship schemes: European Commission opens infringements against Cyprus and Malta for "selling" EU citizenship, Press Release 20 October 2020, available on: https://ec.europa.eu/commission/presscorner/detail/en/ip_20_1925, Access on 25 March, 2024

418 Government of Malta, The Government of Malta notes the Reasoned Opinion from the European Commission. 06/04/2022

On 29 September 2022, the European Commission decided to refer Malta to the European Court of Justice under Article 258 (2) of the Treaty on the Functioning of the European Union:[419]

> Article 258 (ex-Article 226 TEC) If the Commission considers that a Member State has failed to fulfil an obligation under the Treaties, it shall deliver a reasoned opinion on the matter after giving the State concerned the opportunity to submit its observations. If the State concerned does not comply with the opinion within the period laid down by the Commission, the latter may bring the matter before the Court of Justice of the European Union.

The decision by the Court will probably enter EU law and principles, but one point still remains interesting to highlight. According to the principle of conferral, if the Union acts beyond its powers, the act will be declared invalid. It may be that the Court will say – if it explores competence – that the act of the European institutions (Commission and Parliament) was invalid because it entered the field of nationality, an exclusive competence of Member States. If that is the decision, Malta will probably be satisfied. However, if the Court says that there was no violation of the principle of conferral, the decision could also be challenged from a competence angle. In this line of argument, the European Court is part of the Union. It is an institution of the Union. If the Court decides on the limits of the Union's power, it is, in a sense, empowering itself. The Union does not have this power, what Germans call *Kompetenz-Kompetz* (the power to confer power on yourself). This could be strange in the eyes of the Constitutional Courts of the countries that have been attacked by criticism from the European institutions. The Constitutional Courts of Germany, Denmark, and Poland have already said that, in their view, the European Court "does not have the final say on this point: the Member State courts do."[420] As the European Court does not

---

419 Investment Migration Council, Malta: European Commission refers Malta to the European Court of Justice against all legal advice. 2022; Available from: https://investmentmigration.org/news/malta-european-commission-refers-malta-to-the-european-court-of-justice-against-all-legal-advice/

420 Hartley, TC. The Foundations of European Union Law: an introduction to the constitutional and administrative law of the European Union. Eighth Edition, Oxford: Oxford University Press, 2014, page, 113.

accept this, the decision of the Court of Justice of the European Union could also be contested regarding the conferral principle.

Other procedures besides the case against Malta could be taken by the Commission. Indeed, although Malta changed its citizenship-by-investment programme in 2020 (the Malta Citizenship by Naturalisation for Exceptional Services by Direct Investment Program) and now requires 12 months or 36 months of residence before receiving a naturalisation certificate,[421] a decision by the Court declaring a violation of the principle of sincere cooperation could affect the current naturalisation scheme in the sense that Malta would end the programme for good, or add new requirements. One such option is presented in the 2022 Resolution of the European Parliament,[422] which proposes that the Commission should commence additional infringement procedures against Member States that offer residence by investment schemes, such as Portugal, if deemed necessary. Should this route be taken, it would potentially impact twelve other Member States that currently have similar investment programmes in place.

Also, due to the fact many of the recipients of investor citizenship programmes are from Russia and Belarus, following the invasion of Ukraine by Russian military forces, the calls from Member States to withdraw citizenship by investment when it has been granted to Russians or Belarussian nationals who are on sanctions lists or who have supported the invasion were intensified.[423] This resulted in Malta and Portugal not allowing applicants from Russia or Belarus since the war of aggression against Ukraine began.[424]

---

421 If the applicant invests EUR 600,000, the requirement is 36 months of residence. In case the investment is EUR 750,000, the residence requirement is reduced to 12 months. Additionally, the applicant must purchase a EUR 700,000 residential home in Malta and retain it for at least five years.

422 European Parliament Resolution of 9 March 2022 with proposals to the Commission on citizenship and residence by investment schemes (2021/2026(INL)), Point 14

423 European Parliament, Russia's war on Ukraine: Reassessing "citizenship by investment" schemes 2022; Available from: https://www.europarl.europa.eu/RegData/etudes/ATAG/2022/729385/EPRS_ATA(2022)729385_EN.pdf

424 Reuters, Malta stops sale of passports to Russians, Belarusians, Available on: https://www.reuters.com/world/malta-stops-sale-passports-russians-belarusians-2022-03-02/ Access on: 25 March, 2024; Portugal.com, Portugal suspends Golden Visas for Russians, available on: https://www.portugal.com/news/portugal-suspends-golden-visas-for-russians/ Access on: 25 March, 2024

Early October 2024 the Advocate General Collins delivered his opinion[425] in the Maltese case, which was very concise in saying the case should be dismissed. The Advocate General reinforced that it is for Member States "alone to determine who is entitled to be one of their nationals and, as a consequence, who is an EU citizen."[426] Related to the Michelleti judgement, which determined that Member States cannot limit the impact of recognising a nationality from another Member State by setting additional requirements for that recognition, the Advocate General also clarified that "the system of compulsory mutual recognition envisioned by this case law implies that Member States do not need to have a uniform understanding of what nationality entails, and their criteria for granting it can vary."[427]

Moreover, while some rulings from the CJEU do place (minimal) limitations on the ability of member states to define who their nationals are, these decisions specifically relate to the loss of nationality, as explained previously in this chapter (Rottmann and Tjbbes case). The Advocate General also explained that there is significantly more case law regarding the revocation of nationality than concerning its granting. This is because "EU law imposes distinct requirements on Member States regarding both aspects." Losing nationality can lead to individuals not only losing their EU citizenship but might also leave them stateless. Since acquiring nationality does not strip individuals of their rights, the precedents regarding revocation of nationality cannot be automatically applied to its acquisition (para 52). In summary, due to these arguments, the Advocate General suggested that the Court should dismiss the case, and the final was released on April 29th 2025.

The Court has found that Malta's investor citizenship scheme (Maltese Citizenship by Naturalisation for Exceptional Services by Direct Investment) is incompatible with EU law, in particular with the principle of sincere cooperation. According to the Court, the Republic of Malta has failed to fulfil its obligations under Article 20 TFEU and Article 4(3) TEU. The Court

---

425 European Court of Justice, Opinion of Advocate General Collins, delivered on 4 October 2024, European Commission vs Republic of Malta, Case C-181/23, available on: https://curia.europa.eu/juris/document/document.jsf?text=&docid=290735&pageIndex=0&doclang=EN&mode=lst&dir=&occ=first&part=1&cid=4084899#Footref62, Access on: 23.11.2024

426 Para 46

427 Para 48

dismissed the case and failed to explore the legal arguments in sufficient depth. It reinforced the assertion that Union citizenship is intended to be the fundamental status of nationals of the Member States. Although it interferes in a field of competence of the Member States, it does so only in relation to the granting of nationality via investment. The Court states that this scheme commoditises Union citizenship, undermining the integrity of that status and constituting a particularly serious infringement of EU law[428].

The Court ruled that a Member State violates the principle of mutual trust when "when it establishes and implements a naturalisation scheme based on a transactional procedure between that Member State and persons submitting an application under that programme, at the end of which the nationality of that Member State and, therefore, the status of Union citizen, is essentially granted in exchange for predetermined payments or investments."[429] Moreover it added that "A programme of that sort amounts to the commercialisation of the granting of the status of national of a Member State and, by extension, Union citizenship, which is incompatible with the conception of that fundamental status that stems from the Treaties."[430] Therefore, the Court based its argument on the assertion that the scheme constitutes a transactional naturalisation mechanism. The commodification of citizenship undermines the very essence of EU citizenship, violating both Article 20 TFEU and the principle of sincere cooperation in Article 4(3).

The decision marks a shift in the debate from the issue of genuine link to that of mutual trust. The Court affirmed that Union citizenship is based on the common values set out in Article 2 TEU and on mutual trust between the Member States. It does not say that the genuine link is a requirement to all naturalisation policies but it states that a Member State breaches the mutual trust principle when it establishes – like Malta did – a naturalisation scheme based on a financial transaction, granting nationality in exchange of a payment. While the focus on the Advocate General Collins of 4 of October 2022 was the argument from the Commission that EU law would require a

428 European Court of Justice, Judgment of 29.04.2025, Case C-181/23 Commission v Malta (Citizenship by Investment), para 43–44

429 European Court of Justice, Judgment of 29.04.2025, Case C-181/23 Commission v Malta (Citizenship by Investment), para 99

430 European Court of Justice, Judgment of 29.04.2025, Case C-181/23 Commission v Malta (Citizenship by Investment), para 100

genuine link between a Member State and its nationals, the Court focused on mutual trust and the principle of sincere cooperation. Indeed, it is wiser not to enter into this debate, as the genuine link is much more political and philosophical than mutual trust. Furthermore, as this dissertation demonstrates, arguing for a genuine link in all naturalisation laws would call into question the many naturalisation policies that do not require proof of residence or knowledge of the member state's language.

The Court also defends the argument that national citizenship laws have "consequences for the functioning of the EU as a common legal order" and explains that EU citizenship confers the right to "enjoy an area of freedom, security and justice without internal frontiers; to move, reside and work within that area; to vote and stand as candidates in EU and municipal elections, and within national political parties; and to receive consular protection from each Member State" (paras. 84–91). In this sense, the Court defends the idea of Union citizenship, based on the common values set out in Article 2 of the Treaty on European Union (TEU) and mutual trust between Member States. The Court argues that, although the exercise of naturalisation law is a Member State competence, it cannot be incompatible with Union citizenship.

In response to the Court ruling, Malta already announced that is undertaking a legislative transition from a Citizenship by Investment (CBI) to a Citizenship by Merit (CBM). This shift is encapsulated in the new full draft[431] of the Maltese Citizenship Amendment Bill, which incorporates recent legal guidance from the European Union and introduces a discretionary route to naturalisation predicated on demonstrable exceptional service in the national interest, in areas such as health, security, science, culture, and innovation. The reform is a direct legislative response to the Court of Justice of the European Union (CJEU) ruling in the European Commission vs Malta (April 2025). The draft legislation formally revokes the previously financial investment pathway to citizenship. The new route is based on genuine and demonstrable contributions to Malta's national interest, assessed on a discretionary basis.

---

[431] Bill No. 140 of 2025, Government of Malta, available on: https://parlament.mt/en/14th-leg/bills/bill-140-maltese-citizenship/ Access on: 18.07.2025

2.12.2 The Commission Recommendations of 28 March 2022 and the Principle of Non-Discrimination

Against the background of the Russia aggression against Ukraine, the European Commission urged Member States to stop all citizenship by investment schemes and to ensure strong checks on investor residence.[432] Besides the repetition of arguments previously presented by the Commission in 2019, the Recommendation made explicit reference to action to limit the sale of citizenship to wealthy Russians connected to the Russian government.[433] It was not only citizenship, but the Commission also requested that Member States that operating investor residence schemes should suspend the issuance of residence permits on the basis of such schemes to Russians and Belarusians.[434] The documents states as follow:

> any Member State that has naturalized Russian or Belarusian nationals based on an investor citizenship scheme should immediately assess, in accordance with the principles resulting from the case law of the Court of Justice of the European Union, including the principle of proportionality and the protection of fundamental rights, whether these individuals' naturalizations should be withdrawn because: – the person concerned is or becomes subject to the EU restrictive measures – or because it is otherwise determined that the person concerned significantly supports by any means the war in Ukraine or other related activities of the Russian government or Lukashenko regime breaching international law.

This step was highly criticised by some scholars, who called it direct discrimination due to nationality.[435] Moreover, Dimitry Kochenov[436] criticised the measure, even calling it something new in global law. For him, withdrawing citizenship based on someone's personal opinion (related to activities of

432 European Commission, Recommendation of 28 March 2022.

433 European Commission, Joint Statement on further restrictive economic measures of 26 February 2022.

434 European Commission, Commission Recommendation of 28 March 2022 on immediate steps in the context of the Russian invasion of Ukraine in relation to investor citizenship schemes and investor residence schemes

435 Sarah Ganty, Why Banning Russians from Schengen Is Unlawful. 2022; Available from: https://verfassungsblog.de/banning-russians/.

436 Kochenov, D. B., Elena, It's All about Blood, Baby! The European Commission's Ongoing Attack against Investment Migration in the Context of EU Law and International Law. Working Paper no. 161 The Centre on Migration, Policy & Society, 2022

the Russian government or the Lukashenko regime) would be a new form of consideration when withdrawing citizenship or residence permits. The implementation of the Recommendation was supposed to be reported to the Commission by the Member States by May 2022, and Malta suspended the scheme for Russian and Belarussian applicants on 2 March, almost a month before the Commission recommendation asserting that "the existent due diligence checks cannot be carried out effectively in the current scenario."[437] Portugal had suspended the residence by investment for holders of Russian passports on 26 February.[438]

Would it be possible in the future that all these passports or residence permits granted via investment could face withdrawal? Lawyers who have clients as investors waiting for residence or citizenship by investment could activate the national courts in case the principle of proportionality is not taken into consideration, but only the future will show whether the matter will be judicialised. The Portuguese lawyer Irina Akhmetova, who had forty-eight golden visas waiting for the procedure to be concluded, affirms the following regarding her clients: "They start to ask if we can take legal action. For them, this is a refusal. For a normal citizen, who is not a lawyer, this is what they understand when the SEF (*Serviço de Estrangeiros e Fronteiras*) says that it suspends the processes. And then they talk about going to court because the government created the expectation that they could invest."[439]

If there are non-discrimination arguments related to possible discrimination against investors, there are also arguments related to discrimination with other migrants who need to follow the traditional path to acquiring residence or citizenship (time of residence + language tests or/and citizenship tests). This was already highlighted in the European Parliament Resolution in 2014: "Concerns exist as regard possible discrimination because these practices by Member States only allow the richest third-country nationals to obtain EU Citizenship, without any other criteria being considered."[440] The argument

---

437 Press Release by the Parliamentary Secretariat for Citizenship and Communities 2022

438 Público. Portugal suspendeu apreciação de "vistos gold" de cidadãos russos. 2022

439 Renascença, R. Vistos Gold. Candidatos russos querem processar Estado português. 2022.

440 European Parliament Resolution on EU citizenship for sale, 2013/2995 (RSP), 16 January 2014, Point K.

is compelling, particularly in light of the disparate treatment experienced by migrant groups lacking the necessary qualifications or financial means to obtain high-skilled visas or engage in investment migration.

Also, in 2022 the European Parliament reinforced this thesis saying that "the advantageous conditions and fast-track procedures set for investors under CBI/RBI schemes, when compared to the conditions and procedures for other third-country nationals wishing to obtain international protection, residence or citizenship, are discriminatory, lack fairness and risk undermining the consistency of the Union asylum and migration acquis."[441]

However, although unfair, the competence to limit or grant residence permits is still a competence of Member States based on the conferral principle. While this is the case, although the schemes of citizenship and residence by investment are a privileged path to such titles, they represent the sovereignty principle of Member States to admit third-country nationals as they wish. There are many unfair or privileged paths to acquiring citizenship and residence but legally they are in accordance with the competence established in matters of nationality and granting of residence permits. More research in philosophy and political science is important to cover this gap and reflect on possible pathways to understanding how the nation-state works.

2.13 The Parliament Resolution on 2022 and the Future of Investment Migration in Europe

The European Parliament debates in 2018 did not advance for a common framework on investment migration within the EU. This led to a second round of debates on 7 March 2022 in Strasbourg. The debate resulted in the Decision by Parliament T-9-0065/2022. The document is the latest stage which CBI/RBI have reached within European Union discussion (statement on 4 June 2024), representing a clear position from the European Parliament to phase out all citizenship by investment programmes by 2025, but also because it presents a possible Union Directive on the topic.

The Parliament suggested that while the programmes are phased out, a financial contribution from the Member States that have CBI/RBI should

441 European Parliament Resolution of 9 March 2022 with proposals to the Commission on citizenship and residence by investment schemes (2021/2026(INL)), point X 6

be made to the European Union as a "concrete expression of solidarity based on Article 80 TFEU."[442] The Article prescribes that "the policies of the Union set out in this Chapter and their implementation shall be governed by the principle of solidarity and fair sharing of responsibility, including its financial implications, between the Member States. Whenever necessary, the Union acts adopted pursuant to this Chapter shall contain appropriate measures to give effect to this principle."[443] The chapter mentioned "policies on border checks, asylum and immigration," which would then include investment migration if this type of mobility is considered migration.

A request to the Commission was made to create a specific category of the Union's own resources, consisting of a "CBI and RBI adjustment mechanism."[444] In other words, the European Union would profit from a part of the investments that the Member States receive, and which they would need to transfer to the Union. The legal base from the Parliament is Article 311 of the Treaty on the Functioning of the European Union: "The Union shall provide itself with the means necessary to attain its objectives and carry through its policies," including the possibility to "establish new categories of own resources or abolish an existing category."[445] This fund would bring a large injection of money into the Commission, as the EPRS EAVA Study estimated that just from 2011 to 2012, the total investment in the Member States via CBI/RBI was EUR 21.4 billion.[446] This option is controversial given the 10 years' worth of attacks by the institutions on residence and/or citizenship by investment programmes. This would be a huge shift from the rhetoric against it, to then gaining economic benefits from these programmes, even if just for a short time.

The Resolution also brings back the genuine link argument: "whereas the Commission has launched infringement procedures against Cyprus and Malta on the grounds that the granting of Union citizenship for predetermined

---

442 European Parliament Resolution of 9 March 2022 with proposals to the Commission on citizenship and residence by investment schemes. 2022, Point 19

443 Treaty on the Function of the European Union

444 European Parliament Resolution of 9 March 2022 with proposals to the Commission on citizenship and residence by investment schemes. 2022

445 Treaty on the Functioning of the European Union. 1958

446 Milieu Law and Policy Consulting, Citizenship by Investment (CBI) and Residency by Investment (RBI) schemes in the EU. 2018

payments or investments without any link with the Member States concerned undermines the essence of Union citizenship."[447] There is no mention of the genuine link argument other than in the paragraph referred to above in quotation marks, which makes it clear that for the European institutions, investments made via residence or citizenship by investment are not considered a genuine link. There are no other legal references or further explanations of the resolution's position on the genuine link argument specifically.

This chapter has shown the various ways that the European institutions (Commission, Parliament, Council, and CJEU) have tried to change or influence the competence over matters of naturalisation and residence in Member States. This framework of opinions and resolutions does not change the competence of the European Union in the sense that the EU begins to have competence over naturalisation matters. The only way to change this would be via a Treaty change, as per Article 48 TEU: "The Treaties may be amended in accordance with an ordinary revision procedure. They may also be amended in accordance with simplified revision procedures."[448] This would need to be done with the unanimity of Member States. At the current stage of the investment migration debate, and in view of the position of many Member States profiting from these schemes, a unanimous decision is unlikely.

---

447 European Parliament, resolution of 9 March 2022 with proposals to the Commission on citizenship and residence by investment schemes. 2022

448 Article 48, Treaty on European Union

The Portuguese and Maltese Schemes Considering the *Nottebohm* Case and International Legal Considerations

From the beginning of the citizenship by investment programme in Malta until today, one of the main reasons for debate and disagreement is the claim of the lack of a genuine link in the case of investors in Malta. Referred to as a principle of international law, this chapter navigates the curiosity of understanding the *Nottebohm* case by applying it to the cases of Malta and Portugal. To guide the reading of this chapter, two questions should be present when reading analysis of the *Nottebohm* case. First, can international law impose limitations on states with respect to citizenship law? The second, more specific question is as follows: could international law impose limitations on the acquisition of citizenship or residence by investment?

In the context of public international law, nationality law has many words connected to what we call citizenship today. The creation of the nation-state through the "Westphalian system" after conclusion of the Treaties of Münster and Osnabrück on 24 October 1648. Words such as "the world state," "sovereignty," "legal personality," "equality," "territorial sovereignty," and "independence" are part of the "nation-state," which we know today. Therefore, the legislative competence of States is an attribute of the sovereignty of states.[449] There is then a presumption "in favour of the full sovereignty of a State over its territory unless a title or rule can be shown under which international law would restrict the sovereignty."[450]

449 Donner, Ruth. The Regulation of Nationality in International Law, 2nd edition, 1994, page 16

450 Delupis, Ingrid; International Law and the Independent State, 1974, 23

The attempt to limit competence over matters of nationality is not new and dates back to the last century. For example, the Permanent Court of International Justice,[451] in its advisory opinion on the Tunis and Morocco (French Zone) Citizenship Decrees, established that a state's discretion could be "restricted by obligations which it may have undertaken towards other states."[452] Although this note may offer space to interpretation that international law could limit nationality regulation, the Court confirmed in the case the "national autonomy" of states with regard to nationality law. The Permanent Court stated as follows:

> The question whether a certain matter is or is not solely within the jurisdiction of a State is an essentially relative question; it depends upon the development of international relations. Thus, in the present state of international law, questions of nationality are, in the opinion of this Court, in principle within this reserved domain."[453]

By "reserved domain" would mean, in the words of Robert Sloane, "nationality falls within a domain of legal competence reserved to internal law, although it may be limited by treaty obligations."[454] Moreover, the PCIJ reinforced this in the case *Lotus*:

> International law governs relations between independent states. The rules of law binding upon states therefore emanate from their own free will as expressed in conversations or by usages generally accepted as expressing principles of law and established in order to regulate the relations between these co-existing independent communities or with a view to the achievement of common aims. Restrictions upon the independence of states cannot therefore be presumed.[455]

---

451 The Permanent Court of Justice was the first permanent international tribunal with general jurisdiction from the League of Nations that existed from 1922 to 1946. International Court of Justice (2023), Permanent Court of Justice. Available on: https://www.icj-cij.org/pcij#:~:text=The%20work%20of%20the%20PCIJ,and%20delivered%2027%20advisory%20opinions. Access on: 27.05.2023

452 P.C.I.J. Nationality Decrees Issued in Tunis and Morocco (Advisory Opinion) [1923] Rep Series B No 4

453 P.C.I.J. Nationality Decrees Issued in Tunis and Morocco (Advisory Opinion) [1923] Rep Series B No 4, page 24

454 Sloane, Robert. Breaking the genuine link: the contemporary international legal regulation of nationality (2009) 500 Harvard International Law Journal 1

455 P.C.I.J, S.S. "Lotus" (France v Turkey) [1927] Rep Series A, No 10, 18, para 44

The first international treaty related to citizenship law was the Hague Convention on Certain Questions Relating to the Conflict of Nationality Law from 1930, initiated by the League of Nations where it also reinforced the competence of the State in Nationality laws. Article 1 provides:

> It is for each State to determine under its own law who are its nationals. This law shall be recognized by other States in so far as it is consistent with international conventions, international custom, and the principles of law generally recognized with regard to nationality.[456]

Article 2 continues:

> Any questions as to whether a person possesses the nationality of a particular State shall be determined in accordance with the law of that State.

Nationality laws are, therefore, competences of states, but Article 1 recognizes that states do not have a duty in international law to recognise foreign nationality legislation if it is not "consistent with international conventions, international custom, and the principles of law generally recognized with regard to nationality." As seen in the previous chapter, the European Commission and the European Parliament claimed the principle of a genuine link as necessary to granting citizenship in Member States. For the former Vice-President of the Commission, "In compliance with the criterion used under public international law, Member States should only award citizenship to persons where there is a 'genuine link' or 'genuine connection' to the country in question."[457]

At the time, Commissioner Reding said that "citizenship should not be for sale and be awarded only where there is a genuine link or connection between the individual and the Member State concerned." The Labour Party of Malta was divided on the issue, with some MEPs being in favour of the programmes and others against. Overall, the resolution of the European Parliament presented back in 2014 against citizenship by investment already

---

456 Convention on Certain Questions Relating to the Conflict of Nationality Laws, 1930

457 Europa Rapid Press Release, Viviane Reding, Vice-President of the European Commission responsible for Justice, Citizenship must not be up for sale, 15 January 2014, SPEECH/14/18.

made reference to a "person's ties" with Europe and Member States as a criterion for naturalisation:

> Notes that EU citizenship implies the holding of a stake in the Union and depends on a person's ties with Europe and the Member States or on personal ties with EU citizens; stresses that EU citizenship should never become a tradable commodity.[458]

On the other hand, some literature argues that the *Nottebohm* case relies on obsolete precedent in arguing that there would be a breach of EU law in citizenship by investment,[459] a jurisprudential illusion,[460] or not relevant for international law.[461] Therefore, the scope of the *Nottebohm* ruling is extremely disputed in the scholarship. I will argue in this chapter that the genuine link doctrine is not the way to interpret a possible violation of public international law in citizenship by investment and that the only possible breach of international law regarding citizenship by investment would be the case of citizenship by investment without consent. In other words, international law prohibits naturalisation without consent, and therefore, when citizenship by investment is awarded without consent, there would be a violation of international law.

In international law, citizenship law is a *domaine reservé*, meaning that, in principle, citizenship is a matter of state sovereignty.[462] The first multilateral international convention on citizenship was the 1930 Hague Convention on

---

458 European Parliament. European Parliament Resolution of 16 January 2014 on EU citizenship for sale (2013/2995(RSP)). 2014

459 Kochenov, D. B., Elena, It's All about Blood, Baby! The European Commission's Ongoing Attack against Investment Migration in the Context of EU Law and International Law. Working Paper no. 161 The Centre on Migration, Policy & Society, 2022, page 32

460 Spiro, Peter, (2019), Nottebohm and Genuine Link: The Anatomy of Jurisprudential Illusion IMC WP 1/2019

461 Macklin, Audrey "Is it time to retire Nottebohm" (2017) 111 American Journal of International Law 492

462 Article 3(1) of the Hague Convention on Certain Questions Relating to the Conflict of Nationality Law (1930), Crwaford, Brownlie's Principles of Public International Law, 8th edition, Oxford University Press, 2010; Sironi, Alice "Nationality of Individuals in Public International Law" in Alessandra Annoni and Serena Forlati (eds), The Changing Role of Nationality in International Law, Routledge, 2013, page 54

Certain Questions Relating to the Conflict of Nationality Laws.[463] Article 1 of the Convention states that "it is for each State to determine under its own law who are its nationals. This law shall be recognised by other States in so far as it is consistent with international conventions, international custom, and the principles of law generally recognized with regard to nationality."[464] States determine who belongs to their citizenry and who do not. In other words, states can do as they want with respect to the allocation of nationality.[465] But could international law limit citizenship law? Or what would be the "in so far as it is consistent" part of the Hague Convention? As the Convention did not specify the limits of "international custom" or "the principles of law generally recognized regarding 'nationality'," the interpretation of these limits remained open in the legal literature.

That is the case of the argument brought by some scholars against Citizenship by Investment, who have found in the *Nottebohm* case of the International Court of Justice the base of an argument: when someone buys a passport, this should create a genuine link with the state from which the person acquires the nationality. A case of international law (*Nottebohm*) has been used against Citizenship by Investment, yet the same international law has been used to argue that these programmes are "readily situated within the scope of sovereign discretion,"[466] and that Citizenship by Investment does not violate international law. What was perhaps attractive for many international lawyers and tribunals in the decades after the decision was the idea that perhaps "it seemed to supply the missing concept to inform the supposedly general international law limits on a state's competence to confer its nationality by internal law."[467]

---

463 Hague Convention on Certain Questions Relating to the Conflict of Nationality Laws (1930)

464 Article 3(1) of the Hague Convention on Certain Questions Relating to the Conflict of Nationality Law (1930)

465 League of Nations Committee of Experts for the Progressive Codification of International Law, Questionnaire No. 1 – Nationality, 1926, 20

466 Spiro, Peter. Investment Citizenship and the Long Leash of International Law. In Citizenship and Residence Sales Rethinking the Boundaries of Belonging Edited by Dimitry Kochenov and Kristin Surak. Cambridge: Cambridge University Press, 2023, page 138

467 Sloane, Robert. Breaking the Genuine Link: The contemporary International legal regulation of nationality, in 50 Harvard International Law Journal 1 (2009), page 25

Along these lines, only one exception is made: the case of the United Arab Emirates. The country bought Comoros Islands citizenship to distribute to its stateless population (known as *Bidoon*) beginning in 2008. As this violated the consent condition of the acquisition of citizenship,[468] this is seen as problematic for Citizenship by Investment to develop this way in the future. Noori Lori explained that the Bidoon did not have a choice regarding receiving citizenship from the UAE or the Comoros.[469] According to her research, Emirati authorities would issue Comoros passport to *Bidoons* with the argument that this was a first step to UAE citizenship. Or that acceptance of the citizenship would facilitate access to basic social services and other forms of documentation. Around 80–120,000 Comoros passports were granted to Bidoon in the UAE. This could set a precedent for other countries seeking a destination for their "unwanted population,"[470] which in terms of stateless people reaches an estimated number of 10 million people worldwide.[471] Kuwait also started to follow UAE's steps, but backed off in the face of criticism.[472] These and other examples are ways of interpreting a violation of international law in relation to naturalisation rules. As referred to by Peter Spiro,[473] there has been little systematic analysis of investment citizenship under international law, which made it essential to devote this chapter to this task using the *Nottebohm* case

468 The requirement of volitional naturalisation is established in international law to mean that states cannot naturalise an individual without his/her consent. Spiro, Peter. Investment Citizenship and the Long Leash of International Law. In Citizenship and Residence Sales Rethinking the Boundaries of Belonging Edited by Dimitry Kochenov and Kristin Surak. Cambridge: Cambridge University Press, 2023, page 143

469 Noori, Lori. Offshore Citizens: Permanent Temporary Status in the Gulf. Cambridge University Press, 2019, page 162

470 Mansour-Ille, Dina. Cash for citizenship: rich Arab countries may pay poor islands to take "stateless" Bidoons. Available on: https://odi.org/en/insights/cash-for-citizenship-rich-arab-countries-may-pay-poor-islands-to-take-stateless-bidoons/ Access on: 05/06/2023

471 United Nations High Commissioner for Refugees. About Statelessness. Available on: https://www.unhcr.org/ibelong/about-statelessness/, Access on: 05/06/2023

472 Human Rights Watch, Kuwait's Plan to Pawn Off its "Stateless." Available on: https://www.hrw.org/news/2015/03/26/kuwaits-plan-pawn-its-stateless Access on: 05.06.2023

473 Spiro, Peter. Investment Citizenship and the Long Leash of International Law. In Citizenship and Residence Sales Rethinking the Boundaries of Belonging Edited by Dimitry Kochenov and Kristin Surak. Cambridge: Cambridge University Press, 2023, page 142

as a reference and to fill the gap in the literature. This final chapter also finalises the argument of this dissertation. While the first chapter explained the object of study of the thesis and its practice, chapters two and three deal with the arguments of both European and international law.

3.1 What is the Genuine Link: The Nottebohm Case

3.1.1 Background and Circumstances of the Case

Friedrich Nottebohm was born in Hamburg on 16 September 1881. Therefore, he was German by birth and possessed German nationality. He moved to Guatemala and was the owner of coffee plantations, spending his whole life in the country. Instead of naturalising as a Guatemalan, he applied, in October 1939 – with the approach of Second World War – for naturalisation in Liechtenstein. For Dimitry Kochenov, this move was done in order first to get rid of his German citizenship but also to hold a super citizenship (Liechtenstein) instead of becoming a victim of citizenship (having a Guatemalan passport would not offer many mobility rights).[474] This argument is well founded. In the closing paragraphs of the decision, the Court states that *Nottebohm* acquired the nationality of Liechtenstein "in order to replace his status as a national of a belligerent State with that of a national of a neutral State, with the sole aim of thus coming into of the protection of Liechtenstein."[475] Having naturalised in Liechtenstein – where his brother lived – had the effect of terminating his German nationality due to German law. It is important to say that his Liechtenstein nationality was "bought" because the standard three-year residence requirement[476] was waived upon the payment of a naturalisation fee and an obligation to pay an annual tax to Liechtenstein.

---

474 Kochenov, Dimitry. Victims of Citizenship Feudal Statuses for Sale in the Hypocrisy Republic in Citizenship and Residence Sales Rethinking the Boundaries of Belonging Edited by Dimitry Kochenov and Kristin Surak. Cambridge: Cambridge University Press, 2023, page 82

475 Nottebohm Case (Liechtenstein v. Guatemala), 1955 I.C.J. 4 (6 April).

476 Section 6 (d) by Liechtenstein Law of Nationality of 10 January, 1934 provides: "Nationality may be conferred upon aliens only if ... they have ordinarily resided in the territory of the Principality of Liechtenstein for at least three Years; that requirement may be dispensed with in circumstances deserving special consideration and by way of exception."

In 1943, Guatemala entered into a state of war with Germany, and this led to Guatemala rejecting the legitimacy of the naturalisation of Mr Nottebohm. It not only detained him but confiscated all his properties in the country. In the same year on 19 October, Guatemala arrested *Nottebohm* and turned him over to the US military, which sent him to the United States. There, he remained in detention for more than two years. Liechtenstein, as a neutral state in the war, tried to intervene with the Guatemalan decision and understood the detention and expropriation as a violation of rights and, therefore, sought to exercise diplomatic protection[477] on behalf of their national. Nottebohm later returned to Liechtenstein and resided there for six years. In 1951, Liechtenstein instituted proceedings at the ICJ on his behalf. This whole story gave rise to the case of *Liechtenstein versus Guatemala*, and the decision is analysed in the next section.

3.1.2 The Decision

The International Court of Justice ruled in 1955's *Nottebohm* decision that nationality constitutes "*a legal bond having as its basis a social fact of attachment, a genuine connection of existence, interests, and sentiments, together with the existence of reciprocal rights and duties*."[478] The majority of the judges also said that,

> Naturalization is not a matter to be taken lightly. To seek and to obtain it is not something that happens frequently in the life of a human being. It involves his breaking of a bond of allegiance and his establishment of a new bond of allegiance. It may have far-reaching consequences and involve profound changes in the destiny of the individual who obtains it.[479]

The Court basically did a "test" of whether Mr Nottebohm's Liechtenstein nationality was "real and effective." In the Court's interpretation, "his actual connections with Liechtenstein were extremely tenuous." On the analysis of

---

477 Under international law, a State is responsible for injury to an alien caused by that State's wrongful act or omission. Diplomatic protection is the procedure employed by the State of nationality of the injured person to secure protection of that person and to obtain reparation for the internationally wrongful act inflicted (Reparations). In John Dugard, Diplomatic Protection Oxford Public International Law Encyclopedia, June 2021

478 Nottebohm Case (Liechtenstein v. Guatemala), 1955 I.C.J. 4 (6 April).

479 Nottebohm Case (Liechtenstein v. Guatemala), 1955 I.C.J. 4 (6 April), page 24

his intentions for the naturalisation, the Court said the act was made with "the sole aim of [...] coming within the protection of Liechtenstein but not of becoming wedded to its traditions, its interests, [or] its way of life." Also, the process "was not based on any real prior connection with Liechtenstein, nor did it in any way alter the manner of life of the person upon whom it was conferred in exceptional circumstances of speed and accommodation. In both respects, it was lacking in the genuineness requisites to an act of such importance."[480]

While the Court ruled on the lack of effect in Mr Nottebohm's naturalisation process, the Court also noted that it was Liechtenstein's competence to define its nationality legislation on the domestic level. Accordingly, the Court stated, "It is for Liechtenstein, as it is for every State, to settle by its own legislation the rules relating to the acquisition of nationality."[481] What the case perhaps leaves open to dubious interpretation is the fact that many countries use the genuine link theory in their naturalisation laws. That was already something recognised in the doctrine back in 1960 after the *Nottebohm* judgement. In Josef Kunz's words, "it is perfectly true that many nationality laws demand previous domicile for granting nationality by way of naturalizing."[482] However, as stated in the judgement, "international law does not, however, require previous residence in the country as a condition for naturalization, nor does it presuppose a subsequent residence there."

Perhaps it is because of these details of the decision that the case resonated almost 70 years later in Brussels regarding citizenship by an investment, since the reading of the decision bears some similarities to the debate about whether there should be a genuine link between the investor and the Member State that offers citizenship by investment. Moreover, the literature has changed greatly over the decades, from scholars favouring the decision to those rejecting the Court's interpretation altogether. The inspiration for the decision to include the genuine link doctrine was present in previous practices of international arbitral tribunals where the Court found several cases of the protection of dual nationals and decided along the same lines as the *Nottebohm* case. That is, in the cases of international arbitrators, preference

480 Nottebohm Case (Liechtenstein v. Guatemala), 1955 I.C.J. 4 (6 April).
481 Nottebohm Case (Liechtenstein v. Guatemala), 1955 I.C.J. 4 (6 April).
482 Kunz, Josef. The American Journal of International Law, 1960, Vol. 54, no 3, page 553

was given to the real and effective link "that which accorded with the facts, that based on stronger factual ties between the person concerned and one of the States whose nationality is involved."[483]

The decision, however, was not unanimous, with three dissenting votes and a vast literature that criticised the case in the majority but also saw the decision as favourable.[484] The next section presents the dissenting justices' counterarguments, something important for the debate about whether or not the *Nottebohm* case is relevant to citizenship and residence by investment.

3.1.3 The Dissenting Opinions

Three judges in the case had dissenting opinions.[485] These are important, especially because dissenting opinions can become the law.[486] These three dissenting opinions from Judge Klaestadt, Read and Guggenheim *(Ad hoc)* resemble the literature from the last 10 years, which criticises the genuine link doctrine. They referred to the fact that many states allow naturalisation "as an exceptional measure" without any connection. In this sense, Judge Read stated,

> In the case of many countries such as China, France, the United Kingdom and the Netherlands, the non-resident citizens form an important part of the body politic and are numbered in their hundreds of thousands or millions. Many of these non-resident citizens have never been within the confines of the home State.[487]

He also observed that the genuine link theory was a peculiar interpretation that the Court made based on late nineteenth and early twentieth-century arbitrations that were answering a different question: whether dual nationals could use one of their nationalities for diplomatic protection against one of

483 Donner, Ruth. The Regulation of Nationality in International Law, 2nd edition, page 60

484 Kunz, Josef. The American Journal of International Law, 1960, Vol. 54, no 3, pages 536–91

485 Judges Klaestad and Read, and *Ad Hoc* Judge Guggenheim

486 Kunz, Josef. The American Journal of International Law, 1960, Vol. 54, no 3, pp. 536–571

487 Dissenting Opinion Judge Read, Nottebohm Case (Liechtenstein v. Guatemala), 1955 I.C.J. 4 (6 April)

their own states of nationality.[488] In international arbitration, the principle of effective nationality (or active or master) is to the effect that "in cases of plural nationality a person is to be considered as having the nationality which they exercise."[489] This principle of effective nationality is well explained in the *Mergé* Case,[490] and it refers to habitual residence of the individual concerned, the centre of one's interests, family ties, one's participation in public life and attachment shown by one for a given country and inculcated in one's children. The case referred to a citizen of the United States who acquired Italian citizenship via marriage. She refers in her application for a new US passport that her legal residence was New York, while in fact she had lived in Italy most of the time. At the Conciliation Commission, the decision was over which nationality was the "effective nationality." The principle also finds legal support in Article 5 of the Convention on Certain Questions Relating to the Conflict of Nationality Law which states the following:

Within a third State, a person having more than one nationality shall be treated as if he had only one. Without prejudice to the application of its law in matters of personal status and of any conventions in force, a third State shall, of the nationalities which any such person possesses, recognize exclusively in its territory either the nationality of the country in which he is habitually and principally resident, or the nationality of the country with which in the circumstances he appears to be in fact most closely connected.[491]

The dominant nationality test may be useful in arbitration cases but using it as a reference for the *Nottebohm* case fails in many aspects. First, the *Nottebohm* case was not a conflict of nationality in arbitration, and Mr Nottebohm had, at the time, only one nationality (Liechtenstein). Second, quoting Judge Read when he stated that the "criteria of dominant nationality designed for cases of double nationality to an essentially different type of relationship (acquisition of nationality, for example)" would be, in my view, a difficult argument to saying it would be possible to "transpose" the argument from international

488 Dissenting Opinion Judge Read, Nottebohm Case (Liechtenstein v. Guatemala), 1955 I.C.J. 4 (6 April)

489 Weiss, P. Nationality and Statelessness in International Law, 1979, Brill

490 Reports of International Arbitral Awards, Mergé Case – Decision No. 55, 10 June 1955, Volume XIV, pp. 236–248

491 Convention on Certain Questions Relating to the Conflict of Nationality Law 1930

arbitration to assume that a criterion – the genuine link – should exist for all cases of acquisitions of nationality.

Also, *ad hoc* Judge Guggenheim remarked:

> International law does not, for example, in any way prohibit a State from claiming as its nationals, as the moment of their birth, the descendants of its nationals, who have been resident abroad for centuries and whose only link with the State which grants its nationality is to be found in descent, without the requirement of any other element connecting them with the State[492]

What the *Nottebohm* case represented was an attempt to replace objective criteria for naturalisation (competence of the states) with a subjective criterion, which would be represented by the genuine link theory. The dissenting opinions highlight this risk. For example, *ad hoc* judge Guggenheim pointed out that the "new rule" is not in accordance with the practice and refers that it would be dangerous to delegate the naturalisation to vague principles that could lead to arbitrary decisions.[493]

3.1.4 The Criticism of the Judgement

From 1955 to the present, legal scholars have criticised the judgement from different perspectives. The criticisms can be divided into four sections: diplomatic protection; whether it imposes some limitation on the acquisition of nationality; its relevance in today's globalised and multi-national world; and whether *Nottebohm* was a case of abuse of rights and not a case of implementation of the genuine link.

In the diplomatic sphere, scholars have said that the judgement imposes limitations on cases where a national acquires their citizenship through naturalisation, when referring to diplomatic protection.[494] Also, the 2006 Draft Articles on Diplomatic Protection (Draft) from the International Law Commission rejected the idea that a genuine link criterion should exist for the exercise of diplomatic protection, as this would exclude millions of persons

492 Dissenting Opinion Judge *Ad hoc* Guggenheim, Nottebohm Case (Liechtenstein v. Guatemala), 1955 I.C.J. 4 (6 April).

493 Dissenting Opinion Judge *Ad hoc* Guggenheim, Nottebohm Case (Liechtenstein v. Guatemala), 1955 I.C.J. 4 (6 April).

494 Donner, Ruth. The Regulation of Nationality in International Law (Transnational Publishers 1994), page 31

living in countries for which they hold no nationality.[495] In its understanding, the International Law Commission argued that "despite divergent views as to the interpretation of the case, the Commission took the view that there were certain factors that served to limit *Nottebohm* to the facts of the case in question" and that the Court "did not intend to expound a general rule applicable to all States, but only a relative rule according to which a State in Liechtenstein's position was required to show a genuine link between itself and Mr Nottebohm in order to permit it to claim on his behalf against Guatemala with whom he had extremely close tie."[496]

As exposed, *Nottebohm* does not create or initiate a new regulation in international law in which it can be said that a genuine link between the individual and the country in which they are naturalising is obligatory. Furthermore, this has not been the reality in several countries since the case was decided, with regard to naturalisation requirements. As Audrey Macklin argues, "among legal scholars who take *Nottebohm* seriously as jurisprudence, there is strong consensus that it was wrong then, and may be even more wrong now."[497] By "now," one should remember all the references already pointed out in the previous chapters: a broader acceptance of dual and multiple citizenship, a globalised world, and elevated numbers of migration all over the world. These social aspects together reinforce how important it is to finally "retire"[498] *Nottebohm*.

On the relevance of the case, Peter Spiro states that the genuine link doctrine had little traction in international forums and has also been rejected in international legal commentaries.[499] He understands the *Nottebohm* case as a "Myth of Genuine Link" but recognises that *Nottebohm* and "genuine link"

---

495 International Law Commission, Draft Articles on Diplomatic Protection (Draft), 2006, available on: https://legal.un.org/ilc/texts/instruments/english/draft_articles/9_8_2006.pdf

496 International Law Commission, "Draft articles on diplomatic protection with commentaries" (2006) UM Doc A/CN 4/L 646, available on: https://legal.un.org/ilc/texts/instruments/english/commentaries/9_8_2006.pdf, Access on: 04.06.2024

497 Macklin, Audrey "Is it time to retire Nottebohm" (2017) 111 American Journal of International Law, page 492

498 Macklin, Audrey "Is it time to retire Nottebohm" (2017) 111 American Journal of International Law, page 492

499 Spiro, Peter. Investment Citizenship and the Long Leash of International Law. In Citizenship and Residence Sales Rethinking the Boundaries of Belonging Edited

hold significant influence within the realm of international legal discourse. The idea that the genuine link should be understood as a general norm of international law, originating from the *Nottebohm* case, according to Robert Sloane[500] is a misreading of the *Nottebohm* case. For him, it is a non-justified romantic view of nationality. He also highlights that the case is not a case of judicial legislation (meaning that the Court would suddenly apply the genuine link to all nationality cases in the world) but a specific case where the Court applied a principle of law, in this case, the principle of abuse of rights.[501] He further defends his idea of abuse of rights instead of genuine link, arguing that Mr Nottebohm "abused the liberal international legal regulation of nationality in an effort to evade the law of war." Why would that be so? One often omitted item of information in the current debate on the genuine link is that Mr Nottebohm was a former Nazi.[502] So, the decision to acquire citizenship from a neutral state (Liechtenstein) and lose his German citizenship was a move that would represent an abuse of rights. Some authors even argue that the fact he was a former Nazi may well have influenced the ICJ's decision.[503]

Finally, "in international law, abuse of rights refers to a State exercising a right either in a way which impedes the enjoyment by other States of their own rights or for an end different from that for which the right was created, to the injury of another State."[504] Here, I can see a less problematic argument against Citizenship by Investment compared to the EU principle of sincere cooperation violation (precisely the *free riders* idea presented in chapter two). What Sloane[505] argued in 2009 was that in the case of *Nottebohm*, it would be

---

by Dimitry Kochenov and Kristin Surak. Cambridge: Cambridge University Press, 2023, page 146

500 Sloane, Robert. Breaking the Genuine Link: The contemporary international legal regulation of nationality, in 50 Harvard International Law Journal 1 (2009), page 04

501 Statue of the International Court of Justice, Article 38 (1), 1945

502 Sloane, Robert. Breaking the Genuine Link: The contemporary international legal regulation of nationality, in 50 Harvard International Law Journal 1 (2009), page 04

503 Kunz, Josef. The American Journal of International Law, 1960, Vol. 54, no 3, pp. 536–540

504 Kiss, Alexandre, Abuse of Rights, in Encyclopedia of Public International Law 1, 4 (Rudolf Bernhardt ed., 1992)

505 Sloane, Robert. Breaking the Genuine Link: The contemporary International legal regulation of nationality, in 50 Harvard International Law Journal 1 (2009)

more reasonable to argue that Mr Nottebohm abused his right to nationality because he wanted to evade the consequences of the international law of war. That could have been one of the arguments from the Court at the time, but the ICJ decided to use the genuine link theory as an argument. This was not in vain, as in the interpretation of the Special Rapporteuer John R. Dugard, the Court did not want to impugn the conduct of Liechtenstein; a sovereign state should decide on matters of naturalisation:

> Faced with the choice between finding that Liechtenstein had acted in bad faith in conferring nationality on Nottebohm and finding that he lacked a "genuine link" of attachment with Liechtenstein, the Court preferred the latter course as it did not involve condemnation of the conduct of a sovereign State.[506]

However, even if the Court had adopted the abuse of rights argument, this idea would not have established a general rule in international law because it is impossible to define – as it was with the genuine link – what this abuse of rights would be. If this were the case, there would be a great risk of countries using this argument against their citizens. Would any naturalisation that had an instrumental bias, as is the case with countless naturalisations around the world, be open to doubt and prosecution by a state that believes the person has abused the right to naturalisation? It does not sound persuasive, but it is extremely dangerous to leave countries free to interpret what this abuse of rights means. Most decisions in international law seek to protect citizens' rights in order – more often than not – to prevent statelessness or reduce laws that promote discrimination.

3.2 The Case's Reception and Application

3.2.1 Nottebohm Dismissed: Flegenheimer Case

The interpretation of the *Nottebohm* case in other international tribunals has had a restrictive interpretation. As Peter Spiro explains, "there are no important decisions from international tribunals which have adopted its

[506] International Law Commission, Dugard, John, First Report on Diplomatic Protection, Document A/CN.4/506, 7 March, 200

rationale."[507] On the contrary, in Flegenheimer's claim,[508] *Nottebohm* was interpreted in the sense that it cannot be invoked to argue against the effectiveness of a person's citizenship. Besides that, *Nottebohm* should be limited to the particular facts of the case. The decision stated that,

> There does not in fact exist any criterion of proven effectiveness for disclosing the effectiveness of a bond with a political collective, and the persons by the thousands who, because of the facility of travel in the modern world, possess the positive legal nationality of a State, but live in foreign States where they are domiciled and where their family and business center is located, would be exposed to non-recognition, at the international level, of the nationality with which they are undeniably vested by virtue of the laws of their national State, if this doctrine were to be generalized.[509]

The 1958 Flegenheimer Case represented the first major consideration of *Nottebohm* in a claim's tribunal. The United States sought to recover assets from Mr Albert Flegenheimer, a US national who was born in Germany but was stripped of his citizenship under German law in 1940. The Italian government argued that Mr Flegenheimer did not qualify as a US national "in view of the fact that, during half a century, the individual concerned was considered as and considered himself to be a German national by his conduct, his sentiments, his interests. The Respondent Party contends that a nationality is not effective when it confines itself to establishing a nominal link between a State and an individual and is not supported by a social solidity resulting from a veritable solidarity of rights and duties between the State and its national."[510]

The Italian attempt to apply the effective/genuine link argument failed in the tribunal. In a clear rejection of the genuine link theory, the decision highlights that "it is doubtful that the International Court of Justice intended to establish a rule of general international law in requiring, in the *Nottebohm* case, that there must exist an effective link between the person and the State in order that the latter may exercise its right of diplomatic protection on

---

507 Spiro, P., Nottebohm and Genuine Link: Anatomy of a Jurisprudential Illusion. IMC Working Papers, 2019 (Investment Migration Working Papers), page 12

508 Flegenheimer (United States v. Italy), 14 RIAA 327 (Italian-US Conciliation Commission 1958), 375

509 53 American Journal of International Law 944 at 957 (1959)

510 United States vs Italy, Flegenheimer Case, Decision no. 182, 1958, Italian-United States Conciliation Commission, page 375

behalf of the former."[511] In this sense, the tribunal limited *Nottebohm* to its facts. Explaining the very limited application of the genuine link theory, the tribunal pointed out the use of it in international private law:

> The theory of effective or active nationality was established, in the Law of Nations, and above all in international private law, for the purpose of settling conflicts between two national States, or two national laws, regarding persons simultaneously vested with both nationalities, in order to decide which of them is to be dominant, whether that described as nominal, based on legal provisions of a given legal system, or that described as effective or active, equally based on legal provisions of another legal system, but confirmed by elements of fact (domicile, participation in the political life, the centre of family and business interests, etc). It must allow one to make a distinction, between two bonds of nationality equally founded in law, which is the stronger and hence the effective one.[512]

Thus, the Flegenheimer case reinforces the refusal to interpret the *Nottebohm* case as a requirement in international law for all naturalisation laws. On the contrary, the case shows the use of the effective nationality theory in cases involving dual national citizens in private international legal disputes. Looking at the dissenting opinions previously presented in this chapter, *Flegenheimer* echoed these dissenting judges and reinforced a more globalised view of nationality, where people have their genuine links less often with their passport but more with countries where they live, work or do business.

3.3 *Nottebohm* Partly Accepted: Iran–US Claims Tribunal & *Mergé* Case (United States v. Italy)

3.3.1 An Iran–United States Claims Tribunal

The Iran–US claims tribunal used the *Nottebohm* case not to apply a "genuine link" requirement broadly but only to refer to the determination of the "real and effective" citizenship in that specific case.[513] However, the case also referred to the genuine link doctrine as something that "radiated throughout

---

511 United States vs Italy, Flegenheimer Case, Decision no. 182, 1958, Italian-United States Conciliation Commission, page 375

512 United States vs Italy, Flegenheimer Case, Decision no. 182, 1958, Italian-United States Conciliation Commission, page 376

513 Iran v. United States, Case No. 32-A/18-FT, 5 Iran–US Claims Tribunal Reporter 251, 263

the international law of nationality."[514] The Iran–United States Claims Tribunal is an international arbitral tribunal created as one of the measures taken to resolve the crisis in relations between the Islamic Republic of Iran and the United States of America arising out of the November 1979 hostage crisis at the United States Embassy in Tehran, and the subsequent freezing of Iranian assets by the United States of America.[515] As explained by the tribunal, there was "much litigation in the courts of the United States brought against Iran by citizens of the United States, often involving judicial attachments of Iranian assets. In order to overcome that obstacle and permit the return of these assets and the termination of that litigation, a new substitute forum – this Tribunal – was established."[516]

In the case A/18, Iran asked the Iran–US Claims Tribunal[517] to decide whether the Algiers Accords invested that Tribunal to deal with questions of dual nationals against Iran. The Tribunal applied the pre-*Nottebohm* tests of "dominant and effective" nationality and in that sense gave a "positive legal authority"[518] to the *Nottebohm* case. The request made by the US was to ask the tribunal to apply customary international law and, in a case involving a dual national "resolve the issue by determining the dominant and effective nationality of the dual national claimant."[519]

In this particular case, it held that dual nationals may sue one of their states of nationality, that is, the non "dominant and effective" state of nationality. In the specific case, the tribunal held that it had jurisdiction "over claims against Iran by dual Iran–United States nationals when the dominant and effective nationality of the claimant during the relevant period from the date the claim arose until 19 January 1981 was that of the United States."[520] In the decision, the tribunal did not contest the rules on acquisition of nationality

---

514 Iran v. United States, Case No. 32-A/18-FT, 5 Iran–US Claims Tribunal Reporter 251, 263

515 Iran–United States Claims Tribunal. Introduction, Iran–United States Claims Tribunal Available on: https://iusct.com/introduction/, Access on: 14.06.2023.

516 Iran v. United States, Case No. 32-A/18-FT, page 19

517 in Introduction, Iran–United States Claims Tribunal Available on: https://iusct.com/introduction/, Access on: 14.06.2023.

518 Sloane, Robert. Breaking the Genuine Link: The contemporary International legal regulation of nationality, in 50 Harvard International Law Journal 1 (2009), page 28

519 Iran v. United States, Case No. 32-A/18-FT, Page 13

520 Iran v. United States, Case No. 32-A/18-FT, Page 25

of Iran or the United States. It merely applied the effective nationality theory to solve a conflict of nationality.

It was not only in *Iran vs United States* that the effective or genuine link theory was applied. Many international arbitral tribunals have done similarly, such as the *Mergé* case (*United States vs Italy*)[521] in the Italian-United States Conciliation Commission, and the Franco-Italian Conciliation Commission in the claims of dual nationals: Rambaldi Claim (*France vs Italy*) 13 R.I.A.A. 786 (1957); Mengui claim (*France vs Italy*) 13 R.I.A.A. 801 (1958) and Lombroso Claim (*France vs Italy*) 13 R.I.A.A. 804 (1958).

3.3.2 B Mergé Case (United States v. Italy)

The *Mergé* case is one example of an arbitration commission applying a "dominant" nationality test in cases where one state of citizenship had a claim against another state of citizenship. In cases where a claimant had legitimate connections with more than one state, tribunals carried out inquiries that focused on factual details to ascertain the state with which the individual had a stronger connection. In the *Mergé* case, the U.S. Italian Conciliation Commission was tasked with property disputes arising out of the Second World War from a United States national. Florence Strunsky-Mergé, a citizen of the United States by birth, entered into matrimony with an Italian government translator. The act of her marriage conferred upon her the status of an Italian national by law.[522] She then lived in different countries (Italy, Japan) and established herself in Italy, living outside of the United States for 20 years. The tribunal found that she could not qualify as a U.S. national for purposes of claiming compensation for loss, as a result of the war, of personal property located at Frascati, Italy. According to the decision in which the dominant nationality principle was applied, the Commission understood that Mrs Mergé could not be considered a predominantly United States national:

> Because the family did not have its habitual residence in the United States and the interests and the permanent professional life of the head of the family were

[521] Mergé Case (United States v. Italy) 14 R.I.A.A.

[522] Mergé Case (United States v. Italy) 14 R.I.A.A., page 237

> not established there. (…) Mrs. Mergé has not lived in the United States since her marriage, (…) stayed in Japan from 1937 until 1946 with her husband (…).[523]

The Conciliation Commission noted that "the conduct of the individual in his economic, social, political, civic and family life, as well as the closer and more effective bond with one of the two States must also be considered."[524] The tribunal emphasised the habitual residence of the individual as a factor for determining the dominant nationality but also referred to the *Nottebohm* case regarding "the center of interests, his family ties, his participation in public life, attachment shown by him for a given country and inculcated in his children, etc.."

It is important to understand that the case is not one of choosing one of the two nationalities, but rather "one of deciding whether in such case the government of the United States may exercise before the Conciliation Commission the rights granted by the Treaty of peace with reference to the property in Italy of United States nationals (Articles 78 and 83)."[525] It is not a case about the acquisition of nationality but a case of representation of a State on behalf of a national in a tribunal.

3.4 The EU Application of the Case

The most important part of the report for this dissertation is the discussion of investor citizenship and EU law, by which the Commission refers to two main cases – *Nottebohm*[526] and *Michelletti*.[527] The Commission defends the genuine link based on two premises: the *Micheletti* case established that while it is for each Member State to lay down the conditions for the acquisition and loss of nationality, they must do so having due regard to Union law.[528] Then, the argument of the genuine link is exposed as due to all Member States, as it was

---

523 Mergé Case (United States v. Italy) 14 R.I.A.A. page 248

524 Mergé Case (United States v. Italy) 14 R.I.A.A. page 247

525 Mergé Case (United States v. Italy) 14 R.I.A.A. page 238

526 Nottebohm Case (Liechtenstein vs Guatemala). 1955, I.C.J. International Court of Justice

527 C-369/90 Mario Vicente Micheletti and Others vs Delegación del Gobierno en Cantabria. 1992, European Court of Justice

528 C-369/90 Mario Vicente Micheletti and Others vs Delegación del Gobierno en Cantabria. 1992, European Court of Justice

established in jurisprudence through *Nottebohm*. "For nationality acquired through naturalization to be recognized in the international arena, it should be granted on the basis of a genuine connection between the individual and the State in question."[529]

The report of the European Commission on Investor and Residence by Investment also provided an argument for what the genuine link is: "a genuine connection with the people of the country (which can be established by descent, origin or marriage) or a genuine connection with the country, established either by birth in the country or by effective prior residence in the country for a meaningful duration."[530] A genuine link is, indeed, for the European Commission, a connection established by blood or another connection after birth (residence, marriage). The report concluded that "each Member State needs to ensure that nationality is not awarded absent any genuine link to the country or its citizens,"[531] by which one can understand that "granting naturalization based on a monetary payment alone" does not qualify as a genuine link.

3.5 Is the Genuine Link the Way Forward?

Martjin van den Brink already posed this question in his article of 2020.[532] When one sees the genuine link principle only from the angle of citizenship by investment, it is easy to intuit that the principle makes sense: EUR 650,000 does not create a link to a country via bank transfer. However, if placed and analysed in a macro sense (across the European Union), a number of arguments can be made against this idea. Even in literature that presents arguments against citizenship by investment, there is an important reference to the fact that the genuine link can "take us closer to nationalism in the

529 Nottebohm Case (Liechtenstein vs Guatemala). 1955, I.C.J. International Court of Justice

530 European Commission, Report on Investor Residence and Citizenship of 23 January 2019.

531 European Commission, Report on Investor Residence and Citizenship of 23 January 2019.

532 Van den Brick, Martijn, Revising Citizenship within the European Union: Is a Genuine Link Requirement the Way Forward?, 2020, EUI Working Papers 2020/76 Robert Schuman Centre for Advanced Studies, GLOBALCIT

domain of citizenship, which defies the purposes of citizenship of the Union as the fundamental status of nationals of EU Member States."[533] Sergio Carrera later reinforces that it is a risk to make this insistence with the genuine link:

> The genuine connection argument has also justified Member States' use of discriminatory practices and naturalization conditions calling upon applicants to show societal ties or assimilation to the receiving country. By insisting mainly on the genuine link standard, European institutions may be fuelling nationalism by Member States in determination of who is or is not an EU Citizen.[534]

There are many examples here. In England, the creation of the so-called "British Overseas Citizens" is a clear example of exclusion of the right to reside in the UK due to a difference regarding genuine connection.[535] In Germany, because citizenship is based on bloodlines (*jus sanguinis*), many German-born Turkish people have been excluded from acquiring citizenship.[536] For Germany, the Turks' failure to naturalise was a demonstration of a lack of attachment to Germany, while Turks mentioned that the requirement of renouncing their Turkish citizenship was the cause for the low naturalisation rate.[537] Turks are the largest ethnic minority group in Germany, numbering nearly three million residents, but only 246,000 hold German citizenship.[538] If in the past, the genuine link already promoted the exclusion of various

---

533 Carrera, Sergio. The Price of EU Citizenship The Maltese Citizenship-for-Sale Affair and the Principle of Sincere Cooperation in Nationality Matters (2014) Maastrich Journal of European and Comparative Law No. 2014-3, page 425

534 Carrera, Sergio. The Price of EU Citizenship The Maltese Citizenship-for-Sale Affair and the Principle of Sincere Cooperation in Nationality Matters (2014) Maastrich Journal of European and Comparative Law No. 2014-3, page 427

535 Government of United Kingdom, Types of British nationality, 2024, Available on: https://www.gov.uk/types-of-british-nationality/british-national-overseas Access on: 12.04.2024

536 McFadden SW. German citizenship law and the Turkish diaspora. *German Law Journal*. 2019;20(1):72–88. doi:10.1017/glj.2019.7

537 McFadden SW. German citizenship law and the Turkish diaspora. *German Law Journal*. 2019;20(1):72–88. doi:10.1017/glj.2019.7

538 *Bevölkerung mit Migrationshintergrund – Ergebnisse des Mikrozensus 2016* [*Population with Migration Background – Results of the Micro census of 2016*], Federal Office of Statistics 63 (2016) https://www.destatis.de/DE/Publikationen/Thematisch/Bevoelkerung/MigrationIntegration/Migrationshintergrund2010220167004.pdf;jsessionid=0646332EA70C5CBB98688BB718A6C657.cae1?__blob=publicationFile

populations, the prognosis that the genuine link could increase nationalism in Member States is already coming true.

The Italian parliament has been discussing a new draft law since 24 January 2024, proposing changes that could affect those of Italian descent seeking to reclaim their heritage through citizenship. Currently, the Italian Citizenship Law (Law No. 91 of 5 February 1992 [New norms on citizenship]) allows the possibility of descendants of Italians, without generational limits, acquiring Italian citizenship and also keeping their home country citizenship. The DDL – *Disegno di Legge* 752, proposed by Senator Roberto Menia from the far-right party *Fratelli d'Italia* – the same party as Prime Minister Georgia Meloni – would change the naturalisation law. The proposal limits naturalisation to great-grandchildren and requires a B1 level of Italian according to the European Framework of References for Language. In the case of more distant ancestors, naturalisation would still be possible as long as the applicant has resided in Italy for at least one year and had a B1 level in the Italian language. I argue that this move is a reflex to the genuine link theory, especially when looking at the proposal, the words used clearly defend a nationalistic perspective. The legislation proposal refers to a necessity of "*un'italianità vissuta e sentita*."[539] An English translation would be a "lived and felt Italianness."

If nationalism is a possible risk related to an application for naturalisation such as the genuine link, in the case of the application, various forms of naturalisation would also need to be modified, as they do not have requirements such as length of residence or language. I will describe four examples of naturalisation that should change if the genuine link were a requirement: Olympic citizenship;[540] Sephardic Jews in Spain and Portugal; reparatory citizenship in Germany; and naturalisation by descent in Ireland, Hungary, and Italy. Before the reader thinks otherwise, I am not arguing that these forms of naturalisation should cease to exist. On the contrary, I believe that they all have their historical value and are fully in line with international law, which states that it is up to each state to decide who its nationals are.

---

539 Italy, *Disegno di Legge No 752, 2023*

540 Shachar, Ayelet "Picking Winners: Olympic Citizenship and the Global Race for Talent." *The Yale Law Journal* 120, no. 8 (2011): 2088–2139. http://www.jstor.org/stable/41149587

My use of these cases only serves to exemplify other forms of naturalisation that do not require proof of knowledge of the language of the country in which one is naturalising, or length of residence, two of the main arguments that serve – or in the case of the Italian bill mentioned above – as to defend a genuine link as a naturalisation rule.

3.5.1 Olympic Citizenship

Several nations speed up naturalisation and eliminate mandatory requirements for individuals who aspire to participate in the Olympic games on behalf of their country. According to Rule 41 of the Olympic Charter, individuals competing in the Olympic games are mandated to hold citizenship of the country they are representing.[541] Many athletes are then naturalised to compete for countries without any language or time of residence requirements. In Olympic citizenship, the country can grant citizenship, or the athlete could acquire citizenship via some distant ancestry.

For example, Becky Hammon is an American basketball player who acquired Russian citizenship in 2008 and represented Russia at the 2008 and 2012 Olympics. As Ayelet Shachar posed, Becky had nothing but the most tenuous ties to Russia before she was granted citizenship in an expedited process.[542] Becky's case one of fast-process citizenship, but there is another practice that athletes follow to be able to represent another country. Many search their family trees for ancestors who can guarantee naturalisation via ancestry. One case here is Chris Kaman, with the NBA's Los Angeles Clippers since 2003, who was born and raised in the United States but guaranteed German citizenship thanks to his great-grandparents. He was contacted by the German sports authorities and granted a German passport in July 2008 in an expedited process, which allowed him to represent Germany in the 2008 Beijing Olympic Games.[543]

---

541 Olympic Charter, available at https://olympics.com/ioc/olympic-charter

542 Shachar, Ayelet "Picking Winners: Olympic Citizenship and the Global Race for Talent." *The Yale Law Journal* 120, no. 8 (2011): 2088–2139. http://www.jstor.org/stable/41149587, page 2091

543 Rosenthal, John, a New German? Olympian Chris Kaman and German Nationality, World Politics Review, 14 August, 2008, Available on: https://www.worldpoliticsreview.com/a-new-german-olympian-chris-kaman-and-german-nationality/ Access on: 19/04/2024

These two examples represent the trend of Olympic citizenship, in which citizenship can be interpreted as a shift towards a more strategic and selective approach to citizenship, where exceptional skills or talents are highly valued over traditional notions of belonging and loyalty.[544] Clearly, it is difficult to say that these modes of acquiring nationality represent a genuine link, in the sense that *Nottebohm* calls for. There is no "*social fact of attachment, a genuine connection of existence, interests, and sentiments, together with the existence of reciprocal rights and duties*"[545] besides the benefits for the athlete of competing in an Olympic games and the possible medals and recognition that the state would receive when winning competitions. If the European Commission's argument holds that a genuine link is needed to grant naturalisation, then Member States that have a form of naturalisation without requirements for athletes should also review this practice, as it does not align with the *Nottebohm* case.

3.5.2 Descendants of Sephardi Jews in Portugal and Spain

A second example of naturalisation that should be modified if the genuine link theory is applied is the naturalisation processes for descendants of Jews who were forced to convert to Catholicism or face expulsion from the Iberian Peninsula in the fifteenth century, who today can apply for Portuguese or Spanish citizenship (only until 2021) if they prove their descent. The connection here would be distant by five centuries, and it is today the main naturalisation route in Portugal, corresponding to 57.5 % of all naturalisations in Portugal by foreigners who did not reside in Portugal in 2022.[546] An interesting fact is that in 2022, the number of newly naturalised people in Portugal had a proportion of people who do not reside in Portugal, with Israel being the country of residence for the vast majority.

544 Shachar, Ayelet "Picking Winners: Olympic Citizenship and the Global Race for Talent." *The Yale Law Journal* 120, no. 8 (2011): 2088–2139. http://www.jstor.org/stable/41149587, page 2094

545 Nottebohm Case (Liechtenstein vs Guatemala). 1955, I.C.J. International Court of Justice

546 Statistics Portugal, Portuguese citizenship acquisition, Demographic Statistics 2022

In the case of Spain, a law approved in 2015[547] offered citizenship to the descendants of Sephardi Jews expelled in 1492. It is important to say that in the "genuine link" logic, before 2015, Spain already allowed Sephardi Jews to become naturalised citizens, except that they had to live in the country for two years. The new law removed this residency requirement.[548] The law was established with a three-year application window and has been extended for another year, ending on 1 October 2019. The Federation of Jewish Communities of Spain, together with the Spanish government, estimated that between 90,000 and 1.5 million descendants would apply for naturalisation. However, only 132,226 Sephardi descendants have applied during the four years in force.[549] While the Spanish law is described as a "reencounter and reconciliation with the global Sephardi community after more than half a millennium, the Portuguese amendment is called a law of return to the homeland."[550] However, neither the Spanish Law 12/2015 or the Portuguese Decree-Law 30-1/2015 mentions reparations for the unjust expulsion of Jews from the Iberian Peninsula, although many authors recognise laws of reparation.[551] The applicants do not need to renounce their current citizenship or establish residence in the new country.

In the case of Portugal, also in 2015, an amendment to Portugal's Nationality Act allowed descendants of Jews who were expelled in the Inquisition to

---

547 Spain, Law 12/2015 of June 24th Granting Spanish Nationality to Sephardi Jews Native to Spain

548 McDonald CA. Rancor: Sephardi Jews, Spanish Citizenship, and the Politics of Sentiment. *Comparative Studies in Society and History*. 2021;63(3):722–751. doi:10.1017/S0010417521000190

549 McDonald CA. Rancor: Sephardi Jews, Spanish Citizenship, and the Politics of Sentiment. *Comparative Studies in Society and History*. 2021;63(3):722–751. doi:10.1017/S0010417521000190

550 Kandiyoti, Dalia and Benmayor, Rina. "Introduction: Sephardi Jews, Citizenship, and Reparation in Historical Context." *Reparative Citizenship for Sephardi Descendants: Returning to the Jewish Past in Spain and Portugal*, edited by Dalia Kandiyoti and Rina Benmayor, New York, Oxford: Berghahn Books, 2023, pp. 1–34. https://doi.org/10.1515/9781800738256-003

551 Aragoneses, Alfons. "Chapter 1 "Reparative Citizenship" Confronting Injustices of the Past or Building Modern Nationalisms?." *Reparative Citizenship for Sephardi Descendants: Returning to the Jewish Past in Spain and Portugal*, edited by Dalia Kandiyoti and Rina Benmayor, New York, Oxford: Berghahn Books, 2023, pp. 37–52. https://doi.org/10.1515/9781800738256-004

become citizens if they "belong to a Sephardic community of Portuguese origin with ties to Portugal."[552] Unlike Spain's law, Portugal's version was less stringent, requiring only a clear criminal record and a verifiable Sephardic certificate. The certificates were produced by the Jewish Community of Lisbon (CIL; *Comunidade Israelita de Lisboa*) and the Jewish Community of Porto (CIP; *Comunidade Israelita de Porto*), the two institutions authorised by the Portuguese government to evaluate proof of ancestry.[553] In 2022, the policy received a lot of attention due to the arrest of Rabbi Daniel Litvak on allegations of fraud and corruption.[554] Approximately 262,000 individuals had applied for naturalisation under the law by the end of 2022, including the Russian oligarch and Chelsea FC owner Roman Abramovich in 2021.[555]

On January 2024, the Portuguese parliament approved the change in the Sephardic Jew naturalisation process and included two cumulative new requirements related to a genuine connection to Portugal: (a) demonstrate a tradition of belonging to a Sephardic community of Portuguese origin, based on proven objective requirements of connection to Portugal, namely surnames, family language, direct or collateral descent; (b) Have legally resided in Portuguese territory for a period of at least three years, consecutive or interpolated.[556] Among the changes is also the suspension of the procedure for acquiring nationality when the applicant is the target of "restrictive measures approved by the United Nations or the European Union."[557]

---

552 Portugal, Decreto Lei no. 30-A/2015 allowing the granting of Portuguese nationality, by naturalisation, to descendants of Sephardic Jews

553 Santos, Teresa and Bento, Heraldo. "Chapter 15 Appendix Certifying Origins for Sephardic Descendants in Portugal: A Snapshot of the Evaluation Process." *Reparative Citizenship for Sephardi Descendants: Returning to the Jewish Past in Spain and Portugal*, edited by Dalia Kandiyoti and Rina Benmayor, New York, Oxford: Berghahn Books, 2023, pp. 295–303. https://doi.org/10.1515/9781800738256-019

554

555 The Guardian, Portugal to change law under which Roman Abramovich gained citizenship. Available on: https://www.theguardian.com/world/2022/mar/16/portugal-nationality-by-descent-law-roman-abramovich-citizenship

556 Portugal, *Lei Orgânica* n. 1/2024 05 March, 2024, available on: https://diariodarepublica.pt/dr/detalhe/lei-organica/1-2024-854130977

557 Portugal, *Lei Orgânica* n. 1/2024, Article 13, para 2, 05 March, 2024, available on: https://diariodarepublica.pt/dr/detalhe/lei-organica/1-2024-854130977

Interestingly, nationality laws have not included other religious groups that were persecuted and expelled from Spain during the years 1609 to 1614. The Moriscos, Muslims converted to Christianity, were forced to leave Spain by the decree of Philipp III in 1609.[558]

What is important here is that the laws, like citizenship by investment, used to not require proof of residence or language. If the genuine link argument is applied to this case, the lack of a genuine link should also be recognised as an argument against the modality, just as it is in citizenship by investment. Perhaps the change presented in 2024[559] is already a reflection of the genuine link theory entering into various naturalisation laws that, by the logic of the argument, affect not only citizenship by investment but other naturalisations that do not require links such as length of residence or knowledge of the language.

3.5.3 Reparatory Citizenship in Germany

Peter Spiro is an American author who has researched dual citizenship for more than 20 years. In his book *At Home in Two Countries*, he explains how he and his kids became German due to the fact his father fled his hometown, Hamburg, in November 1939. His father had his German citizenship stripped because he was Jewish. His kids had never been to Germany, and he hadn't been there in years. They also did not speak German. As he defined it, "my motivation was instrumental" and he can "hardly call myself a German in any real way."[560] This was possible thanks to the Section 15 of the German Nationality Act, which makes individuals who surrendered, lost or were denied German citizenship between 30 January 1933 and 8 May 1945 due to

558 Allard, Elisabeth Bolorinos. "Chapter 6 'Spanish Jews' and 'Friendly Muslims' The Historical Absence of a Citizenship Campaign for Muslims of Iberian Descent." *Reparative Citizenship for Sephardi Descendants: Returning to the Jewish Past in Spain and Portugal*, edited by Dalia Kandiyoti and Rina Benmayor, New York, Oxford: Berghahn Books, 2023, pp. 137–152. https://doi.org/10.1515/9781800738256-009

559 Portugal, Assembleia da República, Projeto de Lei 28/XV/1, Determines that the system for granting Portuguese nationality on the grounds of descent from Sephardic Jews expelled from Portugal in 1496 will cease to apply, available on: https://www.parlamento.pt/ActividadeParlamentar/Paginas/DetalheIniciativa.aspx?BID=121369, Access on: 04.06.2024

560 Spiro, Peter, At home in two countries, New York University Press, New York, 2016, page 2–3

persecution on political, racial or religious grounds entitled to naturalisation. The legal avenue to reclaim citizenship already existed after the adoption of the Basic Law in 1949, under Article 116 (paragraph 2):

> (2) Former German citizens, who, between 30 January 1933 and 8 May 1945, were deprived of their citizenship on political, racial or religious grounds and their descendants shall, on application, have their citizenship restored. They shall be deemed never to have been deprived of their citizenship if they have established their domicile in Germany after 8 May 1945 and have not expressed a contrary intention.[561]

For more than six decades, numerous descendants of German-born ancestors have faced obstacles that have prevented them from claiming their right to German citizenship. However, a recent bill was introduced to parliament in March and has now been passed, which provides the opportunity for a significant number of descendants of Nazi victims to obtain German citizenship.[562] Although German law has different objectives in relation to investment citizenship legislation, in one respect, they are similar: they do not require prior residence or proof of knowledge of the country's language. These two criteria have been defended as the European Commission's genuine link in the case of citizenship by investment. Again, this is another example of how the genuine link argument could collide with other forms of naturalisation that do not require length of residence or proof of knowledge of the language of the country in which one is naturalised. Moreover, Germany is competent to decide which policies of naturalisation the country wants to establish, and the risk of a genuine link theory is a possible collision of arguments between what is being argued as a genuine link (time of residence, proof of language certificate) and other forms of naturalisation that do not require these two requirements.

3.5.4 Ancestry Naturalisation in Ireland, Hungary and Italy

Many Member States use the policy of authorising the naturalisation of descendants of their nationals, often with an unlimited generational gap, as

561 German Basic Law, Article 116, paragraph 2

562 Deutsche Welle, Germany eases citizenship for Nazi victims' descendants, 03.04.2024, available on: https://www.dw.com/en/germany-new-law-eases-citizenship-for-descendants-of-nazi-victims/a-56977454

is the case in Italy. Ireland allows descendants of Irish individuals living anywhere in the world to naturalise as long as they have one grandparent who was born in Ireland.[563] In cases of Irish descent, the conditions for naturalisation most likely to be dispensed with relate to residence and the intent to reside in the state after naturalisation.[564] Here it is not only the lifting of the residence requirement that is similar to citizenship by residence, but Peter Spiro also highlights that acquiring "Irish citizenship may well reflect an important identity, but many will also be interested in the benefits of European Union citizenship that come with it."[565] Even though many may not support this policy, Joseph Weiler pointed out that hundreds of thousands of EU citizens were "born" to parents, grandparents or – in some other Member States – even beyond by virtue of the *jus sanguinis* provisions and countries like Ireland legitimately value this important understanding of itself.[566]

Hungary is another example of naturalisation policy without the requirement of time of residence or an intermediate level of Hungarian language. The country has naturalised 1,000,000 non-resident individuals since it opened its naturalisation to any descendants of persons who were citizens of Hungary before 1920 or between 1941 and 1945. The change in the law in 2010, defined as "ethnically" preferential naturalisation policy,[567] also included knowledge of the Hungarian language. This knowledge is very basic.[568] Although the Hungarian case requires a minimum command of the language, it is also similar to citizenship by investment in the sense that it does not require a

---

563 Irish Nationality and Citizenship Act, 1956, Article 16, a

564 Handoll, Josh, Country Report Ireland EUDO Citizenship Observatory, European University Institute, 2012, Page 13, available on: https://cadmus.eui.eu/bitstream/handle/1814/19618/RSCAS_EUDO_CIT_2012_2.pdf?sequence=3&isAllowed=y

565 Spiro, Peter, At home in two countries, New York University Press, New York, 2016, page 137

566 Weiler, Joseph H. H.: *Citizenship for Sale (Commission v Malta): Who of the Two is Selling European Values?*, *VerfBlog*, 2024/4/14, https://verfassungsblog.de/citizenship-for-sale/, DOI: 10.59704/f3c2e8cfd7fcbbe7.

567 Pogonyi, S. (2022). The right of blood: "ethnically" selective citizenship policies in Europe. *National Identities*, *24*(5), 523–538. https://doi.org/10.1080/14608944.2021.2013185

568 Harpaz, Y. (2019). Citizenship 2.0: Dual nationality as a global asset. Princeton University Press.

period of residence in the country in which one is naturalised, and the process can be carried out in its entirety as a non-resident.

Finally, Italy is an example of a country that offers naturalisation by descent without generational limits, as long as the naturalised person's connection to the ancestor is proven in documents (certificates of births, marriage, death and certificate of non-naturalisation of the ancestor in the country where the descendant established themself after leaving Italy). Knowledge of the Italian language is also not a requirement. If it followed the logic of the lack of a genuine link (with the exception of recognising that blood is a genuine link), the Italian naturalisation law could also be scrutinised by European law in terms of genuine link criteria, something already defended by some critics.[569]

As presented, these four examples do not require criteria (time of residence or language proficiency) that are justified as lacking in the case of citizenship by investment. If the genuine link argument is interpreted as a requirement for all members of the European Union, this same argument could jeopardise other forms of naturalisation that are the competence of Member States described according to the conferral principle, Article 4 and 5 TEU.

3.6 Limitations on States with Respect to Citizenship Law in International Law

If the genuine link principle, in addition to being misinterpreted because it is believed to be a requirement and not merely a guideline, demonstrates risks in terms of nationalism and possible breaches of European law for other forms of naturalisation by Member States, the following question arises: are there any other rules of international law that could limit naturalisation rules and if so, are there any that could have any influence on citizenship and residence by investment? Historically, the field of international law has not provided much guidance regarding how states decide who can be a citizen and how they define the boundaries of citizenship. However, thanks to globalisation, international human rights law and increased dual or multiple citizenship,

569 Costica Dumbrava, "External Citizenship in EU Countries" (2014) 37 Ethnic and Racial Studies 2340; Panascì, Maria Antonia. "Breaking the Ancestral Silence: Recognition of Citizenship by Descent Despite the Great Brazilian Naturalization," *The Italian Review of International and Comparative Law* 3, 1 (2023): 157–168, doi: https://doi.org/10.1163/27725650-03010010

there are a few areas in which international law limits citizenship law. The next three sections present three themes in which international law has had an influence on citizenship and whether there is possible interference in citizenship by investment. The three sections are statelessness, discrimination, and voluntary acquisition of citizenship.

3.6.1 Statelessness

One area in which international law has affected citizenship law is statelessness. Following the 1954 UN Convention relating to the Status of Stateless Persons, a "stateless person" is defined as "a person who is not considered as a national by any State under the operation of its law."[570] Article 15 of the Universal Declaration of Human Rights states: (1) Everyone has the right to a nationality; (2) No one shall be arbitrarily deprived of his nationality nor denied the right to change his nationality.[571] However, much legislation worldwide promotes statelessness: loss or deprivation of citizenship; emergency of new states and changes in borders; gender inequality in citizenship law; discriminatory criteria against a specific minority in citizenship law, among other things.[572] The Hague Codification Conference, the resulting Convention on Certain Questions Relating to the Conflict of Nationality Laws (Hague Convention), indeed contained articles that addressed the consequences of sex discrimination, for example, women who would end up stateless by marrying a foreigner[573] or situations giving rise to the statelessness of children.[574] Nevertheless, state discretion in nationality remained the main rule.[575]

Citizenship by Investment concerns the acquisition of nationality, and most restrictions in international law on statelessness concern the loss of nationality. In particular, cases already presented in chapter two (*Rottmann, Tjebbes*) have shown how the Court influences the loss of nationality and international law. However, as the acquisition of nationality by investment

[570] United Nations Convention Relating to the Status of Stateless Persons, 1954
[571] Universal Declaration of Human Rights
[572] Stiller, Martin, Statelessness in International Law: A Historic Overview 37 DAJV Newsl/ 94 (2012), available on: https://heinonline.org/HOL/LandingPage?handle=hein.journals/dajvnws2012&div=41&id=&page= Access on: 25 April, 2024
[573] Hague Convention on Nationality, Articles 8–9
[574] Hague Convention on Nationality, Articles 13–16
[575] Hague Convention on Nationality, Article 1

allows people to have two or more citizenships, this type of naturalisation does not offer limitations on the issue of nationality acquisition and possible statelessness.

3.6.2 Non-discrimination

A large number of international instruments regulate non-discrimination laws. Article 2 of the Universal Declaration of Human Rights declares as follows:

> Everyone is entitled to all the rights and freedoms set forth in this Declaration, without distinction of any kind, such as race, colour, sex, language, religion, political or other opinion, national or social origin, property, birth or other status. Furthermore, no distinction shall be made on the basis of the political, jurisdictional or international status of the country or territory to which a person belongs, whether it be independent, trust, non-self-governing or under any other limitation of sovereignty.[576]

Moreover, Article 15 (1) UDHR, prohibits any discrimination regarding obtaining and keeping or changing one's citizenship:

1. Everyone has the right to a nationality.
2. No one shall be arbitrarily deprived of his nationality nor denied the right to change his nationality.[577]

Although the UDHR is not binding, the Charter has influenced numerous binding instruments that have comparable guarantees against discriminatory practices, such as the International Covenant on Economic, Social and Cultural Rights,[578] alongside several regional treaties, such as the European Charter of Fundamental Freedoms,[579] the African Charter on Human and People's Rights,[580] and the American Convention on Human Rights. At the European level, Article 14 of the European Convention on Human Rights prohibits discrimination on the grounds of sex, race, skin colour, language,

---

576 United Nations, Universal Declaration of Human Rights
577 United Nations, Universal Declaration of Human Rights
578 ICCPR, Articles 2 and 26
579 CFREU, Article 21
580 African Charter on Human and Peoples' Rights (Banjul Charter), adopted 27 June 1981, entered into force 21 October 1986

religion, political or other opinion, national or social origin, association with a national minority, property, birth or any other status.[581]

Citizenship by investment programmes do not target a specific ethnicity, race, or religion; therefore, it would be difficult to invoke a form of discrimination. However, if countries decided to impose restrictions on certain nationalities, this could be challenged before national or international tribunals by the argument of non-discrimination. Malta does not allow citizens from Afghanistan, Belarus, Congo, Iran, North Korea, Russia (since 2022), Somalia, South Sudan, Sudan, Syria, Venezuela, and Yemen. Countries in the Caribbean also impose restrictions on some nationalities. Antigua and Barbuda restrict Citizenship by Investment from citizens of Afghanistan, Belarus, Iran, North Korea, Russia, Somalia, Sudan, and Yemen. Egypt does not allow citizens of Israel to apply for citizenship by investment.[582]

In all cases, the aim and proportionality of these policies would need to be assessed to confirm whether they would be in accordance with international legal standards of non-discrimination. However, restrictions to some countries could be justified due to difficulties in carrying out due diligence checks on applicants. This could be a justifiable reason to impose restrictions, as some countries require the proof of the absence of a criminal record from the applicant's country of origin.

3.6.3 Voluntary Acquisition of Nationality

The acquisition of a new nationality must be voluntary. Circumstances of long-term residence outside country of nationality or marriage to a foreign national may be examples of an individual wanting to change their nationality. This right is protected by Article 15 of the Universal Declaration of Human Rights, which protects not only the right to a nationality but also the right to change nationality.[583] If it is not voluntary, international law is violated. As explained by Barbara von Rütte, "states shall not impose their

---

581 European Convention on Human Rights

582 Citizenship by Investment, Banned Nationalities, 2024, available on: https://www.imidaily.com/overview-of-restricted-nationalities-lists-of-citizenship-by-investment-programmes/

583 United Nations. Human Rights Council, Report 25/28 (n93) para 8

nationality on individuals without their consent."[584] This is derived from the prohibition of forced naturalisation, which means "the conferment of nationality against the will of the individual concerned."[585] The International Law Commission also reinforces that naturalisation should correspond to the explicit will of the person concerned or a person acting on their behalf.[586]

This international law norm was established due to a series of cases in Latin American states that naturalised nationals of United States and European countries without their consent, just because they had residence in the countries. Moreover, the laws were used to deprive the nationals of their first nationality.[587] Other examples are when a person concerned may have been conferred a new nationality without their consent or even knowledge (through state succession or when marriage or adoption confers automatic nationality).[588] Paul Weis describes the compulsory imposition of nationality without consent of the person concerned as comparable to an arbitrary arrest or forced marriage.[589] The consent requirement was imposed because it was seen as impeding the sovereignty of the state of initial nationality and not due to any concerns regarding human rights.[590]

With the development of international human rights law, the requirement for consent has also been defended as an expression of human dignity.[591] It would, therefore, be a violation of the right to a nationality if a state conferred nationality to individuals without their consent. This has happened

---

584 Von Rutte, Barbara, Defining the Right to Nationality, in The Human Right to Citizenship, Brill, 2022,

585 Von Rutte, Barbara, Defining the Right to Nationality, in The Human Right to Citizenship, Brill, 2022, page 262

586 International Law Commission, Report on Nationality, Including Statelessness (International Law Commission 1952) UM Doc. A/CN.4/50 7

587 Spiro, P., Nottebohm and Genuine Link: Anatomy of a Jurisprudential Illusion. IMC Working Papers, 2019 (Investment Migration Working Papers), page 4

588 United Nations. Human Rights Council, Report 25/28 (n93) para 9

589 Weis, Paul. Nationality and Statelessness in International Law, 2nd edition, Sijthoff & Noordhoff 1979

590 Peters A, "Extraterritorial Naturalizations: Between the Human Right to Nationality, State Sovereignty and Fair Principles of Jurisdiction" (2010) 53 German Yearbook of International Law 623.

591 Peters A, "Extraterritorial Naturalizations: Between the Human Right to Nationality, State Sovereignty and Fair Principles of Jurisdiction" (2010) 53 German Yearbook of International Law, page 659

in the case of citizenship by investment in the case of United Arab Emirates and Kuwait. As Jelena Dzankic has argued, "in an extreme case of avoidance of responsibility towards a non-citizen population, the governments of the United Arab Emirates (UAE) and Kuwait purchased the Comorian passports for Bidoons living in their respective countries."[592] She explains the situation of *Bidoons* in UAE and Kuwait as,

> mostly descendants of nomadic tribes from the Arabian peninsula. For a variety of reasons, they have not been registered as citizens in these Gulf countries, rendering them (and their children) stateless. From the mid-1980s, the situation of the Bidoons has been aggravated as they have been officially designated as "illegal residents." The UAE and Kuwait maintain that the Bidoons have settled in their territories illegally to make claims to welfare and social protection. As a result, this sizeable population has been deprived of many basic rights, including healthcare, education and even the possession of property.[593]

Therefore, citizenship by investment should not be a solution to the problem of statelessness. If countries grant nationality without an individual's consent, these cases could be challenged in court as violations of international law. Forced naturalisation is questionable from an individual rights perspective, as it does not consider the will of the individual concerned, thus interfering with the negative right not to be forcibly given a nationality.[594]

3.7 Genuine Link is Guidance, Not a Rule

Regarding the genuine link, it would be a misconception to understand that the *Nottebohm* decision imposes that all states should have a genuine link requirement in their nationality laws. As seen, the scope of the *Nottebohm* judgement is extremely contested. It is unlikely that international law can constrain the development of citizenship by investment. The maximum states

---

592 Dzankic, Jelena, Investor citizenship must not be used as a remedy for statelessness, 2019, available on: https://www.statelessness.eu/updates/blog/investor-citizenship-must-not-be-used-remedy-statelessness, access on: 08/05/2024

593 Dzankic, Jelena, Investor citizenship must not be used as a remedy for statelessness, 2019, available on: https://www.statelessness.eu/updates/blog/investor-citizenship-must-not-be-used-remedy-statelessness, access on: 08/05/2024

594 Von Rutte, Barbara, Defining the Right to Nationality, in The Human Right to Citizenship, Brill, 2022, page 262

can do is to use their discretionary power on visa-free entry to nationals of other states. That was what Canada did with nationals of St Kitts and Nevis, which previously did not need a visa to enter Canada. Because of "concerns about the issuance of passports and identity management practices within its Citizenship by Investment Program,"[595] Canada requires a visa for citizens of St Kitts and Nevis. On the other hand, St Kitts Citizenship by Investment has become more attractive since the European Union included the country in its visa-free list in 2009. This move was seen as influenced by the private company Henley, which had the head of the company named the country's honorary consul in Switzerland.[596] Therefore, if a state believes another state's investor citizenship programme to be suspicious or not following adequate due diligence, it can revoke visa-free entry and affect the programme's success. In 1960 the doctrine already stated that the genuine link theory is not required by international law[597] and it makes even more sense now to agree with that, having in mind the globalised and dual-and-multiple citizenship world in which we live. That is why I believe there is no violation of international law regarding the Portuguese residence by investment scheme and the Maltese Citizenship by Investment (in the two schemes). It is a mercantilist practice that should receive exemplary punishment in cases of corruption, or other possible crimes connected to the naturalisation process. However, sovereignty remains more important than any other principle in nationality law. As explained with the various other forms of naturalisation, despite having different objectives, they would not fit the genuine link criterion defended by the European Commission and some authors. If the genuine link rule is applied, many other naturalisation policies would be in danger and should be questioned. Also, as seen in other arbitration court decisions, the principle of effective nationality is applied when there are two nationalities and a decision must be made on a specific issue, but it has never referred to requirements for acquiring nationality, which is the case with citizenship by

595 Government of Canada. St Kitts and Nevis citizens now need a visa to travel to Canada. 22 November, 2014. Available on https://www.canada.ca/en/immigration-refugees-citizenship/news/notices/notice-kitts-nevis-citizens-need-visa-travel-canada.html Access on: 06.06.2023

596 Abrahamian, Atossa Araxia. The Cosmopolities: The Coming of the Global Citizen, Columbia Global Reports, 2015, page 82

597 Kunz, Josef. The American Journal of International Law, 1960, Vol. 54, no 3, page 560

investment. In the legal field, with the current state of international law and jurisprudence, added to the high number of dual citizens and globalisation, to defend the genuine link is to reinforce nationalism and call into question various other practices that are the competence of Member States, which could be questioned for lacking a genuine link. However, the concerns of political scientists deserve space so that they can be properly added to the debate. This is the function of the next section.

3.8 Political-Theoretical Considerations

Many political theorists argue against residence and citizenship by investment. They fear these schemes undermine "participation, co-governance, and a degree of solidarity."[598] Ayelet Shachar describes three arguments against citizenship by investment: exacerbating inequality; the intrusion of the market; and the character of citizenship. In her first argument, citizenship by investment can "contribute to perpetuating and deepening patterns of global inequality in contemporary mobility regimes and citizenship allocation." She also argues that "placing a tag on citizenship signifies a transformation of the criteria of membership from a political to an economic metric, contributing to broader processes of commodification that erode the promise of equality among existing members of the political community."[599]

The second critique considers the interference of the market into the political realm. In her analysis, citizenship is about political relations, and she expects participation, co-governance, risk-sharing, and some measure of solidarity among those constituting the body politic. Although she recognises that this is an idealised vision of citizenship, it is difficult to follow this argument for citizenship since the reality of the law does not require this participation.[600] Look at the non-compulsory voting in the majority of Member States or the low numbers of political participation in the European Parliament elections, some with merely 13 % participation.

---

598 Shachar and Hirschl, Ran, On Citizenship, States, and Markets, 2014, 22 (2) Journal of Political Philosophy 231, 247

599 Shachar, Ayelet, Citizenship for Sale? In Ayelet Shachar et al. (Eds), Oxford Handbook of Citizenship (OUP), pages 804–805

600

The third critique relates to the character of citizenship. Citizenship by investment can "detach the notion of citizenship from any kind of connection – be it residence, attachment, commitment – the political community."[601] Moreover, when citizenship is put on sale, it "is not just the price of the membership, but its substantive content as well."[602] Again, the problem with the political arguments is that they do not correspond with the reality of other forms of naturalisation presented in this chapter, which also do not require residence time or knowledge of the language. Also, the obligations that arise after someone acquires citizenship by investment are the same as for any other citizen who acquires citizenship by means other than investment. The responsibility to vote, if mandatory, and to pay fees, will be the same. CBI promotes inequality but there are other unequal means that Member States use to attract money, talent, and scientists. Entering into a logic of argument about what is fairer or unfairer does not change the existing requirements in the naturalisation processes of Member States.

Michael Sandel has argued that there are "moral limits of markets" and that not all goods should be commodified.[603] Although he does not include citizenship in his analysis, several politicians have spoken about whether or not a country's nationality should be put up for sale. An interesting exercise is to ask if the same arguments I analysed in chapter one and two (EU law, genuine link) could be used for the case of investment migration in other parts of the world. The answer would obviously be no in relation to EU law, since these principles apply only to members of the European Union. With regard to the genuine link principle, the case is not about establishing an international requirement for naturalisation, but about the recognition by other states of nationality acquired through investment. Understood as a *requirement*, it does not correspond to several nationality laws and would force the genuine link criterion to be something standardised in the naturalisation process all over the world.

---

601 Shachar, Ayelet, Citizenship for Sale? In Ayelet Shachar et al. (Eds), Oxford Handbook of Citizenship (OUP), page 807

602 Shachar, Ayelet, Citizenship for Sale? In Ayelet Shachar et al. (Eds), Oxford Handbook of Citizenship (OUP), page 809

603 Sandel, Michael, What Money Can't Buy, Farrar, Straus and Giroux 2012

While theorists of citizenship have tended "to focus on the injustices and harms suffered by refugees, the stateless, and migrant workers, often to propose remedies or to advocate specific state policies,[604] legal scholars are there to interpret what legal actors have decided about the law. Citizenship and Residence by Investment certainly do not promote equality. They just reinforce the unequal world that already exists. Ayelet Shachar, for instance, refers to the fact that cash-for-passports "poisons the political ideal of a common enterprise committed to promoting equality, rights, and collective decision-making through processes of deliberation and participation."[605]

In the instrumentalisation discussion from the German sociologist Christian Joppke, it is clear that citizenship by investment is a case of instrumentalism on both sides. States sell citizenship because they want revenue and individuals who apply for passports are looking for mobility rights.[606] A Maltese passport allows the holder to travel visa-free to 166 countries, while a Chinese passport allows travel to only forty-four countries and a Russian passport to eighty-six countries. Although it is a mercantilist practice, legally, because of the competence of the Member States, it is not convincing for the focus to be on a genuine link, because this theory is dangerous in terms of increasing nationalism and excluding populations. On the contrary, the focus – if so in political science – should be in assuring and the defending political participation from those who are excluded for decades from political participation in the country where they live, even though they pay taxes and contribute to the economy. Political scientist Michael Walzer argues that "once people are admitted as residents and participants in the economy, they must be entitled to acquire citizenship, if they wish."[607]

---

604 Balot, Ryan. Revisiting the Classical Ideal of Citizenship in The Oxford Handbook of Citizenship, (2017) Edited by Ayelet Shachar, Rainer Bauböck, Irene Bloemraad and Maarten Vink, page 16

605 Shachar, Ayelet, Citizenship for Sale? In Ayelet Shachar et al. (Eds), Oxford Handbook of Citizenship (OUP), page 811

606 Joppke, Christian, Citizenship by Investment: a case of instrumental citizenship in Citizenship and Residence Sales Rethinking the Boundaries of Belonging Edited by Dimitry Kochenov and Kristin Surak, Cambridge, 2023, page 251

607 Walzer, Michael, Spheres of Justice 60–61 (1983); see also Joseph H. Carens, Immigrants and the Right to Stay (2010)

3.9 Solutions: EU Regulation or Phase Out

Although this dissertation does not have a normative focus in the sense of recommending solutions, it is important to mention possible resolutions, as they have already been presented in the literature of European institutions.

First, the last report of the European Parliament recommended five policy measures to address contested modes of acquisition of residence or citizenship by investment. The first would be to ban citizenship by investment and residence by investment schemes. In this case, the first notable impact is the negative economic consequence in countries with CBIs or RBIs. For some countries like Malta, the programme represented 2.1 % of GDP and brought in EUR 1.2 billion between 2014 and 2019.[608] In Portugal, the golden visa was an important source of funding, similar to Foreign Direct Investment, and this would also mean ending one of the options for investment in older buildings.[609] Although this is the desired option of the European institutions, it will likely not happen. While most Member States claim that the competence for issuing residence permits and citizenship is the competence of those Member States, a possible ban on the programmes does not seem close to happening. What may occur is more coordinated actions of the European Union with other Member States to pressure a Member State to end its programme, which has had an effect in some countries (Bulgaria and Cyprus, for example).

A second policy option presented is an EU tax on CBI and RBI schemes. Two options would arise. First, a 100 % tax would go directly to the EU, leaving the country which grants the CBI or RBI without any benefit and, consequently, mostly likely to end their programme. The second option would be a win-win solution for the EU and the Member States. From the investment, a percentage – for example 20% – would be deducted to the EU and the rest would stay with the Member State. This probably would mean an increase in the programme price as the country would mostly increase the tax price to keep the same revenue as before.[610]

608 Surak, Kristin. Citizenship and Residence by investment schemes – State of play and avenues for EU action. Anex II in Avenues for EU action on citizenship and residence by investment schemes: European added value assessment. Meenakshi Fernandes, Cecilia Navarra, and David de Groot with María García Muñoz, 202, page 401

609 Ibid., page 41

610 Ibid., page 42

The third option would be regulation. This would entail regulating the caps, the approval process, due diligence, investments, and the migration industry. Regulating the number of applicants seems to me to only increase the programme's desirability, as it turns this asset into something that is likely to end. I have never understood the exact number of 1,800 main applicants from Malta. Is this some mathematical accounting so that it does not look like "mass naturalisation"? Is 1,800 a low number or a large number for a total population of 500,000? Claiming that it is possible to have more regulation through a specific or smaller number is yet to be empirically researched and proven. The approval process should be done by several public servants to avoid corruption. Also, excluding the possibility of discretionary authorities would be a way to combat possible loopholes in the system, which should be transparent and systematic.

The fourth policy option would be introducing minimum physical presence requirements for Residence by Investment schemes. The Portuguese investment programme, for instance, requires seven days of physical presence in the first year and fourteen days per year in the subsequent years. This is different from the reading of the Long-Term Residence Directive (2003/109/EC), which states that "Member States shall grant long-term resident status to third-country nationals who have resided legally and continuously within its territory for five years" and that "the acquisition of long-term resident status should be certified by residence permits."[611] There is room for the Commission to argue against Portugal regarding the physical presence and the Long-term Directive, as there is a breach of the national regulation and the European regulation which can be understood to violate principles of fairness and discrimination.[612] The option then would be to amend the Long-Term Residence Directive (2003/109/EC) to exclude beneficiaries of RBI schemes. Debates and this possibility were part of the recast discussions on the new Long-Term Residence Directive in 2024 but were ceased after resistance from some Member States.[613] In order to establish this policy it would be necessary

611 Long-term Residence Directive (2003/109/EC)

612 European Parliament Research Service (EPRS), Avenues for EU action on citizenship and residence by investment schemes. 2021, page 61

613 Investment Migration Council, Europe, Revised EU long-term residence Directive Negotiations Cease, 2024, available on: https://investmentmigration.org/news/

to have an EU-level definition of RBI, which could be done via Article 79 (2) (a) and (b) of the Treaty on the Functioning of the European Union:

> Article 79
>
> (2). For the purposes of paragraph 1, the European Parliament and the Council, acting in accordance with the ordinary legislative procedure, shall adopt measures in the following areas:
>
> (a) the conditions of entry and residence, and standards on the issue by Member States of long-term visas and residence permits, including those for the purpose of family reunification;
>
> (b) the definition of the rights of third-country nationals residing legally in a Member State, including the conditions governing freedom of movement and of residence in other Member States.[614]

In this case, the policy should be made in the form of a directive, and it would place applicants for residence by investment on an equivalent level with other migrants who are required to adhere to residency criteria when applying for citizenship after five years.[615]

The fifth policy suggestion is to regulate access to the EU by countries that have CBI/RBI schemes and that are in the EU accession process and/or regulate access to the EU of third countries with visa-free agreements with the EU. For the first option, the EU would establish a condition for EU accession countries (candidate and potential candidates) that have CBI/RBI schemes to align their vetting and due diligence measures with those already established at the European level, as well as physical presence requirements.[616] For example, Montenegro has been a candidate state since 2010. The country also had a citizenship by investment programme in which applicants made investments of EUR 450,000 to development projects in the capital of Podgorica or the coastal region, or an investment of EUR 250,000

europe-breaking-revised-eu-long-term-residence-directive-negotiations-cease/, Access on: 14/05/2024

614 Treaty on the Functioning of the European Union

615 European Parliament Research Service (EPRS), Avenues for EU action on citizenship and residence by investment schemes. 2021, page 62

616 European Parliament Research Service (EPRS), Avenues for EU action on citizenship and residence by investment schemes. 2021, page 64

to development projects in northern or central Montenegro, excluding Podgorica.[617] Although Montenegro's citizenship-by-investment programme ended on 31 December 2022, creating a policy alignment for potential EU members would make it easier for these countries to either give up on launching citizenship-by-investment programmes given the high costs of including high levels of due diligence and vetting, or to include this cost in their programme fees, passing the final cost on to the applicant, which would result in a less attractive scheme. North Macedonia and Turkey are other examples of countries that have citizenship by investment and could be affected by this policy.

The second option in this category would focus on visa-free agreements that the EU has. For example, countries with citizenship by investment programmes could be removed from the Annex II of Regulation 2018/1806 which lists the countries exempt from visa requirement to Schengen visa. Countries such as Antigua and Barbuda, St Kitts and Nevis, and Montenegro[618] have or had citizenship by investment and are except from visa requirements for the Schengen area. This policy could have an impact on these countries in case the requirement for a visa is implemented, reducing the attractiveness of the scheme.

3.10 Conclusion of the Chapter

This chapter presented the *Nottebohm* case and its application and implications for citizenship and residence by investment. Through a thorough analysis of the case involving dissenting votes and doctrine, it was shown that the case is more about diplomatic representation than a requirement in international law that can be a rule for all countries. It is rather a guide to how nationality could be, but not how it must be.

The second part of the chapter looked at other forms of naturalisation that also do not require the traditional requirements argued by the European Commission or some authors: length of residence or command

617 Montenegrin Government, Citizenship by Investment, available on: https://www.gov.me/en/documents/9dad5bba-64f9-453e-ac3b-b2e7fde109ac, Access on 14/05/2024

618 The exception from the visa requirement shall only apply to holders of biometric passports.

of the language of the country in which you are naturalising. Cases of naturalisation due to historical reparations, such as the case of descendants of victims of persecution in Portugal, Spain or Germany, as well as cases of naturalisation due to ancestry in Ireland, Italy and Hungary, show that the decision on who will be part of the population is a matter for the country itself and not for some plurinational entity or international rule unless it is decided by the country itself.

The third part of this chapter looked at other possible considerations regarding citizenship and international law. International law had an important impact on citizenship law, mostly focusing on protecting individual rights (in the case of deprivation of nationality) or reducing statelessness with the development of international human rights law.

The fourth part of the chapter also aimed to present the arguments arising from political and non-legal considerations in the literature. Although these arguments are not the focus of the chapter, as they are separate from legal arguments and provide normative perspectives, it was necessary to present them to provide a broad view of the context in which citizenship and residence-by-investment programmes are discussed. Again, political arguments are dangerous because they seek to implement a citizenship model that requires participation, which is not required in various naturalisation programmes throughout the European Union.

Finally, in connection with the previous section on regulatory proposals regarding citizenship and residence by investment, an attempt was made to present solutions already put forward by the literature of European institutions to contextualise the moment in which these schemes find themselves and possible solutions to the various arguments against these programmes.

CHAPTER 4

Conclusion

This dissertation has sought to analyse the extent to which residence and citizenship by investment programmes in the European Union (with Malta and Portugal as case studies) are in accordance with European law and international law. To answer the question, a wide range of normative sources were used, such as the Treaties (TFEU, TEU), general principles of EU law (sincere cooperation), authoritative sources (such as the case of the CJEU, ICJ and international arbitral tribunals), transcriptions from the European Parliament, Portuguese and Maltese debates, and both legal and social scientific scholarship. In the second chapter, describing the law in Portugal and Malta, several sources for the respective legal systems were used: in Portugal, *leis, portarias, despachos* and meetings of the parliament *(Reunião Plenária)*; in Malta, reports from the Individual Investor Programme regulator, Citizenship Act, and Legal Notices.

Malta and Portugal are two examples of investment migration. The first chapter of this dissertation explained how their policies work regarding citizenship and residence by investment. While Malta is the only remaining example of citizenship by investment in the European Union, Portugal is an example of residence by investment that received a large number of applications. Since I started my project in 2020, many policies and much legislation have changed on the topic. Ireland stopped offering investment visas. Portugal almost ended its golden visa programme in 2023. Bulgaria and Cyprus have stopped their investment citizenship programmes. Several actions by the European institutions have taken place, including the denunciation of Malta by the Commission to the Court of Justice of the European Union, which is scheduled to be heard by the CJEU sometime in 2024. While researching an issue that was on the front pages of the news was interesting, the challenge was greater because it was a topic to follow not only at a national level (Portugal and Malta) but also at the EU level and international level.

I was able to see various opinions in the literature on the topic and the evolution of the debate from the *Nottebohm* case to the change of the Maltese programme in 2020 and the failed attempt to end the Portuguese programme in 2023. While I did not envision a possible change in the founding Treaties of the European Union, which would require a genuine link to the harmonisation of rules on the acquisition of nationality at the EU level, I was able to see that the genuine link is mostly misinterpreted and is to be understood as guidance but not as a rule. With the current jurisprudence of the Court of Justice of the European Union, as well as an analysis of the principles of European law (conferral and sincere cooperation) and other case law of international and arbitral tribunals, the answer to my research question is that these models of naturalisation and granting of investment visas are (mostly) in accordance with European and international law, since it is the competence of the Member States and there is no overlapping of other principles with the principle of sovereignty and competence of legislation in matters of naturalisation and admission of third-country nationals via residence permits.

Despite being a utilitarian and mercantilist practice, the granting of nationality or residence permits via investment touches on a concept of belonging, or the question of who can or should be part of the nation, and for this reason, at first glance – as at the beginning of my research – one imagines that these practices would be prohibited by European or international law. It was with this curiosity that my research process first investigated how this legislation works in the two countries selected for analysis (Portugal and Malta). After understanding their requirements, the dissertation sought to understand whether there were any possible restrictions in European law, in particular via the main arguments put forward by the European Commission: violation of the principle of sincere cooperation and concerns about the link between the naturalised person and the country: the genuine link theory.

The analysis of the cases of the European Court of Justice made it clear that in this jurisprudential evolution, a timeline from the *Micheletti* case to *JY v Wiener Landesregierung* was necessary to understand how the CJEU has analysed possible limitations regarding EU citizenship and its relationship with naturalisation legislation in Member States. In the *Micheletti* case, besides rejecting the genuine link theory, the Court argued that it is not permissible for the legislation of a Member State to restrict the effects of the grant of the nationality of another Member State by imposing an additional condition for recognition of that nationality with a view to exercising the fundamental freedoms provided for in the Treaty. Later, in 2010 in the *Rottmann* case, the Court ruled that it is for each Member State, having due regard to EU law, to lay down conditions for the acquisition and loss of nationality, stating that EU law and especially its principles have to be part of the assessment of rules of nationality. In *Tjebbes vs Minister van Buitenlandse Zaken*, in 2019, the Court's decision followed up on the *Rottmann* case. The Court analysed the matter of loss of nationality and reinforced that when it comes to the loss of nationality of a European citizen, the process must be in accordance with EU law and follow principles such as proportionality. More recently, in *JY vs Wiener Landesregierung*, the Court went one step further and not only confirmed the proportionality test when a Member State withdrew nationality but also for the first time conducted a proportionality assessment itself.

The third chapter analysed the compatibility of investment migration with international law. Having the genuine link as the focus in line with the *Nottebohm* case, the chapter presented the case, its divergent opinions and implementation or non-implementation in other courts, especially arbitration courts that applied the effective nationality test. Here, the 1958 *Flegenheimer* case dismissed the *Nottebohm* case and its genuine link theory. The Commission's use of this theory appears erroneous, given that there are several Member States that grant naturalisation without any criteria to athletes, artists, and other people who make an excellent cultural or economic contribution to the country. If the requirement were to be applied in a binding manner, the Commission's criticisms should also address these discretionary forms without a genuine link so that there is coherence in placing a possible requirement at European level.

Most of the arguments against investment migration highlight the fact that the applicant has no ties to the state in which they are naturalising. This link is usually defended as length of residence or knowledge of the country's language. In fact, many countries not only require a level of knowledge of the language for naturalisation – B1 in the European framework – but some also require a knowledge test about the country, a citizenship test. However, many countries also grant citizenship without proof of length of residence or knowledge of the language through the *ius sanguinis* criterion. Chapter three gave the examples of Ireland, Italy, and Hungary and their legislation, which could be attacked by the genuine link requirement if the criticisms of citizenship by investment were transplanted to the criteria required for acquiring nationality. In other examples from Portugal and Germany, the practices of reparations for the past also do not require knowledge of the language or length of residence. These examples show how the genuine link theory is dangerous and can also lead to Member States using the same theory to reinforce nationalism. One example is the far right's proposal to require knowledge of Italian and restrict the generational distance required for applications – currently, there is no generational limit – for citizenship if the link to an Italian ancestor is proven.

Looking at all the cases, it seems that the competence of Member States to decide who should be part of their polity is legally unshakeable. This is a competence not only provided for in the founding Treaties of the European Union, by the conferral principle, but also demonstrated in chapter three by the analysis of international treaties. It is for each state to decide its naturalisation legislation. Most of the restrictions on citizenship concern the advancement of the protection of fundamental rights and the defence of the right to citizenship against possible revocations of citizenship that are disproportionate and could result in statelessness.

The genuine link, however, is not so black and white that the Court will say whether this theory is a requirement or mere guidance. Ideally, the Court would define what the genuine link is. It seems that the idea of seeking a definition through residency or language tests is risky, because it opens up the possibility of a "hunt for the non-genuine," whatever that might entail in a Europe increasingly full of nationalisms that can divide its citizens and promote discrimination on the basis of nationality. Of course, the answer is not simple, but a guide from the Court in which, for example, the Court defines that *only ius soli, ius sanguinis* and *ius residenti* (naturalisation by length of residence) are genuine links would make it clear that *ius pecuniae* (investment migration) is not a genuine link.

If it was not just for these risks, there is a risk that the Commission would in fact be entering into a competence clearly established as belonging to the Member States and not the European Union. As much as it is inconvenient, and I personally think there is nothing to celebrate when it comes to citizenship by investment, the final decision on who should be part of a polity should not rest with the European Union, nor its institutions, but rather the states that are part of this community, through their legislative, institutional procedures. The third chapter, however, also gave one example of violation of international law that could have an impact on national naturalisation laws. This is the case of forced naturalisation or the principle of consent. If a country grants nationality, bought from another country to its own citizens without their consent, this would be a violation of international law. The example in the chapter is of the Bidoon ethnic group in the UAE, and demonstrates that there are possible risks, of which countries are aware: Kuwait did not continue with the idea of buying citizenship for a specific group due to international criticism.

The differentiation between residence by investment and citizenship by investment in the realm of investment migration has been reinforced by this research. While the former has received relatively less criticism from European institutions, the latter has sparked strong debates not only in the literature but also at the EU level. However, it is worth noting that Residence by Investment is not exempt from criticism, as it provides a clear path to acquiring citizenship after a period of residence and poses serious risks when due diligence is weak. It presents, in fact, more risks because more than twelve Member States have residence by investment programmes, but the Commission has decided to pursue a fight against one Member State regarding citizenship by investment, which is a decision that makes the arguments from the Commission less reasonable; it would be more logical to also address the issue of residence by investment with all the relevant Member States.

In the area of residence, the EU enjoys competence to define the conditions third-country nationals must have to qualify for residence and free movement rights. Although EU law does not regulate residence by investment directly, it does indirectly regulate a restriction of rights for investors as it does not allow them to settle in other Member State than the one which granted the residence by investment. It allows only free movement for 90 days in other Member States within a period of 180 days. If the Portuguese immigration service grants a long-term residence permit to an investor who does not have all the requirements of the Directive of Long-term residents, this would violate EU law; for example, the period of physical presence. Moreover, according to Article 79 of TFEU,[619] the EU has competence to adopt legislation against an investor residence scheme if Member States decide for it. However, as it seems unlikely that twelve out of twenty-seven Member State would agree to phase out their source of income via residence by investment, I doubt that any action will result in a proper harmonisation of the topic.

As the topic is recent – having in mind that while in the Caribbean they started in 1980s, in Europe CBI and RBI started to receive more attention after the 2008 crisis when many Member States implemented residence by investment, and the Maltese case was implemented in 2013 – the literature is still growing as the challenges and countries implementing investment migration grow all over the world. There is still future work to be done on countries that have investment programmes but are located in different parts of the world besides Europe. A focus on consequences of wars and their effects on dual citizens, as well as a global harmonisation of rules on naturalisation, would be important recommendations for future work on the topic.

This dissertation showed with examples how the genuine link theory could affect – if understood as a requirement – various other forms of naturalisation that are the competence of Member States. It is also one of the few works that has delved deeply into two case studies – Malta and Portugal – in order to address and exemplify the legislative process and context of the implementation of residence and citizenship by investment. As Peter Spiro said, there is a huge gap in the analysis of these schemes in relation to international law, something that this work contributes to with the analysis in the third chapter, by addressing possible limits in international law in relation to citizenship by investment.

619 Article 79 TFEU 1. The Union shall develop a common immigration policy aimed at ensuring, at all stages, the efficient management of migration flows, fair treatment of third-country nationals residing legally in Member States, and the prevention of, and enhanced measures to combat, illegal immigration and trafficking in human beings.

Bibliography

Abrahamian, Atossa Araxia. The Cosmopolities: The Coming of the Global Citizen, Columbia Global Reports, 2015

Agnew, John. Globalization and Sovereignty (Lanham: Rowman and Littlefield Press, 2009)

Allard, Elisabeth Bolorinos. "Chapter 6 'Spanish Jews' and 'Friendly Muslims' The Historical Absence of a Citizenship Campaign for Muslims of Iberian Descent." Reparative Citizenship for Sephardi Descendants: Returning to the Jewish Past in Spain and Portugal, edited by Dalia Kandiyoti and Rina Benmayor, New York, Oxford: Berghahn Books, 2023, pp. 137–152. https://doi.org/10.1515/9781800738256-009

Ammann, Odile, Passports for Sale: How (un) meritocratic are citizenship by investment programmes? European Journal of Migration and Law, 2020, 22, p. 309–337

Amnesty International, Malta is ramping up "despicable and illegal" migrant pushbacks – new report by Amnesty International. Available on: https://www.amnesty.org.uk/press-releases/malta-ramping-despicable-and-illegal-migrant-pushbacks-new-report Access on: 03.07.2023

Andersson, Ruben (2016). Europe's failed "fight" against irregular migration: ethnographic notes on a counterproductive industry. Journal of Ethnic and Migration Studies, 42(7), 1055–1075. https://doi.org/10.1080/1369183X.2016.1139446

Aragoneses, Alfons. "Chapter 1 'Reparative Citizenship' Confronting Injustices of the Past or Building Modern Nationalisms?." Reparative Citizenship for Sephardi Descendants: Returning to the Jewish Past in Spain and Portugal, edited by Dalia Kandiyoti and Rina Benmayor, New York, Oxford: Berghahn Books, 2023, pp. 37–52. https://doi.org/10.1515/9781800738256-004

Armstrong, Chris. The Price of Selling Citizenship. EUI Working Papers, Robert Schuman Centre for Advanced Studies: Should Citizenship be for Sale? 2014

Arton Capital, "Fast-track to permanent residency in the EU in 4 weeks," 2016, https://www.artoncapital.com/industry-news/press-releases/fast-track-permanent-residency-eu-4-weeks/.

Balot, Ryan. Revisiting the Classical Ideal of Citizenship in The Oxford Handbook for Citizenship, edited by Ayelet Shachar, Rainer Bauböck, Irene Bloemraad and Maarten Vink, Oxford, Oxford University Press (2017)

Bauböck, Rainer. Global, European and National Questions about the Price of Citizenship. EUI Working Paper RSCAS 2014ª (Should Citizenship be for Sale?)

Bauböck, Rainer. What is wrong with selling citizenship? It corrupts democracy! In Should be Citizenship be for Sale? EUI Working Papers. Robert Schuman Centre for Advanced Studies EUDO Citizenship Observatory, 2014

Bauböck, Rainer; Paskalev, Vesco. Citizenship Deprivation: A Normative Analysis, ÇEPS Paper in Liberty and Security in Europe no. 82 (2015), available on: https://www.ceps.eu/ceps-publications/citizenship-deprivation-normative-analysis/, Access on: 11/07/2023

Bellamy, Richard. On Mushroom Reasoning and Kostakopoulou's Argument for Eurozenship in Orgad, Liav and Lepoutre, Jules (2019). Should EU Citizenship Be Disentangled from Member State Nationality? Robert Schuman Centre for Advanced Studies Research Paper No. RSCAS 2019/24

Belton, Kristy A., Comparative regional report on citizenship law: Anglophone Caribbean, [Global Governance Programme], GLOBALCIT, Comparative Reports, 2020/03, [Global Citizenship] – https://hdl.handle.net/1814/66909, Access on: 29.05.2024

Bernitz, Hedvig Lokrantz. Country Report: Sweden. Robert Schuman Centre for Advanced Studies: EUDO Citizenship Observatory, 2012, Available on: https://ec.europa.eu/migrant-integration/library-document/eudo-citizenship-observatory-country-report-sweden-0_en, Access on: 15.06.2023

Berton, Raul. Citizenship for those who invest into the future of the state is not wrong, the price is the problem. In Should Citizenship be For Sale? EUI Working Papers, Robert Schuman Centre for Advanced Studies, 2014

Blyth, Mark (2013) Austerity: the History of a Dangerous Idea. Oxford University Press, New York

Boatca, Manuela. Commodification of Citizenship: Global Inequalities and the Modern Transmission of Property, in Overcoming Global Inequalities, C.C.-D. Immanuel Wallerstein, Christian Suter, Editor 2015, Paradigm Publishers.

Boatca, Manuela, The Colonial Institution of Citizenship in Citizenship and Residence Sales Rethinking the Boundaries of Belonging Edited by Dimitry Kochenov and Kristin Surak, 2023, Cambridge

Bogdandy, Armin von, Founding Principles of EU law A Theoretical and Doctrinal Sketch, Revus 12 (2010), 35–56

Bogdandy, Armin von; and Schill, S. Art 4EUV, in E. Grabitz, M. Hilf, and M. Nettescheim (eds), Das Recht der Europäische Union, Kommentar, Vol. II (Munich: Beck, 2011)

Borg, Ian. The length of stay of foreign workers in Malta, 2019, available on: https://ideas.repec.org/p/mlt/ppaper/0119.html, CBM Policy Papers, PP/01/2019, Central Bank of Malta. Access on: 22.05.2024

Boynton, Elspeth. 2015. Protectionism and national migration policy in South Africa. University of Cape Town

Brick, Martijn van den, Revising Citizenship within the European Union: Is a Genuine Link Requirement the Way Forward?, 2020, EUI Working Papers 2020/76 Robert Schuman Centre for Advanced Studies, GLOBALCIT

Brink, Martijn van den, Investment Residence and the concept of residence in EU law: interactions, tensions, and opportunities. IMC Working Papers, 2017 (Investment Migration Working Papers)

Bulc, Violeta, Member of the Commission, Debate on the European Parliament on EU Values and the proliferation of corruption and crime through golden visas, 30th May 2018

Canada. Government of Canada. St Kitts and Nevis citizens now need a visa to travel to Canada. November 22, 2014. Available on https://www.canada.ca/en/immigration-refugees-citizenship/news/notices/notice-kitts-nevis-citizens-need-visa-travel-canada.html Access on: 06.06.2023

Carens, Joseph; Immigrants and the Right to Stay (2010), The MIT Press

Carrera, Sergio. The Price of EU Citizenship The Maltese Citizenship-for-Sale Affair and the Principle of Sincere Cooperation in Nationality Matters (2014) Maastrich Journal of European and Comparative Law No. 2014-3

Chamber of Advocates, Malta. The Maltese Legal System. Available on: https://www.avukati.org/public/law-system-in-malta/ Access on: 03.07.2023

Christians, Allison, Buying in: Residence and Citizenship by Investment, 2017, 62 Saint Louis University Law Journal 51

Convention on Certain Questions Relating to the Conflict of Nationality Laws, 1930

Corrado, Mark, Marsh, Kim. Investment Migration and the Importance of Due Diligence. Examples of Canada, Saint-Kitts and Nevis, and the EU in Citizenship and Residence Sales Rethinking the Boundaries of Belonging Edited by Dimitry Kochenov and Kristin Surak. Cambridge: Cambridge University Press, 2023

Craig, Paul; de Búrca, Gráinne. EU Law Text, Cases, and Materials, Seventh Edition (2020) Oxford, Oxford University Press.

Dalli, Adonia. 2020, An analysis of the determinants influencing labour migration: a gravity model approach: Malta's case (Master's dissertation), University of Malta, available on: https://www.um.edu.mt/library/oar/handle/123456789/66730 Access on: 22.05.2024

Davies, Gareth. The entirely conventional supremacy of Union citizenship and rights in EUI Working Papers RSCAS 2011/62 Has the European Court of Justice challenged member state sovereignty in nationality law?

DeBono, Daniela, Access to Electoral Rights, EUDO Citizenship Observatory, Robert Schuman Centre for Advanced Studies, Florence, June 2013

DeBono, Daniela. Naturalization Procedures for Immigrants Malta, EUDO Citizenship Observatory, Robert Schuman Centre for Advanced Studies, March 2013

DeBono, Daniela; Buttieg, Eugène. Country Report on Citizenship Law: Malta, EUDO Citizenship Observatory (2015)

Delupis, Ingrid; International Law and the Independent State, 1974

Demoy, Catarina; Vicente Rua, Patricia, REUTERS, Portugal's revamped golden visa scheme to boost investment funds, January 9, 2024, available on: https://www.reuters.com/markets/europe/portugals-revamped-golden-visa-scheme-boost-investment-funds-2024-01-09/, Access on: 16.04.2024

Deutsche Welle, Germany eases citizenship for Nazi victims' descendants, 03.04.2024, available on: https://www.dw.com/en/germany-new-law-eases-citizenship-for-descendants-of-nazi-victims/a-56977454

Diener, Alexander. Re-scaling the Geography of Citizenship in The Oxford Handbook of

Citizenship, Oxford, Edited by Ayelet Shachar, Rainer Bauböck, Irene Bloemraad, Maarten Vink, 2017

Directive 2003/109/EC concerning the status of third-country nationals who are long-term residents [2004]

Directive (EU) 2018/843 of the European Parliament and of the Council of 30 May 2018 amending Directive (EU) 2015/849 on the prevention of the use of the financial system for the purposes of money laundering or terrorist financing, and amending Directives 2009/138/EC and 2013/36/EU.
Donner, Ruth. The Regulation of Nationality in International Law, 2nd edition, 1994
Dugard, John; Diplomatic Protection Oxford Public International Law Encyclopedia, June 2021
Dzankic, Jelena, Investment-based citizenship and residence programmes in the EU. RSCAS EUI Working Papers, 2015. 2015/08: p. 5–6
Dzankic, Jelena, Investor citizenship must not be used as a remedy for statelessness, 2019, available on: https://www.statelessness.eu/updates/blog/investor-citizenship-must-not-be-used-remedy-statelessness
Dzankic, Jelena, The Global Market for Investor Citizenship. 1 ed. Politics of Citizenship and Migration. 2019: Palgrave Macmillan
Eco. Mais de 60 % dos "vistos gold" estão caducados, 2023. Available in: https://eco.sapo.pt/2022/10/13/mais-de-60-dos-vistos-gold-estao-caducados/ Access on: February 2023
Enríquez, Carmen et al., The EU performance in the global competition for highly skilled migrants. Available on: https://www.realinstitutoelcano.org/en/analyses/the-eu-performance-in-the-global-competition-for-highly-skilled-migrants/, Access on: August 14, 2023
Esquerda, Bloco, Projeto de Lei N. 920/XIII/3, 2018
EU observer, "EU institutions attack Malta passport scheme," 16 January 2014.
EUR-Lex, Division of competences within the European Union, Available on: https://eur-lex.europa.eu/EN/legal-content/summary/division-of-competences-within-the-european-union.html, Access on: 29.08.2023
Europe, Investigate. Augusto, Dieogo; Bersi, Eurydice; Pena, Paulo. Golden Visas: Europe for Sale? Investigate Europe, 2023. Available in: https://www.investigate-europe.eu/en/2023/golden-visas-europe-for-sale/, Access on: February 14, 2023.
European Commission, Europa Rapid Press Release, Viviane Reding, Vice-President of the European Commission responsible for Justice, Citizenship must not be up for sale, 15 January 2014, SPEECH/14/18
European Commission, Infringement Procedure 2023-4012), Available on: https://ec.europa.eu/commission/presscorner/detail/en/inf_23_4367, Access on: November 8, 2023

European Commission, Investor citizenship schemes: European Commission opens infringements against Cyprus and Malta for "selling" EU Citizenship. Available on: https://ec.europa.eu/commission/presscorner/detail/en/ip_20_1925 Access on: 06/04/2023

European Commission, Joint Press Statement of 29 January 2014 issued by the European Commission and the Maltese authorities, Available on: https://ec.europa.eu/commission/presscorner/detail/en/MEMO_14_70, Access on: 05/07/2023

European Commission, Malta: New policy denies asylum seekers from safe countries the right to work, 11/06/2021, Available on: https://ec.europa.eu/migrant-integration/news/malta-new-policy-denies-asylum-seekers-safe-countries-right-work_en, Access on: 03/04/2023

European Commission, Questions and Answers on the Report on Investor Citizenship and Residence Schemes in the European Union, 2019, Available on: https://ec.europa.eu/commission/presscorner/detail/ro/MEMO_19_527 Access on: 04.07.2023

European Commission, Report on Investor Residence and Citizenship of 23 January 2019

European Convention on Nationality, 1997

European Court of Justice, Case, European Commission vs Republic of Malta, (C-181/23) [2023]

European Court of Justice, Case, European Commission vs Republic of Malta, (C-181/23) [2023] Opinion of Advocate General Collins, delivered on 4 October 2024, available on: https://curia.europa.eu/juris/document/document.jsf?text=&docid=290735&pageIndex=0&doclang=EN&mode=lst&dir=&occ=first&part=1&cid=4084899# Footref62, Access on: 23.11.2024

European Court of Justice. Case, Federal Republic of Germany v European Parliament and Council of the European Union, (C-380/03), [2006], ECR 2006 I-11573

European Court of Justice. Commission of the European Communities v Council of the European Communities. European Agreement on Road Transport, (Case 22-70) [1971]

European Court of Justice. Gerardo Ruiz Zambrano v Office national de lémploi (ONEm) [2001] ECR 2011 I-01177

European Court of Justice. Ingrid Boukhalfa vs Bundesrepublik Deutschland (Case C-214/94) [1996] ECR 1996 I-02253

European Court of Justice. Janko Rottmann v Freistaat of Bayern (C-135/08) [2010], ECR 2010 I-01449

European Court of Justice. JY v Wiener Landesregierung (C-118-20) [2022], ECLI:EU:C:2022:34
European Court of Justice. M. G. Tjebbes and Others v Minister van Buitenlandse Zaken (C-221/17) [2019] ECLI:EU:C:2019:189
European Court of Justice. Mario Vicente Micheletti v Delegación del Gobierno em Cantabria (Case C-369/90) [1992] ECR I-4239
European Court of Justice. Protocol (No 3) On the Statute of the Court of Justice of the European Union, Consolidated Version, 5 May 2019
European Court of Justice. Rudy Grzelczyk v Centre public d'aide sociale d'Ottignies-Louvain-la-Neuve (Case C-184/99), [2001] EU:C:2001:458
European Economic Community. Treaty establishing the European Economic Community (Rome, 25 March 1957)
European Parliament (2022), Members, Bodies and activities, Available on: https://www.europarl.europa.eu/portal/en, Access on: 26/04/2023
European Parliament Research Service (EPRS), Avenues for EU action on citizenship and residence by investment schemes. 2021
European Parliament "Resolution on Union Citizenship," 14 June 1991
European Parliament, 127. Democrats, S.a. Who we are – Our Members. 2023; Available from: https://www.socialistsanddemocrats.eu/who-we-are/our-members/meps
European Parliament, About US: EPP. 2023; Available from: https://www.eppgroup.eu/.
European Parliament, EU values and the proliferation of corruption and crime through golden visas, 2018
European Parliament, Russia's war on Ukraine: Reassessing "citizenship by investment" schemes 2022; Available on: https://www.europarl.europa.eu/RegData/etudes/ATAG/2022/729385/EPRS_ATA(2022)729385_EN.pdf.
European Parliament; European Parliament Resolution of 16 January 2014 on EU citizenship for sale (2013/2995(RSP)). 2014
European Parliament's Resolution on CBI and RBI programmes (2021/2026(INL))
European Union, Treaty on European Union. 1993
European Union, Treaty on the Functioning of the European Union
Fagerlund, Jessica, Brander, Sampo, Country report: Finland, [GLOBALCIT], EUDO Citizenship Observatory, 2010/12, Country Reports – https://hdl.handle.net/1814/19612 Access on: 15.06.2023

Fajon, Tanja. on behalf of the S&D Group. Debate on the European Parliament on EU Values and the proliferation of corruption and crime through golden visas, 30th May 2018
Financial Action Task Force, "Who We Are," Financial Action Task Force 2019, available on: https://www.fatf-gafi.org/en/the-fatf/who-we-are.html, accessed August 8, 2023.
Frost, Lillian. Report on Citizenship Law: Jordan. Country Report 2022/2, Global Citizenship Observatory, available on: https://cadmus.eui.eu/bitstream/handle/1814/74189/RSC_GLOBALCIT_CR_2022_2.pdf?sequence=1, Access on: 29.05.2024
Ganty, Sarah. Why Banning Russians from Schengen is Unlawful, 2022; Available in: https://verfassungsblog.de/banning-russians/ Access on: February 14, 2023
Gaspar, Sofia; de Haro, Fernando (2020) Buying Citizenship? Chinese Golden Visa Migrants in Portugal. International Migration, Vol. 58 (3)
Germany. AufenthalhG, Section 51, 7
Germany. Basic Law for the Federal Republic of Germany
Get Golden Visa Research Team, 2024 Report regarding Portugal's Golden Visa Funds in a Post-Real Estate Era, available on: https://media.licdn.com/dms/document/media/D4D1FAQGw26LTGIeEXw/feedshare-document-pdf-analyzed/0/1706712693685?e=1717027200&v=beta&t=dvlNL3VwNFoDdxuJyePPkGgOlUrr7d2zXk-RKaVqlXI, Access on: 16.05.2024
Gil, Ana Rita. Princípios de Direito da Nacionalidade. O Direito, 142 (2010)
Gil, Ana Rita; Piçarra, Nuno. Report on Citizenship Law Portugal. February 2020, European University Institute (GLOBALCIT)
GLOBALCIT, Webinar Investor Citizenship: a challenge for Citizenship or a Sign of its transformation, 2021, 20:13.
Grabitz, E. Art 5 EWGV, in E. Grabitz (ed.) Kommentar zum EWG-Vertrag, Munich: Beck, 1991, para 1
Grima, Dr Godwin, First Annual Report on the IPP Programme of the Government of Malta, October 2014
Groot, Geard-René De, the relationship between the nationality legislation of the Member States of the European Union and European Citizenship. In European Citizenship: An Institutional Challenge: European Forum (Vol. 3, pp. 115–147). Kluwer Law International, 1998
Guastaferro, Barbara. Sincere Cooperation and Respect for National Identities. In Oxford Principles of European Union Law Volume I:

The European Union Legal Order Edited by Robert Schütze and Takis Tridimas Oxford, Oxford University Press, 2018

Hague Convention on Certain Questions Relating to the Conflict of Nationality Laws (1930)

Handoll, Josh, Country Report Ireland EUDO Citizenship Observatory, European University Institute, 2012, Page 13, available on: https://cadmus.eui.eu/bitstream/handle/1814/19618/RSCAS_EUDO_CIT_2012_2.pdf?sequence=3&isAllowed=y

Harpaz, Yossi. Citizenship 2.0: Dual Nationality as a Global Asset. (2019) Princeton University Press

Harpaz, Yossi. Citizenship and Residence Rights as Vehicles of Global Inequality in

Citizenship and Residence Sales Rethinking the Boundaries of Belonging Edited by Dimitry Kochenov and Kristin Surak, 2023, Cambridge

Harpaz, Yossi. Compensatory Citizenship: Dual Nationality as a Strategy of Global Upward Mobility, 2019, 45(6) Journal of Ethnic and Migration Studies

Hartley, TC. The Foundations of European Union Law: an introduction to the constitutional and administrative law of the European Union. Eighth Edition, Oxford: Oxford University Press, 2014

Heater, Derek. What is Citizenship, Wiley 1999

Henley & Partners, Passport Index 2023, Available on: https://www.henleyglobal.com/passport-index, Access on: 31st July 2023

Henriques, Ana. Vistos de residência para imigrantes: renovação online voltou e abrange os gold, Público, available on: https://www.publico.pt/2023/01/15/sociedade/noticia/vistos-residencia-imigrantes-renovacao-online-voltou-abrange-gold-2035132, Access on: 28.05.2024

Horspool, Margot; Humphreys Matthew; Wells-Greco Michael. European Union Law 11th edition (2021) Oxford, Oxford University Press.

Human Rights Watch, Kuwait's Plan to Pawn Off its "Stateless." Available on: https://www.hrw.org/news/2015/03/26/kuwaits-plan-pawn-its-stateless Access on: 05.06.2023

Idealista, Governo cria novo visto gold "solidário" para apoiar imigrantes, 04.06.2024, available on: https://www.idealista.pt/news/financas/investimentos/2024/06/04/64269-governo-cria-novo-visto-gold-solidario-para-apoiar-imigrantes, Access on: 06.06.2024

Identity Malta, Citizenship has moved to a new agency. 11/12/2020, Available in: https://www.identitymalta.com/citizenship-moved-to-new-agency/, Access on: 29/03/2023

Iglesias, Gil Carlos Rodríguez. Reflections on the General Principles of Community Law, 1998 Cambridge Yearbook of European Legal Studies, 1, 13–14

International Arbitral Awards, Reports of International Arbitral Awards, Mergé Case – Decision No. 55, 10 June 1955, Volume XIV, pp. 236–248

International Court of Justice, (2023), Permanent Court of Justice. Available on: https://www.icj-cij.org/pcij#:~:text=The%20work%20of%20the%20PCIJ,and%20delivered%2027%20advisory%20opinions. Access on: 27.05.2023

International Court of Justice; Nottebohm Case (Liechtenstein v. Guatemala), 1955 I.C.J. 4 (6 April)

International Law Commission, Draft Articles on Diplomatic Protection (Draft), 2006, available on: https://legal.un.org/ilc/texts/instruments/english/draft_articles/9_8_2006.pdf

International Law Commission, Report on Nationality, Including Statelessness, 1952, UN Doc. A/CN.4/50 7, available on: https://legal.un.org/ilc/documentation/english/a_cn4_50.pdf Access on: 7 May, 2024

International Law Commission, "Draft articles on diplomatic protection with commentaries" (2006) UM Doc A/CN 4/L 646, available on: https://legal.un.org/ilc/texts/instruments/english/commentaries/9_8_2006.pdf, Access on: 04.06.2024

International, Transparency. Vistos Gold: Investimento ou Branqueamento? 2018: Available in: https://transparencia.pt/vistos-gold/, Access on: 13 February, 2023

Investment Migration Council, About the IMC. 2022; Available from: https://investmentmigration.org/about/about-the-imc/

Investment Migration Council, Europe, Revised EU Long-Term Residence Directive Negotiations Cease, 2024, available on: https://investmentmigration.org/news/europe-breaking-revised-eu-long-term-residence-directive-negotiations-cease/

Investment Migration Council, Malta: European Commission refers Malta to the European Court of Justice against all legal advice. 2022; Available from: https://investmentmigration.org/news/malta-european-commission-refers-malta-to-the-european-court-of-justice-against-all-legal-advice/

Investment Migration Council, Statement by the Investment Migration Council concerning the European Commission's case against Malta. 2022

Investment Migration Council, Transitioning to a Regulated Environment Yearbook 2021/2022, 4, Editor. 2021
Investment Migration Council, What is Investment Migration? 2022; Available on: https://investmentmigration.org/about/what-is-investment-migration/
IOM, International Migration Law: Glossary on Migration, 2019
Iran v. United States, Case No. 32-A/18-FT, 5 Iran–US Claims Tribunal Reporter 251
Irish Nationality and Citizenship Act, 1956
Italian-US Conciliation Commission, 1958, Flegenheimer (United States v. Italy), 14 RIAA 327 (Italian-US Conciliation Commission 1958), 375
Joppke, Christian, Citizenship by Investment: a case of instrumental citizenship in Citizenship and Residence Sales Rethinking the Boundaries of Belonging Edited by Dimitry
Kochenov and Kristin Surak, Cambridge, 2023, page 251
Kandiyoti, Dalia and Benmayor, Rina. "Introduction: Sephardi Jews, Citizenship, and Reparation in Historical Context." Reparative Citizenship for Sephardi Descendants: Returning to the Jewish Past in Spain and Portugal, edited by Dalia Kandiyoti and Rina Benmayor, New York, Oxford: Berghahn Books, 2023, pp. 1–34. https://doi.org/10.1515/9781800738256-003
King, Russel; Anthony Fielding & Richard Black, "The international migration turnaround in Southern Europe," in Southern Europe and the New Immigrations, eds. R. King & R. Black, Sussex Academic Press, Brighton, 2007, pp. 1–25
Kiss, Alexandre, Abuse of Rights, in Encyclopedia of Public International Law 1, 4 (Rudolf Bernhardt ed., 1992)
Klamert, Marcus, The Principle of Loyalty in EU Law, Oxford: Oxford University Press, 2014
Kochenov, Dimitry. Citizenship. 2019 Cambridge: The MIT Press
Kochenov, D. B., Elena, It's All about Blood, Baby! The European Commission's Ongoing Attack against Investment Migration in the Context of EU Law and International Law. Working Paper no. 161 The Centre on Migration, Policy & Society, 2022
Kochenov, Dimitry and Lindeboom, Justin (eds), Kälin and Kochenov's Quality of Nationality Index, Hart Publishing 2019.
Kochenov, Dimitry. EU Citizenship without Duties, European Law Journal, Vol. 20, No 4, July 2014, pp. 482–498

Kochenov, Dimitry. Victims of Citizenship Feudal Statuses for Sale in the Hypocrisy Republic in Citizenship and Residence Sales Rethinking the Boundaries of Belonging Edited by Dimitry Kochenov and Kristin Surak. Cambridge: Cambridge University Press, 2023

Komárek, Jan, Legal Reasoning in EU Law, in The Oxford Handbook of European Union Law, Oxford, Oxford University Press, 2015

Kostakopoulou, Dora. Who Should Be a Citizen of the Union? Toward an Autonomous European Union Citizenship in Orgad, Liav and Lepoutre, Jules (2019). Should EU Citizenship Be Disentangled from Member State Nationality? Robert Schuman Centre for Advanced Studies Research Paper No. RSCAS 2019/24

Kudryashova, Sofia. The Sale of Conditional EU Citizenship: The Cyprus Investment Programme under the Lens of EU law. IMC Working Papers, 2019 (Investment Migration Working Papers)

Kunz, Josef. The American Journal of International Law, 1960, Vol. 54, no 3

Kwai, Isabella. Cyprus Ends "Golden Passport" Program After Corruption Accusations. The New York Times, 2020, Available on: https://www.nytimes.com/2020/10/15/world/europe/cyprus-golden-passports-corruption.html, Access on: 24.05.2026

Kymlicka, Will, Norman, Wayne. Return of the Citizen: A survey of recent work on Citizenship Theory. Ethics, January 1994, Vol. 104, No 2, pp. 352–381, The University of Chicago Press

LaHaye, Laura (2008). Mercantilism. In: The New Palgrave Dictionary of Economics. Palgrave Macmillan, London. https://doi.org/10.1057/978-1-349-95121-5_838-2

Larguesa, Antônio. "Vistos gold não têm nada a ver com o aumento dos preços das casas," dizem investidores imobiliários" 2022. Available in: https://eco.sapo.pt/entrevista/vistos-gold-nao-tem-nada-a-ver-com-o-aumento-dos-precos-das-casas-dizem-investidores-imobiliarios/, Access on: 14 February, 2023.

League of Nations Committee of Experts for the Progressive Codification of International Law, Questionaire No. 1 – Nationality, 1926

Leydet, Dominique, "Citizenship," The Stanford Encyclopedia of Philosophy (Fall 2017 Edition), Edward N. Zalta (ed.), URL = <https://plato.stanford.edu/archives/fall2017/entries/citizenship/>.

Li, L.v.d. B.a.H, Wealth Influx, Wealth Exodus: Investment Migration from China to Portugal. IMC Working Papers, 2018/1 (Investment Migration Working Papers)

Liechtenstein Law of Nationality of 10 January, 1934
Lindeboom, Justin & Meunier Sophie, In the shadow of the Euro Crisis Foreign Direct Investment and Investment Migration Programmes in the European Union, in Citizenship and Residence Sales Rethinking the Boundaries of Belonging Edited by Dimitry Kochenov and Kristin Surak, 2023, Cambridge
Lutterbeck, D. 2006, Policing migration in the Mediterranean. Mediterranean Politics 11(1): 59–82
Lécuyer, Bruno. LinkedIn Post on February 18th, 2023
Macklin, Audrey "Is it time to retire Nottebohm" (2017) 111 American Journal of International Law 492
Magni-Berton, R. Citizenship for Those Who Invest into the Future of the State is not Wrong, the price is the problem. EUI Working Paper RSCAS, 2014 (Should Citizenship be for Sale?)
Mainwaring, C. (2012), Constructing a Crisis: the Role of Immigration Detention in Malta. Popul. Space Place, 18: 687–700. https://doi.org/10.1002/psp.1721
Malta Today, Malta says yes to budget, no to sale of citizenship. 11/11/2013, Available on: https://www.maltatoday.com.mt/news/data_and_surveys/31360/maltatoday-survey-budget-citizenship-20131111#.ZCWTB-xBzpA, Access on: 30/03/2023
Malta Today, "Immigration is 'national crisis', 84 % say," available on: http://archive.maltatoday.com.mt/2009/04/05/t1.html 05.04.2009
Malta, The Maltese Citizenship by Naturalization for Exceptional Services by Direct Investment Handbook. 2021
Malta, Times of. Over 1,500 people became Maltese citizens through golden passports scheme. Available in: https://timesofmalta.com/articles/view/1500-people-maltese-citizens-golden-passport-scheme.1013883 Access on: 27/03/2023
Malta, Times of. PM defends Citizenship-on-sale scheme. 9 October 2013. Available on: https://timesofmalta.com/articles/view/20131009/local/Citizenship-on-sale-in-scheme-to-net-30m.489548#.UlZ44Ba8KWd, Access on: 30 March, 2023
Malta. Highly qualified worker, 2024, available on: https://immigration-portal.ec.europa.eu/malta-highly-qualified-worker_en, Access on: 22.05.2024
Malta. Legal Notice 47, 2014, 3 (1), Individual Investor Programme of the Republic of Malta Regulations
Malta. Legal Notice 437 (2020) Granting of Citizenship for Exceptional Services Regulation

Malta. Legal Notice 450/2013, Maltese Citizenship Act Chapter 188, Individual Investor Programme of the Republic of Malta Regulations

Malta. Malta Permanent Residence Programme, Residency Malta Agency, available on: https://residencymalta.gov.mt/the-mprp-programme/ Access on: 22.05.2024

Malta. "Due Diligence," website Acquisition of Citizenship for Exceptional Services by Direct Investment 2023, https://komunita.gov.mt/en/services/acquisition-of-citizenship/#ForExceptionalServices, accessed 8 August, 2023

Maltese Citizenship Act, Chap. 188

Mamo, Suzanne, "Maltese and Gozitans: a social identity approach" (Dissertation, University of Malta 2012)

Mansour-Ille, Dina. Cash for citizenship: rich Arab countries may pay poor islands to take "stateless" Bidoons. Available on: https://odi.org/en/insights/cash-for-citizenship-rich-arab-countries-may-pay-poor-islands-to-take-stateless-bidoons/ Access on: 05/06/2023

Marshall, T. H. Class, Citizenship, and Social Development Essays by T. H. Marshall, Doubleday & Company, 1964.

Marx, K., On the Jewish Question, in Marx-Engels-Reader, R. C. Tucker, Editor 1972, Norton: New York. P. 24–51

Mavelli, L. Citizenship for Sale and the Neoliberal Political Economy of Belonging. International Studies Quarterly (2018. 62: p. 482–493)

McDonald CA. Rancor: Sephardi Jews, Spanish Citizenship, and the Politics of Sentiment. Comparative Studies in Society and History. 2021;63(3):722–751. doi:10.1017/S0010417521000190

Menendes, Agustin. "Which Citizenship? Whose Europe? The Many Paradoxes of European Citizenship" (2014) 15 German Law Journal 907, 913

Milanovic, Blanko, Global Inequality: a New Approach for the Age of Globalisation, Harvard University Press, 2016

Milieu Law and Policy Consulting, Factual Analysis of Member States' Investor Schemes granting citizenship or residence to third-country nationals investing in the said Member State. 2018: Brussels

MIPEX, Key Findings Malta 2019, Available on: https://www.mipex.eu/malta, Access on: March 2023

Missing Migrants Project, IOM, 2023. Available on: https://missingmigrants.iom.int/ Access on: 03.07.2023

Montenegrin Government, Citizenship by Investment, available on: https://www.gov.me/en/

documents/9dad5bba-64f9-453e-ac3b-b2e7fde109ac, Access on 14/05/2024

National Statistics Office, 2006, World Refugee Day News Release 2006. National Statistics Office: Malta

Netherlands, The. Rijkswet op het Nederlanderschap (Law on Netherlands Nationality), 1985

Noori, Lori. Offshore Citizens: Permanent Temporary Status in the Gulf. Cambridge University Press, 2019

Nunes, Flávio (2023), Costa admite acabar com os vitos gold. Available in: https://eco.sapo.pt/2022/11/02/primeiro-ministro-admite-acabar-com-os-vistos-gold/ Access on: 23rd February, 2023.

Observador. Vistos Gold: 11 detidos por suspeitas de corrupção. Available in: https://observador.pt/2014/11/13/diretor-nacional-sef-detido-por-suspeitas-de-corrupcao-na-atribuicao-dos-vistos-gold/ Access on: March 27, 2023

OCCPR A Portuguese Crusader Seeks to Tap the Brakes on Golden Visas, 5 March 2018, Available on: https://www.occrp.org/en/goldforvisas/a-portuguese-crusader-seeks-to-tap-the-brakes-on-golden-visas Access on: 04.07.2023

Office of the Regulator Individual Investor Programme (ORiip), Second Annual Report on the IPP Programme of the Government of Malta, October 2015, p. 22

Oltermann, Philip. Switzerland votes to ease citizenship process. Available on: https://www.theguardian.com/world/2017/feb/12/switzerland-votes-immigrants-citizenship-rights-islamophobia Access on: 26/04/2023

Orgad, Liav and Lepoutre, Jules (2019). Should EU Citizenship Be Disentangled from Member State Nationality? Robert Schuman Centre for Advanced Studies Research Paper No. RSCAS 2019/24

Pace, Roderick. A Small State and the European Union: Malta's EU Accession Experience. (2009) South European Society & Politics

Panascì, Maria Antonia. "Breaking the Ancestral Silence: Recognition of Citizenship by Descent Despite the Great Brazilian Naturalization," The Italian Review of International and Comparative Law 3, 1 (2023): 157–168, doi: https://doi.org/10.1163/27725650-03010010

Panayotova, Monika, Debate on the European Parliament on EU Values and the proliferation of corruption and crime through golden visas, 30th May 2018

Parker, Owen, Commercializing Citizenship in Crisis EU: the Case of Immigrant Investor Programmes. Journal of Common Market Studies, 2016. 55

Parliament of Malta, Motion 93 for the Repeal of Legal Notice 450 of 2013, available on: https://parlament.mt/en/12th-leg/motions-12th/motion-no-093/?page=1&numItems=10&text=&number=93&totalItems=1&isPrivate=0&isFirst=0 Access on: 21.05.2024

Parliament of Malta, Motion 115 for the Repeal of Legal Notice 47 of 2014, available on: https://parlament.mt/en/12th-leg/motions-12th/motion-no-115/?page=1&numItems=10&text=&number=115&totalItems=1&isPrivate=0&isFirst=0, Access on: 21.05.2024

Peers, Steve; Barnard, Catherine, European Union Law Third Edition, (2020), Oxford, Oxford University Press

Pegg, David et al. Corrupt Brazilian tycoon among applicants for Portugal's Golden Visas, The Guardian, 2018. Available on: https://www.theguardian.com/world/2017/sep/18/portugal-golden-visas-corrupt-brazilian-tycoon-among-applicants Access on: 24.05.2023

Pela Terra, available on: https://pelaterra.com/welcome/, Access on: 16.05.2024

Permanent Court of International Justice; Nationality Decrees Issued in Tunis and Morocco (Advisory Opinion) [1923] Rep Series B No 4

Peters Anne, "Extraterritorial Naturalizations: Between the Human Right to Nationality, State

Sovereignty and Fair Principles of Jurisdiction" (2010) 53 German Yearbook of International Law 623.

Pogonyi, Szabolcs. (2022). The right of blood: "ethnically" selective citizenship policies in Europe. National Identities, 24(5), 523–538. https://doi.org/10.1080/14608944.2021.2013185

Portugal, Conselho de Ministros – Plano de Ação para as Migrações, 03.06.2024, available on: https://www.youtube.com/watch?v=wKZeFodMryo&ab_channel=Rep%C3%BAblicaPortuguesa, Access on: 06.06.2024

Portugal, Costa, Antonio, Conferência de imprensa do Conselho de Ministros. Available in: https://www.youtube.com/watch?v=iuGquiU7BAo&t=881s Access on: 23rd February, 2023

Portugal, Decreto Lei no. 30-A/2015 allowing the granting of Portuguese nationality, by naturalization, to descendants of Sephardic Jews

Portugal, Gabinetes dos Ministros de Estado e dos Negócios Estrangeiros e da Administração Interna. Despacho n. 11820-A/2012, 03/09/2012.

Portugal, Law No. 29/2012, which changed Law No. 23/2007 (conditions and procedures for the entry, stay, exit and removal of foreign citizens from Portuguese territory)

Portugal, Lei Orgânica n. 1/2024 05th March, 2024, available on:https://diariodarepublica.pt/dr/detalhe/lei-organica/1-2024-854130977

Portugal, Novo Serviço de renovação automática do título de residencia, 27.07.2020, available on: https://eportugal.gov.pt/noticias/novo-servico-de-renovacao-automatica-do-titulo-de-residencia, Access on: 28.05.2024

Portugal, Portuguese Nationality Act Law 37/81, of 3 October. 1981

Portugal. Applying for Residence in Portugal Article 90-A – Residence Permit for Investment

Purposes. 2022; Available from: https://imigrante.sef.pt/en/solicitar/residir/art90-a/.

Portugal. Assembleia da República, Comissão de Assuntos Constitucionais, Direitos, Liberdades e Garantias. Parecer da Proposta de Lei n. 50/XXI/1 (Gov), 2012.

Portugal. Autorização de Residência para Investimento, Serviço de Estrangeiros e Fronteiras, in https://www.sef.pt/pt/Documents/JAN_2023_ARI_CUMULATIVO.pdf, Access on 13 February, 2023

Portugal. Ministério Público. Nota para Comunicação Social: Vistos Gold – Acusação. Available in: https://www.ministeriopublico.pt/sites/default/files/documentos/pdf/nota_comunicao_social_vistos_gold-acusacao.pdf Access on: 27 March, 2023

Portugal. Presidência do Conselho de Ministros de Portugal, Proposta de Lei 50/XII, 2012

Portugal. Statistics Portugal, Portuguese Citizenship Acquisition, 16th November, 2023

Prak, Maarten. Citizenship for Sale in Pre-modern Europe. In Citizenship and Residence Sales Rethinking the Boundaries of Belonging Edited by Dimitry Kochenov and Krisitn Surak, Cambridge 2023

Prats, Elena. Are Citizenship by Investment Programs Legitimate? Suggesting Some Assessment Methods, in Money Matters in Migration, W. M. Tesseltje de Lange, Annette Schrauwen, Editor 2021, Cambridge University Press: Cambridge

Público. Portugal suspendeu apreciação de "vistos gold" de cidadãos russos. 2022

Renascença, R. Vistos Gold. Candidatos russos querem processar Estado português. 2022.

REUTERS, France offers citizenship to Malian immigrant who scaled Building to save child, 28th May, 2018. Available on: https://www.reuters.com/article/us-france-hero/france-offers-citizenship-to-malian-immigrant-who-scaled-building-to-save-child-idUSKCN1IS0UF/#:~:text=France%20offers%20citizenship%20to%20Malian%20immigrant%20who%20scaled%20building%20to%20save%20child,-Reuters&text=PARIS%20(Reuters)%20%2D%20France%20on,balcony%2C%20President%20Emmanuel%20Macron%20said. Access on: 18. December 2023

Rotaeche, Cristina. Identity, Member States Nationality and EU Citizenship. In The Reconceptualization of European Union Citizenship Edited by Elspeth Guild, Cristina

Rotaeche and Dora Kostakopoulou. Brill/Nijhoff, Leiden: 2014

Sandel, Michael, What Money Can't Buy, Farrar, Straus and Giroux 2012

Sarmiento, Daniel, EU Competence and the Attribution of Nationality in Member States. IMC Working Papers, 2019/2 (Investment Migration Working Papers)

Sarmiento, Daniel; Van den Brink, Martijn. EU Competence and Investor Migration in Citizenship and Residence Sales Rethinking the Boundaries of Belonging Edited by Dimitry Kochenov and Kristin Surak, Cambridge, 2023

Schütze, Robert, EU Competences: Existence and Exercise in The Oxford Handbook of European Union Law Edited by Anthony Arnull and Damian Chalmers, Oxford: Oxford University Press, 2015, page 77

Schütze, Robert, European Constitutional Law, Cambridge University Press, 2012

Shachar, Ayelet, Dangerous Liasons: Money and Citizenship in Should be Citizenship be for Sale?, Robert Schumann Centre for Advanced Studies, EUDO Citizenship Observatory, (2014).

Shachar, Ayelet. "The Race for Talent: Highly Skilled Migrants and Competitive Immigration Regimes," N.Y.U.L. Reviwq 148 (2006)

Shachar, Ayelet. Citizenship for Sale?, in The Oxford Handbook of Citizenship 2017, Oxford University Press: Oxford

Shachar, Ayelet. "Picking Winners: Olympic Citizenship and the Global Race for Talent." The Yale Law Journal, vol. 120, no. 8, 2011, pp. 2088–139. JSTOR, http://www.jstor.org/stable/41149587. Accessed 18 Dec. 2023.

Shachar, Ayelet.; Hirschl, Ran. On Citizenship, States, and Markets, 2014. Journal of Political Philosophy, Volume 22, 2, Pages 231–57

Shachar, Ayelet; Bauböck, Rainer; Bloemraad, Irene; Vink, Maarten. Introduction: Citizenship – Quo Vadis? In The Oxford Handbook of Citizenship (2017), Oxford, Oxford University Press

Shaw, Jo. EU Citizenship: Still a fundamental status? In Debating European Citizenship, Rainer Bauböck (Editor), IMISCOE Springer Open, 2018

Shearer, Ivan and Opeskin, Brian "Nationality and Statelessness" in Brian Opeskin, Richard Perruchoud and Jillyanne Redpath-Cross (eds.), Foundations of International Migration Law (Cambridge University Press, 2012)

Sherwin-White, Adrian, the Romand Citizenship, 2nd ed. Oxford/ Clarendon Press 1973

SIC notícias, Marcelo formaliza demissão do governo, 07.12.2023, available on: https://sicnoticias.pt/pais/2023-12-07-Marcelo-formaliza-demissao-do-Governo-6b1ce3d6, Access on: 06.06.2024

Sloane, Robert. Breaking the genuine link: the contemporary international legal regulation of nationality (2009) 500 Harvard International Law Journal 1

Sonne, Kirstin (2021) Learning to "belong": processes of inclusion and exclusion in Malta's migrant integration programme. Master's Dissertation, Erasmus Mundus International Master in Adult Education for Social Change (IMAESC)

Spain, Law 12/2015 of 24th June Granting Spanish Nationality to Sephardi Jews Native to Spain

Spiro, Peter., Nottebohm and Genuine Link: Anatomy of a Jurisprudential Illusion. IMC Working Papers, 2019 (Investment Migration Working Papers)

Spiro, Peter. Cash-for-passports and the end of citizenship (2014), in Should Citizenship be for Sale? Robert Schuman Centre for Advanced Studies, EUDO Citizenship Observatory.

Spiro, Peter. Investment Citizenship and the Long Leash of International Law. In Citizenship and Residence Sales Rethinking the Boundaries of Belonging Edited by Dimitry Kochenov and Kristin Surak. Cambridge: Cambridge University Press, 2023

Statue of the International Court of Justice, art. 38 (1), 1945

Stiller, Martin, Statelessness in International Law: A Historic Overview 37 DAJV Newsl/ 94 (2012), available on: https://heinonline.org/HOL/LandingPage?handle=hein.journals/dajvnws2012&div=41&id=&page= Access on: 25th April, 2024

Strumia, F. New-generation Skilled Migration Policies and the Changing Fabric of Membership: Talent as Output and the Headhunting State. IMC Working Papers, 2016/4 (Investment Migration Working Papers)

Surak Kristin., "What Money Can Buy: Citizenship by Investment on a Global Scale," In Fassin D., ed. Deepening Divides: How Borders and Boundaries Drive Our World Apart. Pluto Press, 2020

Surak, Kristin. Global Citizenship 2.0 The Growth of Citizenship by Investment Programs. IMC Working Papers, 2016/3 (Investment Migration Working Papers)

Surak, Kristin. Millionaires and Mobility: inequality and Investment Migration Programs, in Money Matters in Migration, W. M. Tesseltje de Lange, Annette Schrauwen, Editor. 2021, Cambridge University Press: Cambridge.

Surak, Kristin and Yusuke Tsuzuki, "Are Golden Visas a Golden Opportunity? Assessing the Economic Origins and Outcomes of Residence by Investment Programmes" (2021) 47 (15) Journal of Ethnic and Migration Studies 3367

Surak, Kristin, Millionaire Mobility and the Sale of Citizenship (2020) 47 (1) Journal of Ethnic and Migration Studies 166

Surak, Kristin. Citizenship and Residence by investment schemes – State of play and avenues for EU action. Anex II in Avenues for EU action on citizenship and residence by investment schemes: European added value assessment. Meenakshi Fernandes, Cecilia Navarra, and David de Groot with María García Muñoz, 2021

Surak, Kristin. Investment Migration: Empirical Developments in the Field and Methodological Issues in Its Study, in Citizenship and Residence Sales Rethinking the Boundaries of Belonging Edited by Dimitry Kochenov and Kristin Surak. Cambridge: Cambridge University Press, 2023

Surak, Kristin. Investment Migration: Empirical Developments in the Field and Methodological Issues in Its Study, in Citizenship and Residence Sales Rethinking the Boundaries of Belonging Edited by Dimitry Kochenov and Kristin Surak. Cambridge: Cambridge University Press, 2023

Suryapratim, Roy. The Streetlight Effect in Commentary on Citizenship by Investment in Citizenship and Residence Sales Rethinking the Boundaries of Belonging Edited by Dimitry Kochenov and Kristin Surak, 2023, Cambridge

Tanasoca, A. (2016). Citizenship for Sale: Neomedieval, not Just Neoliberal? European Journal of Sociology / Archives Européennes De Sociologie, 57(1), 169–195. doi:10.1017/S0003975616000059

The Guardian, Portugal to change law under which Roman Abramovich gained citizenship. Available on: https://www.theguardian.com/world/2022/mar/16/portugal-nationality-by-descent-law-roman-abramovich-citizenship

Thwaits, Rayner. The Life and Times of the Genuine link (2018) 49 Victoria University Law Review 645, 657

Torpey, John, Unseemly, Perhaps, but ... : Should Citizenship be for Sale? In Citizenship and Residence Sales Rethinking the Boundaries of Belonging Edited by Dimitry Kochenov and Kristin Surak, Cambridge 2023

Transparency International, Daphne Caruana Galizia Foundation Joins Transparency International Movement as Official Malta Representative. Available on: https://www.transparency.org/en/press/daphne-caruana-galizia-foundation-joins-transparency-international-movement-as-official-malta-representative, Access on: 10.05.2023

Transparency International, Ending Corrupt Abuse of EU Golden Passports & Visas. Available on: https://www.transparency.org/en/campaigns/ending-corrupt-abuse-european-union-golden-passports-visas Access on: 10.05.2023

Transparency International, European Getaway: Inside the Murky World of Golden Visas, 2018

United Nations High Commissioner for Refugees. About Statelessness. Available on: https://www.unhcr.org/ibelong/about-statelessness/, Access on: 05/06/2023

United Nations. Human Rights Council, Report 25/28 2013, Human Rights and arbitrary deprivation of nationality – Report of the Secretary-General

United Nations. United Nations Convention Relating to the Status of Stateless Persons, 1954

United Nations. Universal Declaration of Human Rights, 10 December 1948

University of Malta. Referenda in Malta, referenda questions and voting results. Available on: https://www.um.edu.mt/r/projects/maltaelections/referenda Access on: 26/04/2023

Urry, John, Mobilities, 2007. Polity Press

Van Hoecke, Mark. Legal Doctrine: Which Method (s) for what Kind of Discipline? In Methodologies of Legal Research Which Kind of Method for What Kind of Discipline? (2013) Oxford: Hart Publishing
Van Oers, Ricky. "Deserving citizenship: Citizenship tests in Germany, the Netherlands and the United Kingdom." Deserving Citizenship. Brill Nijhoff, 2013
Vink, Maarten and others, The international diffusion of expatriate dual citizenship, Migration Studies, Volume 7, Issue 3, September 2019
Von Rutte, Barbara, Defining the Right to Nationality, in The Human Right to Citizenship, Brill, 2022
Walker, Neil; The Philosophy of European Union Law, in The Oxford Handbook of European Union Law, Oxford, Oxford University Press
Walzer, Michael, Spheres of Justice 60–61 (1983), Blackwell Publishers
Weiler, J. The Constitution of Europe, Cambridge University Press, 1999
Weiler, Joseph H. H.: Citizenship for Sale (Commission v Malta): Who of the Two is Selling European Values?, VerfBlog, 2024/4/14, https://verfassungsblog.de/citizenship-for-sale/, DOI: 10.59704/f3c2e8cfd7fcbbe7.
Tratnik, M. and Weingerl, P. Investment Migration and State Autonomy: a Quest for the Relevant Link. IMC Working Papers, 2019/4 (Investment Migration Working Papers)
Weiss, P. Nationality and Statelessness in International Law, 1979, Brill
Young, Alexia. The duty of sincere cooperation and its implications on the acquisition of citizenship by investment. Thesis presented in partial fulfilment of the requirements for the degree of Master of Arts in European Legal Studies, Department of European and Comparative Law, Faculty of Law, University of Malta, 2022

Appendices

APPENDIX A – Portugal – Raw Data – Lei n. 56/2023, 6 October, 2023

Diário da República, 1.ª série

N.º 194 | 6 de outubro de 2023 | Pág. 39

Artigo 19.º

[...]

1 — [...]

a) [...]
b) [...]
c) [...]
d) O requerimento de apoio judiciário é processado com caráter de urgência.

2 — [...]

Artigo 20.º

[...]

1 — [...]
2 — O procedimento de injunção em matéria de arrendamento tem natureza urgente.»

Artigo 40.º

Alterações sistemáticas ao Decreto-Lei n.º 1/2013, de 7 de janeiro

São introduzidas as seguintes alterações sistemáticas ao Decreto-Lei n.º 1/2013, de 7 de janeiro:

a) O capítulo II passa a ter como epígrafe «Balcão do Arrendatário e do Senhorio».
b) A secção III do capítulo III passa a ter como epígrafe «Decisão de desocupação do locado e pedido de pagamento de rendas, encargos ou despesas».

Artigo 41.º

Sistema integrado de acesso à informação

O Governo implementa, no prazo de 60 dias, um sistema integrado de acesso à informação relativa ao arrendamento, na ótica do senhorio e do arrendatário.

CAPÍTULO V

Autorizações de residência para atividade de investimento

Artigo 42.º

Autorizações de residência para atividade de investimento

1 — Não são admitidos novos pedidos de autorização de residência para atividade de investimento, concedidos ao abrigo do disposto nas subalíneas *i*), *iii*) e *iv*) da alínea *d*) do n.º 1 do artigo 3.º da Lei n.º 23/2007, de 4 de julho, na redação anterior à entrada em vigor da presente lei, nos termos previstos no seu artigo 90.º-A, a partir da data da entrada em vigor da presente lei.

2 — O disposto no número anterior não prejudica a possibilidade de renovação das autorizações de residência para atividade de investimento quando essas autorizações tenham sido concedidas ao abrigo do regime legal aplicável até à data da entrada em vigor da presente lei.

3 — O disposto no número anterior é igualmente aplicável à concessão ou renovação de autorizações de residência para reagrupamento familiar previstas no artigo 98.º da Lei n.º 23/2007, de 4 de julho.

4 — O disposto no n.º 2 é ainda aplicável aos cidadãos titulares de autorização de residência para atividade de investimento e seus familiares que cumpram os requisitos previstos no artigo 80.º

Diário da República, 1.ª série

N.º 194 6 de outubro de 2023 Pág. 40

da Lei n.º 23/2007, de 4 de julho, e pretendam requerer a concessão de uma autorização de residência para atividade de investimento permanente, excecionando a este regime o previsto na alínea *b*) do n.º 2 e nos n.os 3 e 4 do artigo 85.º do mesmo diploma.

5 — Nos casos previstos nos números anteriores, a renovação determina a conversão da autorização de residência numa autorização de residência para imigrantes empreendedores, nos termos do n.º 4 do artigo 89.º da Lei n.º 23/2007, de 4 de julho, devendo os seus titulares cumprir o prazo mínimo de permanência de sete dias, seguidos ou interpolados, no primeiro ano e de 14 dias, seguidos ou interpolados, nos subsequentes períodos de dois anos.

Artigo 43.º

Pedidos de autorização de residência para atividade de investimento pendentes

1 — Mantêm-se válidos os pedidos de concessão e de renovação de autorização de residência para atividade de investimento previstos nas subalíneas *i*), *iii*) e *iv*) da alínea *d*) do n.º 1 do artigo 3.º da Lei n.º 23/2007, de 4 de julho, na redação anterior à entrada em vigor da presente lei, solicitados ao abrigo do disposto nos n.os 1 e 2 do artigo 90.º-A da Lei n.º 23/2007, de 4 de julho, que se encontrem a aguardar decisão junto das entidades competentes na data de entrada em vigor da presente lei.

2 — O disposto no número anterior é ainda aplicável aos pedidos que se encontrem pendentes de procedimentos de controlo prévio nas câmaras municipais, na data da entrada em vigor da presente lei.

3 — Aos pedidos referidos nos números anteriores aplica-se, com as necessárias adaptações, o previsto no n.º 5 do artigo 42.º

4 — Para efeitos do disposto no número anterior, devem as entidades competentes verificar a adequação do investimento ao respetivo projeto empreendedor.

5 — São competentes para a verificação da adequação do investimento ao respetivo projeto empreendedor, consoante a matéria:

a) A Agência para o Investimento e Comércio Externo de Portugal, E. P. E.;
b) O Banco Português de Fomento, S. A.;
c) O IAPMEI — Agência para a Competitividade e Inovação, I. P.;
d) A Agência Nacional de Inovação (ANI);
e) O Gabinete de Estratégia, Planeamento e Avaliação Culturais (GEPAC);
f) Outras entidades que se revelem adequadas em razão da matéria.

Artigo 44.º

Alteração à Lei n.º 23/2007, de 4 de julho

Os artigos 3.º, 77.º e 85.º da Lei n.º 23/2007, de 4 de julho, passam a ter a seguinte redação:

«Artigo 3.º

[...]

1 — [...]

a) [...]
b) [...]
c) [...]
d) [...]

i) *(Revogada.)*
ii) [...]
iii) *(Revogada.)*

Diário da República, 1.ª série

N.º 194 6 de outubro de 2023 Pág. 41

iv) (*Revogada.*)
v) [...]
vi) [...]
vii) Transferência de capitais no montante igual ou superior a 500 000 €, destinados à aquisição de partes de organismos de investimento coletivo não imobiliários, que sejam constituídos ao abrigo da legislação portuguesa, cuja maturidade, no momento do investimento, seja de, pelo menos, cinco anos e, pelo menos, 60 % do valor dos investimentos seja concretizado em sociedades comerciais sediadas em território nacional;
viii) Transferência de capitais no montante igual ou superior a 500 000 €, destinados à constituição de uma sociedade comercial com sede em território nacional, conjugada com a criação de cinco postos de trabalho permanentes, ou para reforço de capital social de uma sociedade comercial com sede em território nacional, já constituída, com a criação de, pelo menos, cinco postos de trabalho permanentes ou manutenção de, pelo menos, dez postos de trabalho, com um mínimo de cinco permanentes, e por um período mínimo de três anos;

e) [...]
f) [...]
g) [...]
i) [...]
j) [...]
k) [...]
l) [...]
m) [...]
n) [...]
o) [...]
p) [...]
q) [...]
r) [...]
s) [...]
t) [...]
u) [...]
v) [...]
x) [...]
y) [...]
z) [...]
aa) [...]
bb) [...]
cc) [...]
dd) [...]
ee) [...]
ff) [...]
gg) [...]
hh) [...]
ii) [...]
jj) [...]
kk) [...]
ll) [...]
mm) [...]
nn) [...]
oo) [...]
pp) [...]
qq) [...]

Diário da República, 1.ª série

N.º 194 6 de outubro de 2023 Pág. 42

rr) [...]
ss) [...]
tt) [...]
uu) [...]
vv) [...]
ww) [...]
xx) [...]

2 — O montante ou requisito quantitativo mínimo da atividade de investimento prevista nas subalíneas *ii*), *v*) e *vi*) da alínea *d*) do número anterior pode ser inferior em 20 %, quando a atividade seja efetuada em territórios de baixa densidade.

3 — Para efeitos do disposto no número anterior, consideram-se territórios de baixa densidade os definidos na Portaria n.º 208/2017, de 13 de julho, com menos de 100 habitantes por km^2 ou um produto interno bruto (PIB) *per capita* inferior a 75 % da média nacional.

4 — As atividades de investimento previstas nas subalíneas *ii*) e *v*) a *viii*) da alínea *d*) do n.º 1 carecem de avaliação a cada dois anos quanto aos seus impactos na atividade científica, cultural e na promoção do investimento direto estrangeiro e criação de postos de trabalho.

5 — As atividades de investimento previstas nas subalíneas referidas no número anterior não se podem destinar, direta ou indiretamente, ao investimento imobiliário.

Artigo 77.º

[...]

1 — [...]
2 — [...]
3 — Pode ser recusada a concessão ou a renovação de autorização de residência a nacionais de países terceiros, alvo de medidas restritivas da União Europeia.
4 — *(Anterior n.º 3.)*
5 — *(Anterior n.º 4.)*
6 — *(Anterior n.º 5.)*
7 — *(Anterior n.º 6.)*

Artigo 85.º

[...]

1 — [...]

a) [...]
b) [...]
c) [...]
d) [...]
e) Se concluir que o seu titular está sujeito a uma medida restritiva da União Europeia.

2 — [...]
3 — [...]
4 — [...]
5 — [...]
6 — [...]
7 — [...]»

APPENDIX B – Malta – Raw Data – Subsidiary Legislation 188.06, Granting of Citizenship for Exceptional Services Regulations, 20th November 2020 – Legal Notice 437 of 2020

SUBSIDIARY LEGISLATION 188.06

GRANTING OF CITIZENSHIP FOR EXCEPTIONAL SERVICES REGULATIONS

20th November, 2020

LEGAL NOTICE 437 of 2020.

Part I
Preliminary

1. The title of these regulations is the Granting of citizenship for Exceptional Services Regulations. Citation.

2. The scope of these regulations is to prescribe the requirements and to regulate the granting of citizenship by naturalisation for exceptional services to the Republic of Malta on the basis of humanity, or on the basis of exceptional interest to the Republic of Malta, in accordance with article 10(9) of the Maltese Citizenship Act. Scope. Cap. 188.

3. In these regulations, unless the context otherwise requires: Interpretation.

"Act" means the Maltese Citizenship Act; Cap. 188.

"Agency" means the Community Malta Agency established by the Community Malta Agency (Establishment) Order; S.L. 595.38.

"applicant" means the person who applies for citizenship of Malta by naturalisation under these regulations and includes a dependent or a person who applies on behalf of another person;

"application" means an application made by the applicant under these regulations;

"Agent" means an agent duly licensed and certified for the purpose of the processing of applications under the Agents (Licences) Regulations; S.L. 188.05.

"authenticated translation" means a translation made by a recognised translator.

"certified copy" means a photocopy of an original document certified to be a true copy of the original by a duly warranted lawyer, notary public, commissioner for oaths, Maltese consular or diplomatic officer, in accordance with such guidelines as the Agency may issue from time to time;

"Commissioner" means the Information and Data Protection Commissioner as defined in the Data Protection Act; Cap. 586.

"dependant" means the family members of those applicants making an exceptional direct investment in terms of Part IV and under the First Schedule and shall include:

(a) the spouse of the applicant in a monogamous marriage or partner in another relationship having the same or similar status to a monogamous marriage, including a civil union, domestic partnership, common law marriage, provided that for the purpose of these regulations, the term "spouse" in these regulations shall be construed as gender neutral, and, saving the discretion of the Minister to authorise, and on a case by case basis, other relationships having a similar status as aforesaid;

(b) a child, of the main applicant or of his dependant as defined in paragraph (a) above including an adopted child, who has not yet attained eighteen (18) years of age at the time when the main applicant submits an application for citizenship by naturalisation under these regulations and is accepted by the Agency;

(c) a child, of the main applicant or of his dependant as defined in paragraph (a) above including an adopted child, who has attained eighteen (18) years of age but has not yet attained twenty-nine (29) years of age, at the time when the main applicant submits an application for citizenship by naturalisation under these regulations and is accepted by the Agency, and who is not married and proves, to the satisfaction of the Minister, that he is wholly maintained or otherwise largely supported by the main applicant;

(d) a parent or grandparent of the main applicant or of his dependant as defined in paragraph (a) above who has attained fifty-five (55) years of age at the time when the main applicant submits an application for citizenship by naturalisation under these regulations and who proves to the satisfaction of the Minister that he is wholly maintained or otherwise largely supported by the main applicant;

(e) a child, of the main applicant or of his dependant as defined in paragraph (a) above, including an adopted child, who at the time when the main applicant submits an application for citizenship by naturalisation under these regulations has attained eighteen (18) years of age, is a qualified person with a disability as defined in the Equal Opportunities (Persons with Disability) Act:

Cap. 413.

Provided that where such child does not have full capacity the provisions of article 21(3) of the Act shall apply.

"designated competent body" means the locally registered entity in Malta, specified in the Third Schedule that is capable to determine whether an individual is recognised in a particular field as a leading talent, or has demonstrated exceptional promise and is likely to become a leading talent;

"due diligence data" shall mean any personal data pertaining to the applicant collected and processed by the Agency as part of the due diligence process, excluding the personal data collected by the Agency directly from the applicant;

"eligibility form" means the prescribed form issued by the Agency by which the applicant signifies his intention to the Minister to apply for citizenship by naturalisation through exceptional contribution or exceptional services by merit or exceptional direct investment;

"Evaluation Board", hereinafter referred to as "the Board", means the group of individuals appointed in accordance with these regulations to evaluate applications made under article 10(9) of the Act and to prepare a reasoned opinion with regard to each application to be referred to the Minister responsible for citizenship;

"exceptional contribution" means manifestly superior and refers primarily to contributions by scientists, researchers, athletes, sports people, artists and cultural performers;

"exceptional direct investment" means the investment requirement in the Maltese economy as defined in the First Schedule ;

"exceptional services by merit" means exceptional services to the Republic of Malta or to humanity or whose naturalisation is of exceptional interest to the Republic of Malta;

"Letter of Approval in Principle" means letter issued following the approval in principle of the citizenship application by the main applicant as provided for in regulation 16(7);

"Minister" has the same meaning as defined in the Act;

"person" shall mean a physical person and where applicable means a legal person;

"police conduct certificate" means a certificate of conduct, report or statement from a national law enforcement authority, or other public authority, in charge of criminal records, on the status of an applicant's criminal record;

"Regulation" shall mean Regulation (EU) 2016/679 of the European Parliament and the Council of 27 April 2016 on the protection of natural persons with regard to the processing of personal data and on the free movement of such data, and repealing Directive 95/46/EC.

Part II
General Provisions applicable to all applications

Administration.

4. The Agency shall process all applications filed in accordance with these regulations.

Qualifications.

5. (1) A person may apply for a certificate of naturalisation under these regulations if that person:

(a) undertakes to take the oath of allegiance to the Republic of Malta and to abide by the Constitution of Malta;

(b) undertakes to promote the fundamental and democratic values of the Republic of Malta;

(c) undertakes to support the Maltese Community in the spirit of social justice and equity;

(d) satisfies the requirements prescribed under these regulations.

(2) In addition to the qualifications set out in regulation 5(1), a person may apply for a certificate under these regulations if that person:

(a) has rendered an exceptional contribution to the Republic of Malta; or

(b) has rendered an exceptional contribution to humanity; or

(c) is of exceptional interest to the Republic of Malta; or

(d) is willing to contribute through an exceptional direct investment in the economic and social development of the Republic of Malta.

Persons who do not qualify to be naturalised for exceptional services.

6. (1) A person is disqualified from applying for the grant of a certificate of naturalisation as a citizen of Malta in terms of these regulations if:

(a) he or any of this dependants is or was indicted of an offence before an International Criminal Court or has been arraigned at any time before an International Criminal Court, whether such person has been found guilty, declared innocent or otherwise acquitted for any reason by such Court;

(b) he or any of his dependants, are listed with the

International Criminal Police Organization (Interpol) or Europol;

(c) he or any of his dependants is an actual or potential threat to national security, public policy or public health of Malta;

(d) he or any of his dependants has, at any time, been charged with or found guilty of crimes, related to:

(i) terrorism,

(ii) money laundering,

(iii) funding of terrorism,

(iv) crimes against humanity,

(v) war crimes,

(vi) crimes that infringe upon such Protection of Human Rights and Fundamental Freedoms as established by the European Convention on Human Rights.

(e) he or any of his dependants has, at any time, been charged or found guilty of any criminal offences that disturb the good order of the family, which offences include, without limitation, the following:

(i) paedophilia;

(ii) defilement of minors;

(iii) rape;

(iv) violent indecent assault;

(v) inducing persons under age to prostitution; and

(vi) abduction;

(f) he or any of his dependants has, at any time, been found guilty of, or at any time during the processing of the application, has been interrogated or is suspected of, or has criminal charges brought against him for any criminal offence punishable with more than one (1) year's imprisonment other than an involuntary offence;

(g) he or any of his dependants is, or is likely to be, involved in any activity which may cause disrepute to the

Republic of Malta;

(h) he or any of his dependants has been denied a visa to a country with whom Malta has visa-free travel arrangements and has not subsequently obtained a visa from that same country;

(i) he or any of his dependants is named or listed in international sanctions applying restrictive measures on them; that the Agency is bound by law, or has opted, to follow.

General requirements. S.L. 188. 01.

7. (1) Applications shall be made on the forms prescribed under the Citizenship Regulations.

(2) The applications and other accompanying documents shall be completed in the English language and, if the original language of a document is not English, the document shall be accompanied by an authenticated translation into English.

(3) All forms shall be signed by the applicant.

S.L. 188.05.

(4) All applications shall be submitted by the applicant through an Agent licensed in terms of the Agents (Licences) Regulations:

Provided that an applicant for naturalisation for exceptional services by merit may file the application directly not through an Agent.

(5) All applications shall only be accepted and processed provided that all forms are properly completed, dated, confirmed on oath and signed, and accompanied by all required documents and fees.

(6) The Agency shall ensure that all applications are complete and correct.

(7) If an applicant makes a false statement or otherwise omits material information, his application may be suspended and/or considered inadmissible.

(8) Where a document is required to be produced under these regulations in support of an application:

(a) such document must be an original document or a certified copy; and

(b) the person certifying the document shall provide the full name, capacity in which the person is acting, residential or business address, telephone number and email address.

(9) The following conditions shall apply to dependants who

are below the age of eighteen (18) years of age:

(a) the forms shall be signed by both parents on behalf of the dependant; and

(b) in the case where one parent has sole custody of a dependant, or another person has legal guardianship of a dependant, the appropriate legal documentation shall be provided to demonstrate that sole custody or guardianship was awarded to the said parent or person, as the case may be, by a court of law or other relevant authority.

Application for the eligibility assessment.

8. (1) The prospective applicant who is desirous to apply for the eligibility assessment shall signify his intention to the Minister on the applicable prescribed forms:

Provided that a prospective applicant who intends to file an application under the provisions of regulation 10 and making the direct investment shall indicate the dependants that will be included in the application for Maltese citizenship:

Provided further that the dependants except in the case of minors shall signify their intention on the applicable forms.

(2) The forms for the eligibility assessment shall be accompanied by the originals or certified copies of the following:

(a) a declaration on the form issued by the Agency, duly filled and certified by the Agent of the applicant, that the applicant and his dependants are fit and proper persons to hold Maltese citizenship:

Provided that in the case that the form is filed by an applicant for naturalisation for exceptional services by merit may file the application directly not through an Agent;

(b) a declaration on the form issued by the Agency, duly filled and certified by a recognised medical practitioner, clinic, hospital, medical or health institute or other health care system attesting that the applicant and his dependants are in good health and are not suffering from any contagious disease and are not likely to become a burden on the Maltese public health system;

(c) a clean police conduct certificate or certificates: the Agency may require the applicant to provide a clean police conduct certificate from the countries where applicant has resided for at least six (6) months during the last ten (10) years;

(d) any other document as may be required by the Agency from time to time.

(3) The applicant shall attach with his applications a sworn declaration made before a commissioner for oaths attesting that the information provided is true and correct;

(4) The applicant shall pay the administrative fees established in the First Schedule.

(5) Applicants for naturalisation for exceptional services by direct investment shall pay the non-refundable due diligence fee established in the First Schedule.

Eligibility assessment.

9. (1) The Agency shall, on behalf of the Minister, administer the due diligence and verification process of the eligibility of the applicant.

(2) The Agency shall cause due diligence checks to be performed also by third parties including one (1) or more internationally recognised specialised due diligence service providers, in respect of every applicant. Such due diligence checks shall be of a four (4) tier nature or more, as the Agency shall determine from time to time and may include security checks to be carried out by law enforcement authorities in line with the Data Protection (Processing of Personal Data by Competent Authorities for the Purposes of the Prevention, Investigation, Detection or Prosecution of Criminal Offences or the Execution of Criminal Penalties) Regulations, who may use available tools for such purposes, as all other checks as regards money laundering and terrorism financing risks by the pertinent Authorities having the necessary authority to conduct such checks.

S.L. 586. 08.

(3) The Applicant shall provide a title to residential property in Malta, except in the case of an applicant who is a minor or in the case of a dependent of an applicant who is filing an application in terms of Part IV or if a waiver has been given by the Minister in accordance with paragraph (b) of sub-regulation (4) of regulation 11.

(4) An applicant may not apply for an eligibility assessment for authorisation to apply for a certificate of naturalisation for exceptional services by direct investment, unless he is eighteen (18) years of age.

(5) The Agency shall ensure that:

(a) all relevant information provided by the applicant has been verified by one (1) or more independent due diligence service providers;

(b) the background of the applicant and his dependants, if any, has been verified by one (1) or more independent due diligence service providers;

(c) the applicant shall attach with his application a

sworn declaration made before a commissioner for oaths, attesting that the information that he has provided is true and correct;

(d) the source of funds of the applicant is legitimate with due regard to anti money laundering and financing of terrorism legislation and guidelines issued by the competent authorities;

(e) an appropriate risk weighting has been carried out as established by the Agency;

(f) all non-refundable due diligence and administrative fees have been made in accordance with the First Schedule.

(6) The Agency shall inform the Minister of its findings for his review and decision.

Minister's decision on eligibility of applicant.

10. (1) If the Minister is satisfied that the applicant meets the necessary criteria he shall authorise the applicant to submit an application for Maltese Citizenship on the prescribed form.

(2) The Agency shall immediately notify the applicant in writing in accordance with the Minister's instructions, that the applicant is authorised to submit a full application for Maltese Citizenship on the prescribed form:

Provided that applications filed in terms of the provisions of Part IV, such notification in writing shall be made to the applicant through his Agent:

Provided further that the applicant shall not submit the application for a certificate of citizenship by naturalisation for exceptional services before he has completed the residence requirement as stipulated in these regulations.

Part III

Special Provisions applicable to naturalisation for exceptional services by merit

11. (1) The Agency shall carry out on behalf of the Minister the processing of applications for a certificate of citizenship of naturalisation for exceptional services by merit.

(2) Every application shall be presented to the Minister through the Agency.

(3) Only applicants authorised by the Agency on the instructions of the Minister are eligible to submit a full application for a certificate of citizenship by naturalisation for exceptional services by

merit.

(4) The application for a certificate of citizenship by naturalisation for exceptional services by merit shall be accompanied by the original documents or certified copies of the following:

(a) proof of residence in Malta for at least eight (8) months in the period preceding the date of application;

(b) proof of title of residential property in Malta, except in the case of an applicant who is a minor:

Provided that where the applicant is still a member of the household of his family, the Minister may, if he is satisfied that the applicant is not in a position to purchase or take on lease such property, waive this requirement;

(c) proof of the exceptional services rendered to the Republic of Malta or to humanity, or if the individual claims that his naturalisation is of exceptional interest to the Republic of Malta, provides an endorsement by the designated competent body.

(d) a recommendation by two people who are qualified to act as sponsors for the applicant for certificate of naturalisation for Maltese citizenship for exceptional services.

(5) Following submission of all the documents by the applicant, the Agency shall:

(a) update its due diligence;

(b) request the applicant to produce any further documentation and information that it may require;

(c) request the applicant to pay any applicable administrative fees established in the First Schedule.

(6) The Agency shall provide the Board with the application and the findings of the due diligence and its verification process.

Evaluation Board.

12. (1) The Evaluation Board shall evaluate applications made under Part III and prepare an evaluation for the Minister.

(2) The composition of the Evaluation Board shall vary in accordance with the nature of the application to be evaluated, and shall comprise:

(a) a Chairperson to be appointed by the Minister, who shall be a person who has practiced the profession of advocate for at least seven years; and

(b) two (2) members to be selected by the Chairperson from amongst the members of three panels to be appointed by the Minister, which panels shall include persons having knowledge of sport, culture and the arts and science and research, respectively.

(3) The Chairperson and the appointed panel members of the Evaluation Board shall hold office for a term of three years and under such conditions as may be set out in their letter of appointment, and shall, on the expiration of the term of their office, be eligible to be reappointed.

(4) The Chairperson and the panel members of the Evaluation Board shall, before commencing to execute their duties, take an oath in the form set out in the Fourth Schedule . Such oath shall be taken before, and shall be deposited with, the Attorney General.

(5) When any vacancy in the Evaluation Board occurs, the Minister shall, as soon as practicable, appoint another person to fill the vacancy.

(6) A member of the Evaluation Board may be removed from office by the Minister, but such member may be removed only for proved inability to discharge the functions of his office (whether arising from infirmity of mind or body or any other cause) or for misbehaviour.

(7) The Chairperson and any member of the Evaluation Board may abstain from sitting or may be challenged for any of the causes mentioned in article 734 of the Code of Organization and Civil Procedure. Cap. 12.

(8) Save as otherwise expressly provided by these regulations, the Evaluation Board may make its own rules and otherwise regulate its own procedure.

(9) The Minister shall appoint a Secretary to the Evaluation Board and such other officers as may be necessary from time to time and shall determine their duties.

(10) The Evaluation Board shall have the power to request such technical advise as it may deem necessary for the proper performance of its functions.

(11) Any notice issued by the Board shall be signed by the Chairperson and counter-signed by the Secretary.

(12) The findings of the Evaluation Board shall, through the Agency, be signed by the Chairperson and by the Secretary and forwarded to the Minister for his consideration.

Evaluation process.

13. (1) The Evaluation Board shall evaluate the applications submitted and prepare an evaluation report. In order to properly carry out the task entrusted to it, the Board may interview the applicant in person and, or the legal representative of the designated competent body endorsing the applicant. The Evaluation Board shall keep a record of its evaluation in writing.

(2) The Evaluation Board shall, through the Agency, provide the Minister with a reasoned opinion containing the findings of their evaluation.

(3) The Minister shall determine whether a certificate of naturalisation as a citizen of Malta shall be granted to the applicant and instruct the Agency to inform the applicant about his decision:

Provided that if the application is filed through an Agent, the notification of the decision shall be made through the Agent of the applicant.

(4) The Agency shall notify the applicant in writing, in accordance with the Minister's instructions, that the application has been:

(a) approved; or

(b) refused:

Provided that if the application is filed through an Agent, the notification of the decision shall be made through the Agent of the applicant:

Provided further that where an application is approved in accordance with paragraph (a), the Agency shall issue a Letter of Approval in Principle to the applicant.

Oath of allegiance.

14. (1) Subject that the conditions of the Letter of Approval in Principle have been satisfied, and all fees are settled, the Agency shall inform the Minister that all requisites for the issue of a certificate of citizenship by naturalisation for exceptional services by merit in the name of the applicant are satisfied.

(2) The applicant shall be required to complete the process and take the oath of allegiance within six (6) months from the approval in Principle by the Minister.

(3) The Agency may suspend or terminate the application process before the applicant takes the oath of allegiance, if he fails to satisfy all conditions or if the Minister is no longer satisfied that the applicant is worthy of Maltese citizenship.

Part IV
Special provisions applicable to naturalisation for exceptional services by direct investment

Processing of applications.

15. (1) The Agency shall carry out on behalf of the Minister the processing of applications for a certificate of citizenship by naturalisation for exceptional services by Direct Investment in the economic and social development in the Republic of Malta.

(2) Every application shall be presented to the Minister through the Agency.

(3) Only applicants authorised by the Agency on the instructions of the Minister are eligible to submit a full application for a certificate of citizenship in terms of regulation 10.

Requisites of the application.

16. (1) The application for naturalisation through exceptional services by direct investment for applicants shall be accompanied by the originals or certified copies of the following:

(a) for the main applicant and dependants aged eighteen (18) and above, proof of residence in Malta, for a period of thirty six (36) months, provided that this period may by exception be reduced to a minimum of twelve (12) months subject to an exceptional direct investment, to be effected prior the issue of the certificate of naturalisation, as provided in the First Schedule;

(b) an undertaking to either purchase, an immovable residential property in Malta having a minimum value of seven hundred thousand euro (€700,000) or to take on a lease of a residential immovable property in Malta for a minimum annual rent of sixteen thousand euro (€16,000), which property shall be adequate and suitable for the applicant and his dependants, for a minimum period of five (5) years from the date of issue of the certificate of citizenship.

(c) an undertaking to carry out an exceptional direct investment in Malta, in accordance with these regulations;

(d) an undertaking to donate, prior to the issue of the certificate of naturalisation, a minimum of ten thousand euro (€10,000) to a registered philanthropic, cultural, sport, scientific, animal welfare or artistic non governmental organisation or society, or as otherwise approved by the Agency.

(2) The applicant may, at any time prior to submitting the citizenship application, apply to include with his application other minor dependants by complying with the requirements under these

regulations, including the submission of eligibility form and due fees.

(3) The dependants of the applicant mentioned in sub-regulations (1) and (2) may submit an application if they have been authorized to do so in accordance with regulation 10.

(4) Following submission of all the documents by the Applicant, the Agency shall:

(a) update its due diligence;

(b) request the applicant to produce any further documentation and information that it may require;

(c) request the applicant to pay any applicable administrative fees established in the First Schedule.

(5) The Agency shall provide the Minister with its findings.

(6) The Minister shall determine whether a certificate of naturalisation as a citizen of Malta shall be granted to the applicant and instruct the Agency to inform the applicant through his Agent about his decision.

(7) The Agency shall notify the Agent in writing, in accordance with the Minister's instructions, that the application has been:

(a) approved; or

(b) refused:

Provided that where an application is approved in accordance with paragraph (a), the Agency shall issue a Letter of Approval in Principle to the applicant:

Provided further that within four (4) months from the issue of the Letter of Approval in Principle the applicant shall submit a certified copy of the contract of purchase or of the lease agreement. The applicant may not dispose of the property for a period of at least five (5) years from the date of the certificate of citizenship but may be authorised by the Agency to substitute the said property by purchasing or leasing another equivalent property. The Applicant shall also provide documentary evidence that the conditions stipulated in this regulation have been satisfied.

Oath of allegiance.

17. (1) Subject that the conditions of the Letter of Approval in Principle have been satisfied, and all investments and fees are settled, the Agency shall inform the Minister that all requisites for the issue of a certificate of citizenship by naturalisation for exceptional services by direct investment in the name of the applicant are satisfied.

(2) The applicant shall be required to complete the process and take the oath of allegiance within six (6) months from the approval in Principle by the Minister.

(3) The Agency may suspend or terminate the application process before the applicant takes the oath of allegiance, if he fails to satisfy all conditions and the Minister is no longer satisfied that the applicant is worthy of Maltese citizenship.

18. During the first five (5) years from the grant of the certificate of Maltese citizenship, the Agency may request the applicant to provide any information or documentation and may also subject the applicant to an interview. First five years.

19. The number of certificates by Maltese Citizenship by Naturalisation for Exceptional Services by Direct Investment granted, excluding dependants, shall not exceed four hundred (400) per annum, and in any case the total accumulated amount of successful applicants excluding dependants shall not exceed one thousand five hundred (1,500). Maximum number of admissions.

Part V
Miscellaneous Provisions

20. (1) Where a document is required to be produced under these regulations in support of an application:

(a) such document must be an original document or, a true copy certified by a lawyer, notary, Maltese consular or diplomatic representative or a Commissioner for Oaths;

(b) the person certifying the document shall provide the full name, capacity in which the person is acting, residential or business address, telephone number and email address; and

(c) any other requirement that the Agency may impose from time to time.

(2) Where a lawyer, notary public or commissioner for oaths certifies a document to be a true copy of the original, that document must be authenticated by:

(a) an apostille in accordance with the provisions of the Hague Convention of 5th October 1961 Abolishing the Requirement of Legalisation for Foreign Public Documents, in the case of a jurisdiction that is a party to that Convention; or

(b) a validation of the certificate of the lawyer, notary public or Commissioner for Oaths by the appropriate government department or other competent authority in the case of a jurisdiction that is not a party to that Convention and a validation of the certificate by a Maltese consular or diplomatic representation in the case of a jurisdiction that is not a party to that Convention.

Non-refundable fees and investment.

21. The due diligence fees, administrative fees and any other fee, investment or charge levied or payable under these regulations are not refundable.

Continuing obligations and annual compliance form.

22. (1) The applicant shall prior to taking the oath of allegiance undertake and confirm in writing that he shall continue to observe and fulfil all obligations in terms of his application and these regulations for a minimum period of five (5) years from the certificate of naturalisation.

(2) The Agency reserves the right to request proof of observation of these obligations and to make its own verifications.

Guidelines.

23. The Agency shall, from time to time, issue procedural guidelines to specify the operational aspects and interpretations under these regulations.

Deprivation of citizenship.

24. (1) Without prejudice to the provisions of article 14 of the Act, the Minister shall have the power to deprive a person of Maltese citizenship granted under these regulations, if an applicant:

(a) fails to comply with any material obligation under these Regulations; or

(b) becomes a threat to national security; or

(c) is involved in conduct which is seriously prejudicial to the interests of the Republic of Malta; or

(d) in the case of an individual who acquired Maltese citizenship in terms of Part III, the said individual fails to use his skills for the benefit of the Republic of Malta.

(2) In such cases the procedure for deprivation of citizenship stipulated in article 14 of the Act and in any regulations made under the Act in respect of such deprivation shall *mutatis mutandis* apply.

Dissemination of information.

25. No person shall, without the Agency's consent, advertise, publish or otherwise disseminate publicity through any means whatsoever on the acquisition of citizenship by naturalisation in terms of these regulations.

Data Protection.. Cap. 586.

26. (1) Nothing in these regulations shall prejudice the applicability of the Regulation and the Data Protection Act and the fundamental rights and freedoms of the data subject.

(2) Where the Agency in its capacity of data controller processes personal data on the applicant or the beneficiary and, or

dependants, as established under these regulations, it shall:

(a) comply with the principles relating to processing of personal data pursuant to Article 5(1) of the Regulation;

(b) apply appropriate technical and organisational measures to ensure a level of security appropriate to the risk posed, and prevent abuse or unlawful access to or transfer of, personal data pertaining to the applicants.

(3) The controller shall retain the personal data of the beneficiary and/or his dependants as long as the certificate issued to the beneficiary and dependants, if any, pursuant to these regulations remains valid:

Provided that where the application is refused, or where the certificate is revoked, such data shall be retained for the purposes of these regulations for a period of five (5) years from the date of the refusal of the application or the revocation of the certificate thereof.

(4) Where the Agency pursuant to its functions under these regulations processes information in relation to the due diligence process, the Agency may restrict the rights and obligations provided for in Articles 14 to 20 and Article 34 of the Regulation in accordance with Article 23 of the Regulation:

Provided that such personal data shall only be restricted in case the Agency refuses the application or revokes the certificate:

Provided further that the Agency's Data Protection Officer designated pursuant to Article 37 of the Regulation shall be consulted as appropriate in a timely manner in the entire process of applying the restriction.

(5) The restrictions under sub-regulation (4) shall only apply in the event that these restrictions are considered as a necessary and proportionate measure to protect the sources and confidentiality of legally privileged information collected in the course of carrying out the due diligence process and to:

(a) safeguard important objectives of general public interest of the Republic of Malta; or

(b) protect national and public security and the obligations of the Agency connected with its functions pursuant to these regulations.

(6) The Agency shall apply the restrictions referred to in sub-regulation (4) for as long as the reasons justifying them remain applicable following a necessity and proportionality test:

Provided that such reasons justifying the restrictions shall be documented and made available to the Commissioner when and as required.

(7) Where the reasons for a restriction no long apply, the Agency shall lift the restriction and inform the data subject concerned accordingly and comply with the rights and obligations provided for in Articles 14 to 20 and Article 34 of the Regulation.

(8) The Agency shall review the application for the restrictions referred to in this regulation every year and depending on the outcome of such review inform the data subject accordingly.

(9) For the safeguard of the rights and freedoms of the data subject, the following conditions and safeguards shall apply to documents, reports and other personal data processed throughout the due diligence process subject to the restrictions in terms of sub-regulation (4):

(a) access to due diligence data by competent authorities other than the Agency shall not be permitted unless provided for by law;

(b) the Agency shall maintain an audit trail record of access to due diligence data by competent authorities, containing at least the date of the access, the identifiable details of the Agency's officer accessing the data, the requesting competent authority and the purpose for the access. Such audit trail record shall be kept for as long as the due diligence data is stored in line with regulation 20(3);

(c) the Agency's Data Protection Officer shall keep a register to record the restrictions applied in relation to the requests made by the applicants. The register shall include the details of the applicants, the right requested to be exercised that was restricted and the purpose for such restriction. Restriction of rights in terms of Article 34 of the Regulation, shall also be recorded in the register; and

(d) the applicants in their capacity as data subjects shall be informed of the application of restrictions to their rights by informing the data subject concerned in reply to the request to exercise any of the rights which are being restricted in terms of these regulations, unless this may be prejudicial to the purpose of the restriction:

Provided that the Agency justifies the prejudice claimed by the Agency to the Commissioner when and where requested.

(10) In this regulation unless the context otherwise requires, Article 4 of the Regulation shall *mutatis mutandis* apply.

27. (1) Other than for the proper discharge of their duties or functions under these regulations and in terms of the Act, including for the purposes of the due diligence checks referred to in regulation 9, or as may be otherwise provided in any other law, the Agency, and the officers and employees of the Agency, shall treat all information furnished in accordance with these regulations and at all times as confidential and shall be solely used by the Agency for the purpose of these regulations, shall treat any information acquired in the discharge of their duties as confidential, and shall not, directly or indirectly, disclose such information to any other person, except with the consent of the person to whom the information relates. For the purposes of this sub-regulation, "employees" and "officials" shall include former employees and officials. Confidentiality.

(2) No person appointed or employed by the Agency in carrying out the provisions of these regulations shall be required to produce in any court, tribunal, board or committee of inquiry any document or to divulge any matter coming under his notice in the performance of his duties under these regulations except as may be lawfully required under any applicable law or for the purpose of carrying into effect the provisions of these regulations, or for the purpose or in the course of any appeal made or proceedings instituted in accordance with these regulations or a prosecution for any offence against any of the provisions of these regulations.

(3) Notwithstanding the provisions of the other sub-regulations of this regulation or of any other law, the Agency shall have the power to furnish to the Commissioner for Revenue, the Financial Intelligence Analysis Unit, the Malta Financial Services Authority and the Commissioner of Police such information, being information obtained by the Agency for any of the purposes of these regulations.

(4) Without prejudice to the foregoing provisions of this regulation, the Agency may, pursuant to a written request, disclose information to local or overseas enforcement or regulatory authorities or police agencies, or a network or grouping comprising such local or overseas enforcement or regulatory authorities or police agencies, or both, for the purpose of preventing, detecting, investigating or prosecuting the commission of acts or omissions that amount to or are likely to amount to a criminal offence under any applicable law or to an offence or breach of a regulatory nature, whether in Malta or overseas.

28. All information obtained through the due diligence process and its sources shall be kept secret. Due diligence to be kept secret.

Protected disclosures.

29. Any person may make a protected disclosure to the Agency:

Provided that a disclosure shall be deemed to be a protected disclosure if it is made in good faith, if the person making the disclosure reasonably believes, at the time of making the disclosure based on the information he has at that moment, that the information disclosed and any allegation contained in it are substantially true and that the information disclosed tends to show an improper practice being committed by a main applicant or any dependants and the disclosure is not made for purposes of personal gain:

Provided further that disclosures shall be made on the grounds of bribery, corrupt practices and improper practice of a main applicant or any dependants.

Fees.

30. (1) The fees set out in the First and Second Schedule, as the case may be, shall be paid for the matters therein respectively specified.

Cap. 35.

(2) The provisions of the Fees Ordinance shall apply to the fees set out in the First and Second Schedule as if they were fees prescribed under the said Ordinance.

Repeal and savings.
S.L. 188. 03.
S.L. 188. 04.

31. (1) The Individual Investor Programme of the Republic of Malta Regulations and the Grant of Citizenship for Exceptional Services Regulations are hereby being repealed:

S.L. 188. 03.

Provided that the Individual Investor Programme of the Republic of Malta Regulations shall remain in force until the maximum amount of applications established in regulation 12 of the said regulations is reached.

S.L. 188. 03.
S.L. 188. 04.

(2) Applications for naturalisation by applicants submitted in terms of the Individual Investor Programme of the Republic of Malta Regulations and the Grant of Citizenship for Exceptional Services Regulations shall remain regulated by the said Individual Investor Programme of the Republic of Malta Regulations and the Grant of Citizenship for Exceptional Services Regulations:

S.L. 188. 03.
S.L. 188. 04.

Provided that any decision, action and notification effected in terms of the Individual Investor Programme of the Republic of Malta Regulations and the Grant of Citizenship for Exceptional Services Regulations shall remain valid.

S.L. 188. 03.
S.L. 188. 04.

(3) The acquisition, deprivation or retention of Maltese citizenship by naturalisation obtained in terms of Individual Investor Programme of the Republic of Malta Regulations and the Grant of Citizenship for Exceptional Services Regulations prior to the coming into force of these regulations shall not in any way be affected.

(4) On the date of coming into force of these regulations, any natural person or legal organisation recognised by law already carrying out the services of an Approved Agent shall be obliged to conform with the Agents (Licences) Regulations within three (3) months from their coming into force, provided that payment of the license fee as established in regulation 5(2) of the Agents (Licences) Regulations is to be paid by the Approved Agent upon the date of its next annual renewal, whenever this may be. S.L. 188.05.

First Schedule
Naturalisation for Exceptional Services Regulations, 2020 Schedule of Fees

1. Naturalisation for exceptional services by direct investment

The following shall constitutes part of the minimum requirements to qualify for citizenship under these regulations:

(a) applicant: six hundred thousand euro (€600,000) , of which a payment of ten thousand euro (€10,000) shall be paid to the Agency as a non-refundable deposit together with the residence application 16(1)(a); whereas the applicant is already a resident of Malta, the non-refundable deposit shall be paid to the Agency together with the eligibility form

(i) without prejudice to regulation 16 where the application is submitted before the completion of thirty six (36) months residence: seven hundred and fifty thousand euro (€750,000), of which a payment of ten thousand euro (€10,000) shall be paid to the Agency as a non-refundable deposit together with the residence application 16(1)(a); whereas the applicant is already a resident of Malta, the non-refundable deposit shall be paid to the Agency together with the eligibility form

(b) for each dependant referred to in the definition of the term 'dependant' in regulation 2: fifty thousand euro (€50,000).

2. Schedule of Fees

The following fees, exclusive of any taxes, shall be payable under each application in terms of the regulations:

Due diligence fees applicable with the eligibility application for exceptional investment applicants

(a) applicant: fifteen thousand euro (€15,000);

(b) for each dependant referred to in the definition of the term 'dependant' in regulation 2: ten thousand euro (€10,000);

(c) for every third party contributing financially to the application: fifteen thousand euro (€15,000).

(3) Administrative fees due together with all eligibility applications:

The following fees are exclusive of any taxes:

(a) administrative fee per applicant: one thousand euro (€1,000);

(4) Notwithstanding the provisions of any other regulations, the fees stipulated in this Schedule shall apply in respect of applications and grants of citizenship under these Regulations and shall include all other fees applicable regarding the applications for naturalization and certificates issued under these Regulations.

(5) Administrative fees due together with all citizenship applications:

The following fees are exclusive of any taxes:

(a) administrative fee per applicant: five hundred euro (€500);

Second Schedule
(Regulation 16)

A fee of five thousand euro (€5,000) exclusive of any taxes shall be applicable in the case of a prospective applicant, and one thousand euro (€1,000), exclusive of any taxes, for each dependant, prior to submitting an application under these regulations for a residence permit may be issued to him in order that he may satisfy the provisions of regulation 16.

Third Schedule
(Regulation 3)

DESIGNATED COMPETENT BODY

In the case of sports:
The National Sports Associations that are registered with SportMalta

In the case of culture and the arts:
The Arts Council Malta or the Superintendence of Cultural Heritage

In the case of science and research:
A recognised tertiary educational institution or the National Council for Further and Higher Education or the Malta Council for Science and Technology.

Fourth Schedule
Form of Oath to be Taken by the Chairperson or a Member of the Evaluation Board

I, ... having been appointed to be Chairperson/Member of the Evaluation Board for the period .... to ...., do swear/solemnly affirm that I will faithfully, fully, impartially and to the best of my ability discharge the trust and perform the duties devolving upon me by virtue of the said appointment.

So help me God.

....

Chairperson/Member

Index

www.ingramcontent.com/pod-product-compliance
Ingram Content Group UK Ltd.
Pitfield, Milton Keynes, MK11 3LW, UK
UKHW020835290926
15470UKWH00004B/1357

9 783631 942154